NO ONE HERE
GETS OUT ALIVE

No One Here Gets Out Alive

By Jerry Hopkins
and Daniel Sugerman

WARNER BOOKS

A Warner Communications Company

Designed by Thomas Nozkowski with William Giersbach

Warner Books, Inc., 75 Rockefeller Plaza, New York, N.Y. 10019

W A Warner Communications Company

Printed in the United States of America

First Printing: June 1980 10 9

LIBRARY OF CONGRESS CATALOGING IN PUBLICATION DATA

HOPKINS, JERRY.
    NO ONE HERE GETS OUT ALIVE.

    DISCOGRAPHY: P.
    BIBLIOGRAPHY: P.
    FILMOGRAPHY: P.
    1. MORRISON, JIM, 1943–1971.   2. ROCK MUSICIANS—
UNITED STATES—BIOGRAPHY.   I. SUGERMAN, DANIEL A.,
JOINT AUTHOR.   II. TITLE.
ML420.M62H7   784'.092'4   [B]   79-26611
ISBN 0-446-97133-2

Erin & Nicky
—Jerry

Alex, Ray, & Jim
—Danny

Let's just say I was testing the bounds of reality. I was curious to see what would happen. That's all it was: just curiosity.

Jim Morrison
Los Angeles, 1969

Foreword

Jim Morrison was well on his way to becoming a mythic
hero while he was still alive—he was, few will dispute, a living
legend. His death, shrouded in mystery and continuing speculation, completed the consecration, assuring him a place in the
pantheon of wounded, gifted artists who felt life too intensely
to bear living it: Arthur Rimbaud, Charles Baudelaire, Lenny
Bruce, Dylan Thomas, James Dean, Jimi Hendrix, and so on.

This book neither propels nor dispels the Morrison myth.
It is simply a reminder that there is more to Jim Morrison (and
the Doors) than legend; that the legend is founded in fact.
Sometimes the content of this book is in sharp conflict with
the myth, sometimes it is indistinguishable from it. Such was
the man.

My personal belief is that Jim Morrison was a god. To
some of you, that may sound extravagant; to others, at least
eccentric. Of course, Morrison insisted we were all gods and
our destiny was of our own making. I just wanted to say I think
Jim Morrison was a modern-day god. Oh hell, at least a lord.

Until now we have had little understanding of the man.

His work as a member of the Doors continues to reach new audiences, while the man's real talent and sources of inspiration are all but ignored. The stories of arrests and feats circulate wider and wilder than ever, while our image of the man himself grows dim.

Morrison changed my life. He changed Jerry Hopkins's life. The truth is Jim Morrison turned a lot of lives around, not only those that were in his immediate orbit, but those he reached as the controversial singer/lyricist of the Doors.

This book is the coverage of Jim's life, not his meaning. Yet we gain insight into the man simply by seeing where he came from and how he got where he was headed.

Getting hip to Morrison in the first place, back in 1967 (which was when most of us first heard from him), was no easy task. It involved more than a bit of soul searching; identifying with Jim meant you were an outsider who *preferred* to look in. Rock and roll has always attracted a lot of misfits with identity problems, but Morrison took being an outsider one step further. He said, in effect, "That's okay, we *like* it here. It hurts and it's hell, but it's also a helluva a lot more *real* than the trip I see *you* on." He pointed his finger at the parents, teachers, and the other authority figures around the land. He did not make vague references. Angered by the fraud, he did not imply—he blatantly, furiously accused. Then he showed us what it was really like: "People are strange when you're a stranger/faces are ugly when you're alone." He showed us what could be: "We could be so good together/I'll tell you about the world we'll invent/wanton world without lament/enterprise/expedition/invitation and invention." He communicated with emotion, rage, grace, and wisdom. He offered very little in the way of compromise.

Getting in was definitely not Jim's concern. Getting past or by was not Jim's concern. Jim's only motivation was to break through it *all.* He'd read about those others who had, and he believed it was possible. And he wanted to take us with him. "We will be inside the gates by evening," he sang. The first few magical years of the Doors' life were little more than

Jim and his band taking their audiences on abbreviated visits to another place—a territory that transcended good and evil; a sensuous, dramatic musical landscape. Of course, the ultimate breakthrough to the other side is death.

You can straddle the fence between life and death, between "here" and "there," for only so long. Jim did it, frantically waving his arm for us to join him. Sadly, he seemed to need us more than we needed him. We surely were not ready for where he wanted to take us. We wanted to watch him and we wanted to follow, but we did not. We couldn't. And Jim couldn't stop. So he went on alone, without us.

Jim didn't want help. He only wanted to help. I do not believe Jim Morrison was ever on the "death trip" so many writers claimed he was on. I believe Jim's trip was about life. Not temporary life, but eternal bliss. If he had to kill himself to get there, or even to get a mite closer to his destination, that was all right. If there was any sadness at the end of Jim's life, it was the grief of instinctive, mortal clinging. But as a lord, as a visionary, he knew better.

The story you are about to read may sound like a tragedy, but for me it is a tale of liberation. No matter what depression and frustration Jim might have endured in his final days, I believe he also knew joy, hope, and the calm knowledge that he was almost home.

It does not matter how Jim died. Nor does it particularly matter that he left us so young. It is only important that Jim Morrison lived, and lived with the purpose birth proposes: to discover yourself and your own potential. He did that. Jim's short life speaks well. And I have already spoken too much.

There will never be another one like him.

Daniel Sugerman
Beverly Hills, California
March 22, 1979

Contents

The
Bow
Is
Drawn

CHAPTER

1

Once, when the snow was packed high in the mountains outside Albuquerque, near Sandia Peak, Steve and Clara Morrison took their children tobogganing. Steve was stationed at nearby Kirtland Air Base where he was the executive officer and number two man at what was called the Naval Air Special Weapons Facility. That meant atomic energy, then still a mysterious subject and one he couldn't discuss at home.

It was the winter of 1955 and Jim Morrison was just a few weeks past his twelfth birthday. In less than a month his sister, Anne, who was turning into a chubby sort of tomboy, would be nine. His brother, Andy, somewhat huskier than Jim, was half his age.

The picture was winter simplicity: in the background the snowy Sangre de Cristo Mountains of New Mexico, in the foreground rosy cheeks, dark wavy hair almost hidden by warm-fitting hats—healthy children in heavy coats, clambering onto a wooden toboggan. No snow was falling, there were only the dry, stinging flurries blown by gusts of mountain wind.

At the edge of the slope Jim placed Andy in the front of the sled. Anne got behind Andy, and Jim squeezed in at the rear. Using their mittened hands, they propelled themselves forward and slid away with a whoosh and whoop.

Faster and faster they went. In the distance, approaching rapidly, was a cabin.

The toboggan rushed downhill like a spaceship tearing the chill of outer space. Andy panicked.

"Bail out!" he cried. "Bail out! Bail out!"

Andy's galoshes were stuck under the front of the toboggan where it curled up and back. He tried to push backward to free himself, but Anne, who was behind him, couldn't move. Jim was pushing forward from the rear, holding them helpless.

The cabin approached rapidly.

"Bail out! Bail out!"

The toboggan was less than twenty yards from the side of the cabin on a certain, horrifying collision course. Anne stared dead ahead, the features on her face numbed by terror. Andy was whimpering.

The toboggan swept under a hitching rail and five feet from the cabin was stopped by the children's father. As the children tumbled out of the sled, Anne babbled hysterically about how Jim had pushed them forward and wouldn't let them escape. Andy continued to cry. Steve and Clara Morrison tried to reassure the younger children.

Jim stood nearby looking pleased. "We were just havin' a good time," he said.

Jim's mother, Clara Clarke, was one of five children, the slightly kooky, fun-loving daughter of a maverick lawyer from Wisconsin who had once run for public office on the Communist ticket. Her mother died when Clara was in her teens, and in 1941, when she was twenty-one and her father had moved to Alaska to work as a carpenter, Clara went to visit a pregnant sister in Hawaii. At a navy dance she met Jim's father, Steve.

Steve had grown up in a small central Florida town, one of

three children, the only son of a conservative laundry owner. As a child, he was given thyroid shots to stimulate his growth, and in high school he was called (by his cousin and best friend) "a campus cowboy: something of a goody-goody—an energetic Methodist but popular with the girls." Steve graduated from the U.S. Naval Academy four months early, in February 1941, after the course of instruction was accelerated to produce a new class of officers for the coming World War.

Steve and Clara met close to the time the Japanese bombed Pearl Harbor. They married quickly, in April 1942, shortly before Steve's mine layer was taken out of dry dock and returned to service in the north Pacific.

The following year he was sent to Pensacola, Florida, for flight training, and just eleven months after that, on December 8, 1943, James Douglas Morrison joined the wartime baby boom, in Melbourne, Florida, near what is now Cape Canaveral.

Jim's father left him at age six months to go back to the Pacific to fly Hellcats from an aircraft carrier. For the next three years Clara and her infant son lived with Steve's parents in Clearwater. The house, right on the Gulf of Mexico, was run in a carefully prescribed fashion and its residents were governed by Victorian clichés: Children should be seen and not heard . . . Ignore something unpleasant and it will go away . . . Cleanliness is next to godliness. Jim's paternal grandparents were raised in Georgia. Neither one drank or smoked.

Clara's behavior during her husband's absence was impeccable, but between the stuffiness of her in-laws and the boredom of Clearwater, she was overjoyed to see Steve return from the Pacific, nearly a year after the war ended, in the humid midsummer of 1946.

The mobility and separation that characterized the Morrison family during the war continued throughout Jim's childhood. His father's first postwar assignment was in Washington, D.C., but he remained there only six months before being sent—for the first of two times—to Albuquerque, where for a year he was an instructor in one of the military's atomic weapons programs. By now, Jim, who was four, had a sister.

It was outside Albuquerque, while traveling with his parents on the highway from Santa Fe, that Jim experienced what he would later dramatically describe as "the most important moment of my life." They came upon an overturned truck, and saw injured and dying Pueblo Indians lying where they had been thrown on the asphalt.

Jim began to cry. Steve stopped the car to see if he could help and dispatched another onlooker to a telephone to call for an ambulance. Jimmy—as his parents called him until he was seven—stared through the car window at the chaotic scene, still crying.

Steve returned to the car and they left, but Jimmy wasn't calmed. He became more and more upset, sobbing hysterically.

"I want to help, I want to help . . ."

While Clara held him in her arms, Steve consoled the boy. "It's all right, Jimmy, it is."

"They're dying! They're dying!"

Finally his father said, "It was a dream, Jimmy, it didn't really happen, it was a dream."

Jim continued to sob.

Years later Jim told his friends that as his father's car pulled away from the intersection, an Indian died and his soul passed into Jim's body.

In February 1948 Steve was sent to sea, a "special weapons officer" aboard another carrier. Now the Morrisons lived in Los Altos in northern California, Jim's fifth home in his four years. It was here that Jim started public school and here that his brother Andy was born.

At age seven, Jim was uprooted again when Steve's career took him once more to Washington. A year later, in 1952, Steve was sent to Korea to coordinate carrier-based air attacks and the rest of the Morrisons returned to California, settling this time in Claremont, near Los Angeles.

Some say that the negative aspects of rootlessness have been greatly overstated, that what a child whose family moves frequently loses in traditional roots he makes up for in variety of experiences. No matter how valid these and other arguments, the special problems remain.

First, a military family knows it will not remain anywhere permanently, and it seldom has much choice about where or when it will make its next move. A navy family knows that even in peacetime there will be long periods when the father is aboard ship and, unlike land-based military people, he cannot take his dependents along. The family members learn to travel light, usually acquiring only essential items, such as furniture, silver, china, and linen. Jim and his brother and sister had toys and books, but not in abundance.

Many families are not so eager to make new friends, knowing the relationship can only last a year or two. Others try extra hard to make friends and either exhaust themselves emotionally or push so hard that they offend the established order.

Of course, the familiarity of military bases and the camaraderie they breed help to offset the strangeness of a new community. An officer's family is always welcome at the officers' country club, for example, where it may mix with others in this highly mobile society. This is especially true in the navy, whose officers constitute a fairly small and intimate group. Over the years many of Steve and Clara's closest friends were other navy officers and their wives whose paths they crossed and recrossed. Children, on the other hand, generally find their friends at school, and navy children must find new ones more frequently.

Psychologists who have studied the highly mobile society of the navy have found a variety of emotional disorders, from alcoholism and marital discord to anomie and a sense of "unconnectedness." Probably the most significant factor is the periodic absence of the father. The mother's role repeatedly changes, depending on whether or not the father is home, and the children often suffer a confusion about and resentment of authority.

When Jim was little Clara and Steve agreed never to raise a hand in anger at their children, to practice some other sort of discipline, to reason with their children, to make it crystal clear when they had erred. Sometimes this discipline took the form of a verbal dressing down, other times a silent freeze.

"What it came down to," says Andy today, "was they tried to make us cry. They'd tell us we were wrong, they'd tell us why we were wrong, and they'd tell us why it was wrong to be wrong. I always held out as long as I could, but they could really put it to you. Jim eventually learned not to cry, but I never did."

By the time Steve reached Korea, in early 1953, Jim was a handsome if slightly chubby boy whose intelligence, natural charm, and good manners made him a favorite of teachers and president of his fifth grade class. But he could startle his elders with braggadocio and shocking language. He rode his bicycle no-hands fashion and got kicked out of the Cub Scouts for sassing the den mother. He persecuted his brother.

Jim shared a room with Andy in the Claremont house, and if there was one thing he hated, it was the sound of heavy breathing, especially when he was reading or watching television or trying to sleep. Andy suffered from chronic tonsillitis, which made it difficult for him to breathe at night.

Sometimes Andy would come awake gasping, desperately trying to catch his breath, to discover his mouth sealed shut with cellophane tape. In the next bed Jim would be feigning sleep or shaking silently with laughter.

After the Morrisons returned to Albuquerque Clara took a part-time secretarial job. Jim was enrolled in Albuquerque's public school system for his seventh and eighth grade years, 1955 to 1957. It is a family member's observation that this was when the three children grew close as a "defense action to moving around so much," but it was also in New Mexico that his parents noticed Jim's withdrawal. It was here that he lost interest in his music lessons, refused to participate in family functions, began his voracious reading, and experienced that dangerous toboggan ride.

In September 1957, after two years in the crisp mountain air of New Mexico, the Morrisons moved again, this time to Alameda in northern California. Alameda is a small island in San Francisco Bay noted for its naval air station, which is the largest industrial complex in the Bay area and the largest U.S. Navy air station anywhere in the world. This was Jim's ninth home town and it was here that he spent his first year and a half of high school.

The only real friend he made was a tall but overweight classmate with a sleepy voice. Fud Ford introduced Jim to the social nuances of Alameda High, telling him it wasn't cool to ride a bicycle (Jim began to walk the mile and a half to school) and that it wasn't acceptable to wear clean Levi's to class.

"My mother washes them every week," Jim said. "Sometimes twice a week."

Fud shrugged hopelessly.

Jim brightened. "I got an idea. I'll leave a second pair next door under Rich Slaymaker's porch. I can change into them after I leave the house."

It was an obvious move to gain acceptance. So, too, were his efforts to draw attention to himself. Once he tied the end of a piece of string around one ear, placed the other end in his mouth, and whenever anyone commented, said he had a tiny bucket hanging down his throat to collect saliva for medical tests. He read *Mad* magazines avidly and adopted several of the catch phrases as his own. He said he was "crackers to slip the rozzer the dropsy in snide."

In an early show of resentment toward authority, something that would become a pattern in his life, when local policemen threw him out of the Alameda Theater one Friday night for being among the noisy rowdies who sat in the front row, he snapped, "Whip out some identification."

He worked out elaborate ways to answer the telephone, reflecting the sick side of *Mad*'s humor or the taint of ethnic slur: "Morrison's Mortuary . . . you stab 'em, we slab 'em" and "Hello, Mo'son's rez-dence, this here's Thelma."

Sometimes Jim was subtler, and more bizarre. When he was caught going up a stairway marked for downward movement only, he was taken before the student "border patrol" and asked, "Do you plead guilty or not guilty?"

"Not guilty," Jim said solemnly, "for, you see, I have no legs."

Jim and Fud were inseparable. They took their first drinks together, sneaking gin from the Commander's bottle and replacing it with water. They faked fights at the officers' club pool that looked and sounded homicidal, then giggled all the way home.

They also shared the pain of sexual awakening. Jim encouraged Fud to join him at Joy Allen's house on the estuary, where they secretly watched Joy and her mother change into their bathing suits. Nearby, where there were houses on fingers of land built into the bay, they peeled off their bathing suits and flashed out of the water on one side, sprinting naked to the other side and back. Jim told Fud he was banging two girls right in his own room when his mother went shopping. Fud shook his head in envy, and told a lie to match.

Many of Jim's afternoons were spent at Fud's, writing dozens of wildly scatalogical and sexually explicit radio commercials about the problems of "butt-picking and masturbation."

Masturbation usually occurs between the ages of twelve and eighteen, although some continue past the age of ninety-three. You may not realize the dangers of masturbation. Often a severe rash will develop around the outer skin of the penis delpisto which in extreme cases might call for amputation. Also, stri-dopsis of the papuntasistula gland may develop, or in lay terms, you might find yourself with a big red prick. No one wants this to happen. But it will occur unless immediate help is obtained. We (at the Society for the Prevention of Masturbation) are equipped with special water-tested machines and our staff of trained nurses are always ready to pitch in and lend a willing hand when needed.

Jim created an elaborate pencil drawing of a man contorting and vomiting: "Neglected kidneys caused this." Another showed a man with a Coca-Cola bottle for a penis, a mean-looking can opener for testicles, one hand held out and dripping with slime, more of the slime hanging from his anus. A third showed a man with an erect penis the size of a baseball bat, a small boy kneeling in front and holding on, licking his pointed teeth in anticipation.

Jim made hundreds of these drawings. When his mood was lighter, he and Fud cut out cartoon characters from the Sunday funnies and rearranged them on strips of paper, giving them new dialogue or captions. Again the themes were sexual, or scatological, but they were imbued with sophistication and subtle humor unusual for someone just fourteen.

Jim sat in his room in the evening, alone. He closed the book that had held him captive for four hours, releasing a deep breath. The next morning he began to read the book again. This time he copied paragraphs he liked into a spiral notebook that he'd started to carry around with him.

The book was Jack Kerouac's novel about the beat generation, *On the Road*, published the same month the Morrisons arrived in Alameda, September 1957. Jim discovered the book that winter, about the same time a newspaper columnist in San Francisco gave the world a new pejorative: *beatnik*.

World headquarters for the beatniks was North Beach, a San Francisco neighborhood that was only forty-five minutes by bus from Alameda. On Saturdays Jim and Fud walked up and down Broadway tirelessly, stopping to browse in the City Lights Book Shop, where a sign in the window read "Banned Books." Once Jim saw one of the owners of the shop, the poet Lawrence Ferlinghetti. Jim nervously said hello, and when Ferlinghetti said hello back to him, Jim fled.

Ferlinghetti was one of Jim's favorites, along with Kenneth Rexroth and Allen Ginsberg. Ginsberg made the greatest impact, for he was the real-life Carlo Marx (one of Kerouac's characters in *On the Road*), "the sorrowful poetic con-man with the dark mind." It was an image that stuck to Jim like paste.

Jim was also fascinated by Dean Moriarty, the "sideburned hero of the snowy west" whose energy gave Kerouac's novel a rush like amphetamine. He was one of Kerouac's "mad ones, the ones who are mad to live, mad to talk, mad to be saved, desirous of everything at the same time, the ones who never yawn or say a commonplace thing, but burn, burn, burn like fabulous yellow roman candles exploding like spiders across the stars and in the middle you see the blue center-light pop and everybody goes 'Awww!' "

Jim began to copy Moriarty, right down to his "hee-hee-hee-hee" laugh.

Time passed slowly in Alameda. Jim took "accidental" falls from the swimming pool at the navy base, listened to his Oscar Brand and Tom Lehrer records over and over, and got into hassles with his mother.

Clara was a "screamer," and when she didn't get her way, she threatened to hold back allowances. Jim laughed at her and once when she came at him in anger he grabbed her and started wrestling her to the floor, pulling out a ball-point pen and scribbling on her arm.

"You don't fight fair," she hollered. "You don't fight fair!"

Jim was laughing. "Hee-hee-hee-hee, ah-hee-hee-hee-hee-hee . . ."

Jim came to Alexandria, Virginia, from California in December 1958, ahead of the rest of the family, to stay with navy friends of his parents who had a son his age. Jeff Morehouse was the slight, bespectacled class "brain" and he introduced Jim to Tandy Martin. Tandy lived only a hundred yards from the spacious home the Morrisons leased in January, when Steve returned to the Pentagon.

The brick-and-stone house was in a hilly, wooded section called Beverly Hills, an upper-middle-class neighborhood whose population included diplomats, high-ranking military officers, cabinet members, doctors, lawyers, and senators. There was a thick floral carpet in a living room filled with functional antiques (one of Clara's brothers was an antique dealer), overstuffed chairs, and a big television set. Bicycles leaned against the outside porch.

Jim and Tandy had lockers near each other at school and usually they walked to and from George Washington High School together.

Jim liked to shock Tandy. "Ah think ah'm gonna go over there and piss on that fire plug," he announced one day, reaching dramatically for the zipper of his chino pants.

"No," cried Tandy, horrified.

In a more laborious plot Jim invited Tandy to watch him play tennis with a cousin who was deaf. For nearly an hour Jim "talked" to his cousin with his hands, translating for Tandy, who stood sympathetically nearby. Suddenly the conversation flared into an argument. Jim's fingers and those of his cousin flew like knitting needles and finally the cousin stalked off.

Jim shrugged and told Tandy he'd walk her home. "What was that all about?" she asked.

"Oh, nothing," Jim said. "He asked if he could come with us when I walked you home and I said no."

Tandy told Jim he was cruel and she burst into tears. "Oh, Jim, how could you . . ."

"Oh, for Christ's sake," said Jim to that, "he's not *really* deaf."

Tandy stopped crying and started screaming with rage. She was Jim's only girlfriend for two and a half years in Alexandria and she suffered most. Jim tested her constantly.

One Saturday they went by bus to the Corcoran Art Gallery in nearby Washington. As they rumbled across the Potomac, Jim dropped to his knees on the floor, grabbing for Tandy's feet.

"Jim!" Tandy said in a mortified hush. "What in the world are you doing? Stop it, now, stop it."

Swifly, Jim removed one of her saddle shoes and began tugging on a white sock.

"Jim, please." Tandy folded her hands in the lap of her pleated skirt, gripping until her knuckles were white. A deep blush colored her cheeks and ran back around her neck under her ponytail.

"All ah want to dooooo is kiss yore presh-ussss feet," Jim said in that "dumb," syrupy voice he put on to annoy her. It was a voice purposely developed so no one would know whether or not he was kidding. Jim raised the naked foot in his hands, give it a peck, then started his snuffing hee-hee laugh.

The bus hissed to a stop a short walk from the gallery half an hour before it opened, so Jim and Tandy went to a nearby park. They came to a large statue of a nude woman, bending from the waist.

Jim whispered in Tandy's ear, "Betcha chicken to kiss that statue's ass."

"Jim . . ."

"Go on, betcha chicken."

"No."

"Are you tellin' me you're 'fraid to approach the buttocks of a simple marble edifice?" he asked, showing off his vocabulary as usual.

"Come on now, Jim." Tandy looked nervously around her. Some tourists were taking pictures of the statue.

"Go on, Tandy, put your orbicular muscle to work. Kiss the gluteus maximus!"

Tandy lost control. *"I will not kiss that statue's whatever you call it no matter what you say!"*

Her wail was followed by silence. Tandy looked around. Everyone was staring at her. Jim was seated several yards away, looking off as if he didn't know who she was, barely able to contain himself from exploding into laughter.

"I asked him why he played games all the time," Tandy says today. "He said, 'You'd never stay interested in me if I didn't.' "

Tandy wasn't the only one subjected to Jim's tests. His teachers suffered, too—especially a naïve and conservative biology teacher well past the retirement age. Jim cheated openly in her class, and once during an exam, he leaped onto one of the lab tables, swinging his arms wildly, causing everyone to look at him.

"Mr. Morrison!" came the teacher's angry voice. "What are you doing!"

"Ahh wuz jus' chasin' a beeeee," Jim said, still standing on the table. The others in the classroom began to laugh.

"The bee has every right to be left alone, Mr. Morrison. Please return to your seat."

Jim dropped to the floor and strode to his chair triumphantly. The classroom settled into silence. Then Jim leaped over the lab table and chased the "bee" up the aisle and out of the room.

When he came to class late, Jim told elaborate stories about being held up by bandits or kidnapped by gypsies, and when he suddenly walked out of a classroom and the teacher rushed after him, he explained that he was to be operated on for a brain tumor that afternoon. Clara was stunned when the principal called the next day to inquire about the operation's outcome.

He approached pretty girls, bowed, recited ten or so lines from a sonnet or eighteenth-century novel that he'd memorized, bowed again, and strolled away. After school he accompanied friends to the golf course (although he didn't play) and walked along the two-inch railing bordering the greens, precariously balanced thirty feet above the rushing Potomac River. In the hallways at school he shouted at pals, "Hey, motherfuckerrr."

Sometimes the stunts rang with bitterness and cruelty. Coming back from Washington on the bus he once caught an older woman staring at him. "What do you think of elephants?" Jim asked her.

She looked away quickly.

"Well," said Jim, "what *do* you think of elephants?"

When the woman didn't respond, Jim bellowed, "What's the matter with elephants?"

By the time the bus reached Alexandria, the woman was whimpering and several adults were telling Jim to leave her alone.

"I was just asking about elephants," he said.

Another time when he and Tandy encountered a paraplegic in a wheelchair, Jim began to twitch and whirl and salivate in mockery.

As unpleasant as Jim sometimes was, he had no difficulty attracting companions. In fact, most of those around him in Alexandria were from the GW elite, including several prominent jocks, the editor of the school magazine (voted "most intelligent" in the class), and the student body president. They all competed for his attention—unconsciously mimicking the way he talked while adopting his favorite expressions: "That's a hot one!" and "Unnnnhhh . . . you got me, right in the gonads!"; urging him to double-date with them (he always refused); trading what came to be called, even then, "Jim Morrison stories." Jim's magnetism was becoming obvious, if not clearly definable.

"We were so goddamned straight," one of his friends and classmates recalls, "that when someone actually did these nervy things, things *we* wanted to do, we felt gratified in a sense, and we gravitated toward Morrison. He was a center for us."

Tandy Martin offers another view. "When you're in high school and you're *different* . . . like, I wanted to join a sorority because I wanted to be 'in,' but I knew it was bullshit, so I couldn't do it. I got bid to the top sorority and I went home and cried all night because I knew I'd have to say no. And I was emotionally damaged. When you think that you're right and everybody else is doing something else and you're only fifteen years old, well, what happens is: your heart breaks. And a scar forms. Everybody wants to belong when they're fifteen. Jim was asked to join AVO—*the* fraternity—and he said no."

Throughout his years at GW Jim maintained an 88.32 grade average with only minimal effort, twice being named to the honor roll. His IQ was 149. In his college boards he scored above the national average in mathematics (528, contrasted with the national 502) and much higher in the verbals (630, compared to the average 478). But statistics tell so little. The books Jim read reveal more.

He devoured Friedrich Nietzsche, the poetic German philosopher whose views on aesthetics, morality, and the Apollonian-Dionysian duality would appear again and again in Jim's conversation, poetry, songs, and life. He read Plutarch's *Lives of the Noble Greeks,* becoming enamored of Alexander the Great, admiring his intellectual and physical accomplishments, while adopting some of the look: ". . . the inclination of his head a little on one side towards his left shoulder. . . ." He read the great French Symbolist poet Arthur Rimbaud, whose style would influence the form of Jim's short prose poems. He read everything Kerouac, Ginsberg, Ferlinghetti, Kenneth Patchen, Michael McClure, Gregory Corso, and all the other beat writers published. Norman O. Brown's *Life Against Death* sat on his bookshelf next to James T. Farrell's *Studs Lonigan,* which abutted Colin Wilson's *The Outsider,* and next to it: *Ulysses* (his English teacher in senior year felt that Jim was the only one in the class who'd read it and understood it). Balzac, Cocteau, and Molière were familiars, along with most of the French existentialist philosophers. Jim seemed to understand intuitively what these challenging minds offered.

It's now twenty years later and Jim's senior-year English teacher still talks about Jim's reading habits: "Jim read as much and probably more than any student in class. But everything he read was so offbeat I had another teacher who was going to the Library of Congress check to see if the books Jim was reporting on actually existed. I suspected he was making them up, as they were English books on sixteenth- and seventeenth-century demonology. I'd never heard of them. But they existed, and I'm convinced from the paper he wrote that he read them, and the Library of Congress would've been the only source."

Jim was becoming a writer. He had begun to keep journals, spiral notebooks that he would fill with his daily observations and thoughts; lines from magazine advertisements; scraps of dialogue; ideas and paragraphs from books; and as he entered his senior year, more and more poetry. The romantic notion of poetry was taking hold: the "Rimbaud legend," the predestined tragedy, were impressed on his consciousness; the homosexuality of Ginsberg and Whitman and Rimbaud himself; the alcoholism of Baudelaire, Dylan Thomas, Brendan Behan; the madness and addiction of so many more in whom the pain married with the visions. The pages became a mirror in which Jim saw his reflection.

To be a poet entailed more than writing poems. It demanded a commitment to live, and die, with great style and even greater sadness; to wake each morning with the fever raging and know it would never be extinguished except by death, yet to be convinced that this suffering carried a unique reward. "The poet is the priest of the invisible," Wallace Stevens said. "Poets are the unacknowledged legislators of the world," wrote Shelley, "... the hierophants of an unapprehended inspiration; the mirrors of the gigantic shadows which futurity casts upon the present."

Rimbaud himself, in a letter to Paul Demeny, put it best: "A poet makes himself a visionary through a long, boundless, and systematized *disorganization* of *all the senses.* All forms of love, of suffering, of madness; he searches himself, he exhausts within himself all poisons and preserves their quintessences. Unspeakable torment, where he will need the greatest faith, a superhuman strength, where he becomes among all men the great invalid, the great accursed—and the Supreme Scientist! For he attains the *unknown!* So what if he is destroyed in his ecstatic flight through things unheard of, unnameable. . . . " The poet as a thief of fire.

Jim had once written what he described as a "ballad type poem" called "The Pony Express," but now he was firing off shorter bursts, filling notebooks that would provide much of the material or inspiration for many of the Doors' first songs. One poem that survived was "Horse Latitudes." Jim wrote it after seeing a lurid paperback cover showing horses being jettisoned from a Spanish galleon that was becalmed in the Sargasso Sea:

> When the still sea conspires an armour
> And her sullen and aborted
> Currents breed tiny monsters,
> True sailing is dead
>
> Awkward instant
> And the first animal is jettisoned,
> Legs furiously pumping
> Their stiff green gallop,
> And heads bob up
> Poise
> Delicate
> Pause

Consent
In mute nostril agony
Carefully refined
And sealed over

Many of Jim's poems, now and later, were about water
and death. Although he was a superb swimmer, his closest
friends maintained that Jim greatly feared the water.

Jim was a junior when Tandy Martin transferred from GW
to the St. Agnes School for Girls, in the same neighborhood.
Jim often saw her as she walked past his house on her way
home and many times he followed her, to share hours of revealing confidences.

"What's your earliest memory?" Tandy asked.

"I'm in a room and there are four or five grown-ups
around me and they're all saying, 'Come to me, Jimmy, come
to me . . .' I'm just learning to walk and they're all saying,
'Come to me . . .'"

"How do you know that isn't something your mother told
you?" said Tandy.

"It's far too trivial. She wouldn't tell a story like that."

"Oh well, Freud says that . . ."

Perhaps Jim did think it trivial, but in the years to come he
would tell of similar memories. Most of these were presented
as dreams, and all of them featured a number of adults who
held out their arms to Jim as a small child.

Tandy and Jim talked about what scared them and what
they shared and hoped to be. He said he wanted to be a writer,
to experience everything. Once or twice he said he wanted to
be a painter and he gave her two of his small oils. One was a
portrait of Tandy in the form of a sun; the second was a self-
portrait, showing Jim as a king.

Jim's painting, like his poetry, was nearly a secret activity.
His allowance was small, so he stole paints and brushes, and
after his paintings were finished, they disappeared as mysteri-

ously as the supplies had arrived. The erotic ones, of course, were hidden, destroyed, or given away. Copies of de Kooning nudes were painted over and the drawings of giant, snakelike penises and fellatio cartoons were slipped into his classmates' textbooks, where Jim knew they'd be seen by the teachers. As usual, Jim noted all reactions, learning what would appall, fascinate, and madden.

Jim's brother once asked him why he painted. "You can't read all the time," he told Andy. "Your eyes get tired."

Andy worshipped his older brother, even when Jim was at his meanest. He remembers two or three occasions when they walked through a field and Jim picked up a rock and said, "I'll give you to ten . . ."

Andy looked in mute terror at Jim, and then at the rock and back at Jim.

Jim said, "One . . ."

"No," Andy cried, "no, no . . ."

"Two . . ."

"Come on, Jim, please, Jim, please . . ."

By "three," Andy was running as Jim shouted, "fourfive-sixseveneightnineten," then aimed and hit him.

Jim was sixteen when he did that, seventeen when he approached Andy malevolently, dog shit held in his hand in a towel. He chased a screaming Andy all over the house. Finally he caught him and rubbed the turd in his face. It was made of rubber. Andy sobbed with relief.

"I don't know how many times I'd be watching TV and he'd come sit on my face and fart," Andy says. "Or after drinking chocolate milk or orange juice, which makes your saliva real gooey, he'd put his knees on my shoulders so I couldn't move and hang a goober over my face, just let that spit roll out of his mouth and down, down, down, until it hung just over my nose . . . and then he'd suck it back up."

When they walked through the neighborhood together and encountered someone older and bigger than Andy, Jim would say, "Hey . . . my brother wants to fight you . . . mah bruther wonts to faht chewwwwww. What-a ya gonna doooooo about it?"

At the zoo in Washington Jim dared Andy to walk the narrow ledge along the deep gorge that separated the animals from the spectators. Another time he goaded Andy into walking a similar ledge that dropped fifty feet to a freeway below.

"If I didn't do it," Andy says, "he'd call me 'pussy' because he wasn't asking me to do anything *he* wouldn't do."

Jim took many such walks, and as with the toboggan ride, he didn't fall or crash. Jim once said, "Well, you either have faith, man, or you fall."

Jim saw little of his sister and parents in Alexandria, often leaving the house in the morning without breakfast, without a word. His sister, Anne, was merely another object of his incessant teasing. His father was what he'd always been: mentally preoccupied or physically absent—visiting Cape Canaveral for the Vanguard space shots, playing golf at the Army-Navy Country Club, flying to keep his wings, and working mathematical puzzles at home rather than paying as much attention to Jim as Jim would have liked.

By now, Jim's mother was the dominant parent. Even when Steve was home, Clara handled the family finances. She was the exemplary navy wife, doing everything well, from polishing the silver to hosting bridge parties. She was what one relative called "the life of the party, the one who'd keep going at one A.M., whereas Steve would've gone to bed by nine." Jim thought his mother was an overprotective nag. She got on his nerves, always harping about the length of his hair or the state of his shirt.

Jim would wear the same shirt for weeks, until it was in very bad condition. At one point a teacher asked him if he needed financial assistance. Once Clara gave Jim five dollars to buy a new shirt and he bought one for twenty-five cents at a Salvation Army store and spent the rest on books. Finally she tried to get Tandy Martin's mother to ask Tandy to speak to Jim. Of course Tandy refused.

One afternoon Tandy was with Jim in his house when they heard his parents returning. Jim suddenly carried Tandy upstairs into his parents' bedroom and threw her onto the bed, mussing the bedcovers. Tandy protested. She got to her feet and made for the door, with Jim behind her. The timing was perfect. Tandy, her blouse pulled out of her skirt from the activity, and Jim tumbled downstairs just as the Morrisons entered the living room.

"Hi, Mom, hi, Dad." Jim grinned.

Clara worried about Jim's "queerness," feared he'd inherited some of the eccentricity that she believed characterized her brothers. She didn't know what to make of it when Jim turned on her and said, "You don't really care about my grades, you only want me to get good grades so you can brag to your bridge club." Another time he shocked everyone when he petulantly dropped his silverware onto his dinner plate and told her, "You sound like a pig when you eat."

Others wondered about Jim's odd manner as well. When he slopped around Alexandria in his Clarke desert boots, chinos, and Banlon shirts, needing a haircut, he seemed cordially distant, idiosyncratic at worst. Other times he was downright mysterious. Seldom permitted the use of the family car, he often had friends take him into downtown Washington, where he struck off on foot, giving no explanation.

Where was he going? What was he doing? Some believe he was seeing a friend he'd met at one of those odd little bookstores he frequented. Others say he was sneaking off to the sleazy bars on old Route 1, near Fort Belvoir, to listen to black blues singers. The latter seems most likely. The music he liked, and played most often in his basement room, were blues and spirituals recorded by the Library of Congress. (At that time he said he hated rock and roll.) He also liked to wander the decaying Alexandria waterfront, talking to the black men fishing from the piers. Sometimes Jim took Tandy there at night to meet these "friends."

Stranger were his moonlight visits to Tandy's house,

where Jim stood in the Martin yard, silently staring at her second-floor bedroom window. Tandy claims she always woke up, but by the time she got downstairs, Jim was gone. When she accused Jim of waking her, he said he hadn't left his bed.

Throughout his senior year his parents pressured Jim to apply to colleges, just as they had badgered him into having his photograph taken for the high school yearbook. When Jim showed no interest, the Morrisons enrolled him at St. Petersburg Junior College in Florida and decided he'd live with his grandparents in nearby Clearwater while he was attending college. Jim submitted with a shrug and then announced he had no intention of showing up at his high school graduation ceremonies. Jim's father was furious, but Jim remained unmoved. So the diploma was mailed, after Jim's name was called and no one stepped forward to pick it up.

Jim's final date with Tandy was Friday night, when they parked by the Potomac River with Tandy's friend Mary Wilson and her date. Jim had a six-pack of beer, and when they went to Mary's house later, he produced a notebook of his poetry. As Tandy read the book, Jim began clowning, bragging that he'd consumed half a bottle of his father's whiskey at the beginning of the evening.

Tandy was annoyed and showed it. "Oh Jim, why must you wear a mask? Do you have to wear it all the time?"

Jim suddenly burst into tears and fell onto Tandy's lap, sobbing hysterically.

"Don't you know," he said finally, "I did it all for you?"

Tandy remembered the Wilsons, asleep upstairs, and she suggested to Jim that he go home.

"Oh," he said, "you're afraid I'll wake the Wilsons, I'm making you nervous, right? You wouldn't know what to do if they found me crying, would you?"

Tandy choked and said, "No."

Jim moved to the door, said good night, and stepped outside, closing the door behind him. Tandy sighed. Then the door flew open and Jim announced loudly, "I've changed my mind!" Then he confessed, "I love you!" Tandy sniffed haughtily, "Sure you do."

"Oh, you're so smug," Jim said, taunting her, using the word that always set Tandy off. She bristled. Jim grabbed her arm and twisted it behind her back painfully. She choked back a cry and listened in horror as Jim told her he thought what he ought to do was to take a sharp knife and cut her face, leaving a nasty scar, "so no one else will look at you but me."

Tandy never related this incident to her mother, but Mrs. Martin was not blind to Jim's changing personality. Nor was Tandy herself. She had thought him innocent and happy when she'd met him in the middle of their sophomore year. Now, just two and a half years later, he seemed bitter, cynical, obsessive, perverse, and she didn't understand the reasons for the change. His tongue was more vicious too, and the knife threat apparently was only one of several even more frightening incidents that happened in quick succession. Mrs. Martin told Tandy he seemed "unclean, like a leper," and urged her not to spend any time with him. An alarmed appraisal, perhaps, but it caused Tandy and her mother to recall an incident of two years earlier, when Jim was new to Alexandria.

He had a problem he couldn't discuss with his parents, Jim said, and Tandy (wishing he would discuss it with her) suggested he talk with the young assistant minister at the Westminster Presbyterian Church who was the head of her youth fellowship and was "cool" with kids. Jim agreed and an appointment was made.

"I don't think I'll go after all," Jim said the day Tandy's mother picked him up at GW.

"Oh yes you will," Tandy said, standing nearby with one of her girlfriends. Together they pushed him into the back seat of the car.

What Jim's problem was and what he told the young pastor are unknown. Apparently Jim never confided in anyone else and the assistant minister recalls nothing of the visit. Now, as Jim's graduation approached, Tandy wondered if the problem of two years earlier was relevant to the "personality change" she and her mother had been witnessing.

The next night Jim called to apologize for the knife incident and asked to see Tandy again. She wanted to see Jim, but months earlier she'd promised someone else she'd go to a formal dance and she didn't think it fair to break the date so late.

"But I'm moving to Florida," he said. "Tomorrow I'm gonna be gone for good."

Tandy was stunned. It was the first she'd heard of the move. Angry and hurt, she said it was too bad he hadn't told her earlier, and just before starting to cry, she hung up the telephone.

Jim ran to her house in a fury, stood under one of the big leafy trees in the Martin yard, and screamed, *"At last I'll be free of you! I'll be free! I'm leaving and I'll never write you . . . I won't even think of you!"*

Jim then demanded that Tandy return the journals she'd borrowed. *Immediately.* Tandy appeared, her mouth and eyes slits as she gave him the notebooks of poetry.

Sunday night Tandy woke up late and knew he was standing in the back garden. She went downstairs and heard the familiar steps fading away. She went to a window and watched the dark figure get into the Morrison car.

The car moved into the night toward Florida.

CHAPTER

2

J im stood on the hot Florida curb, peeling off his black suit coat, ripping open the tab collar of his clean white shirt, tearing away the red stripe tie: the uniform of St. Petersburg JC. The "upcounty bus" that took him home threw open its doors.

Jim slumped into a seat about midway back and began whistling, then produced two or three long low belches, a noisy, self-conscious prelude to one of the rambling, sorry jokes and tall tales that he liked to tell.

"I had this friend who wanted to buy a duck-hunting dog," Jim announced, "so he went to an old-timer and asked how he could be sure he got a good one. The old-timer told my friend to look at the dog's asshole, because you need a dog with a tight asshole so when he jumps into the water all the water won't run in and make him sink. So my friend goes to the local kennel, where he's shown a number of dogs and told the price is seventy-five dollars apiece. My friend tells the kennel owner he'd like to examine the dogs closely . . ."

When Jim began the story it seemed he was talking to

himself. But soon everyone near him was straining to hear.

"... and he goes over to a big friendly looking dog and lifts up his tail. 'Uh-oh,' my friend says, 'big asshole,' and he moves to another dog. The kennel owner comes over at that, pointing to the first dog. 'What the fuck are you doing to my dog?' he says. 'Well,' says my friend, 'I just been looking at the dog's asshole and it's pretty big, see, so when he jumps in the water after the duck, the water will run in and he'll sink.' The kennel owner takes a look and says, 'Yeah, the asshole *is* big, isn't it?' And he reaches out, grabs the ol' dog's balls and gives 'em about a half turn and that ol' asshole cinches up tight. 'Sorry,' the kennel owner says to my friend, 'I had that dog adjusted for quail.' "

Jim went into his long hee-hee-hee laugh and started another story, ignoring the groans and stony silences. Soon the other students on the bus were listening intently again.

The school bus dropped Jim three blocks from where he lived. It was a short walk but long enough to devise some means of hassling his "Grandmommy" Caroline and "Grandpa" Paul. Both the elder Morrisons were teetotalers, and although Paul had a weakness for the dog races, the prevailing attitudes in the comfortable home in the older section of town were fundamentalist. Jim mocked them.

He ignored their pleas to get a haircut, to shave, to change his clothes, to go to church. He threatened to bring a "nigger girl" home and he left empty wine bottles in his room. Sometimes he said nothing for days; he came into and left their daily schedule like black smoke.

"He hated conformity, he'd always get some queer slant on things," his grandmother recalls. "He'd try to shock us. He loved to do that. He'd tell us things that he knew would make us feel queer. We just didn't understand him, any of us. There were so many sides to Jimmy. You'd see one, then get a glimpse of another. You never knew what he was thinking."

Jim walked through his academic year at JC anonymously, ignoring all extracurricular activities. His first-semester grades were unspectacular: one A, two B's, one C, and a D.

More interesting were the findings of the personality tests given all new students. On these, Jim was adjudged impulsive, happy-go-lucky, and excitement-loving, as opposed to disciplined and self-controlled ... but paradoxically he was also judged to be shy *and* interested in overt activity as well as thinking ... extremely hypercritical of social institutions ... given to self-pity ... and surprisingly macho considering his leanings toward literature and his strength in composition and communication as shown in his records from Alexandria.

Jim was capable of stunts of intellectual virtuosity. When friends visited his room he challenged them, "Go ahead, pick a book, any book." His voice was boastful, but he toed the carpet of his bedroom: the shy magician. "Pick any book, open it to the beginning of any chapter, and start reading. I'll keep my eyes closed and I'll tell you what book you're reading and who the author is."

Jim swept one arm around the room at the hundreds and hundreds of books on top of the furniture and stacked everywhere against the walls.

He never missed!

More generous but no less memorable was the time he helped a friend with her term paper, instantly and expertly analyzing a sizable bulk of poetry. For another friend he wrote a thirty-page essay on Lord Essex, one of Queen Elizabeth's paramours, and provided a lengthy bibliography, all off the top of his head.

"I had to write and give a speech on 'Moral Integrity: Imperative for Our Survival,' " says Jim's brother Andy. "I didn't even know what the fuck that meant. My parents wouldn't let me leave the house for Easter vacation until I finished it, and Jim wanted me to go out with him. I worked on it a couple of days and Jim finally took it and rewrote it for me, throwing in a lot of his own stuff at the end. The speech was pretty good, and it ended: 'We are drifting in blind orbits, helpless, alone.' There were three or four sentences in a row like that, and although it wasn't quite my style, I got an A on the speech."

Jim fell in with a small band of graduates of Clearwater High School, with whom he drank. He got drunk at dances and stood in the corner, pretending to be a tree; he got drunk at parties and once cut himself badly, but was so belligerent and insulting that the doctor at a local hospital refused to treat him.

Jim wasn't yet into heavy, steady drinking. As one classmate observed, "It was as if he drank *only* to get drunk; otherwise he didn't drink at all." For Jim, getting intoxicated was a special occasion. But already it was an apparent form of relief.

One significant occasion came on his eighteenth birthday in December, when he registered for the draft. Jim hated the military with a desperate fury, fearing its awesome grip of authority. In 1961 there was no popular antiwar movement. Jim never heard the words "conscientious objector." So he registered and then he went out and got roaring drunk. Members of the family say an uncle who lived in Clearwater extricated him from a sticky situation that night that could have resulted in an injurious scandal. It was so embarrassing to them, apparently, they still won't reveal what it was.

About the same time Jim found a refuge: an old hotel in the palmetto wilderness between Clearwater and St. Petersburg, the Renaissance Gallery and Coffeehouse, a rabbit warren of studios, stages, and patios that was on the junior college's unofficial "off limits" list. That's probably what attracted Jim, but it was the poetry readings, folksinging contests, and prevailing bohemianism that held him.

The Renaissance was run by a garrulous, middle-thirtyish homosexual named Allen Rhodes. Half an hour after meeting him, Jim was given the verbal equivalent of an epic novel, a thicket of information that included stories of ancestors who'd done the engineering of St. Petersburg in the nineteenth century, wildly exaggerated adventures of sexual conquest during the blackouts of wartime London, tales of Rhodes's days with Red Shawn's All-Male Dance Troupe, the family origin and sexual proclivity of every cat prowling the gallery labyrinth, knowing references to the Garden of Eden nudist camp north of Tampa—every declaration introduced with the expression, "You won't believe this, you'll drop dead."

Allen remembers telling Jim how Jim had "it," just like Elvis. And he recalls saying that when he was in London during the war and went cruising for whatever he might attract on the streets, he never wore any underpants.

"Show your meat is what I told everybody. I never knew it to fail."

Jim visited his family, now living in a suburb of San Diego, at the end of the school year. When he returned to Clearwater in July, he finally met someone to take over Tandy Martin's role as girlfriend and confidante.

Mary Frances Werbelow was almost sixteen, just over five feet tall, had long brown hair, and was a runner-up in that summer's Sun N Fun Beauty Contest. She had just finished her junior year at Clearwater High when Jim met her at a party.

"Hey, hey, ever'body, look-a there!" a voice warned.

Jim was balanced on one foot on the balcony railing of an apartment building, teetering twenty feet above the ground.

"Hey, y'all been drinkin', boy?"

Laughter.

Jim placed his right foot down on the railing and lifted his left, slipped, and began beating his arms. He was falling. The boy and girl standing closest to him grabbed him and pulled him back into the party.

"You should'na done that," Jim said to the girl. "S'long it's you, it's okay though." He gave her an irresistible boyish smile.

Mary was a Catholic and had once considered becoming a nun. She was quiet, like Jim, and it gave her an air of maturity. She told Jim she taught part time at the local Fred Astaire

Dance Studio, said she wanted to be a dancer in movies some-day. She warmed immediately to Jim when he said he wanted to write and direct movies.

"Do you write poetry?" Jim asked.

"Sometimes. But I don't ever show it to anybody."

"I've got some poems . . ."

"You do?"

In the final week of summer vacation Jim became an influence in Mary Frances's life. At his urging, she began wearing sunglasses, in defiance of local convention. She tried alcohol for the first time. Then she told her parents that she was going to visit Jim for weekends when he started classes at Florida State University in Tallahassee in September.

Every night Jim stood in his underwear in the middle of the small bedroom and stretched, reaching for the ceiling on his toes. He told his roommate he did it to make himself taller, and he appeared to believe it worked. Jim weighed 132 pounds and was five feet eight and three-quarter inches tall when he left Alexandria, and he said he'd grown more than an inch since.

He was sharing a modern three-bedroom house a mile from the FSU campus with five other students. He had known only two of them previously; the others were housemates of convenience. As was his custom, he began "testing" his roomies immediately. He had become obsessed about Elvis Presley and insisted upon silence whenever Presley's records were played on the radio, turning the volume up full, and sitting in front of the radio mesmerized. When his grandparents sent him an electric blanket, he refused to pay his share of the heating bill. On Halloween Jim embarrassed everyone by greeting the young trick-or-treaters dressed only in a large cape, which he threw open once they came inside the house for the candy he offered them.

Jim also caused trouble on the buses that he and his

housemates took to class. Once he gave the driver a twenty-dollar bill and argued belligerently when the driver told him he had no change. Another time he walked to the rear of the bus and noisily insisted that all the blacks move to the front. Then one day he sat behind the driver next to a ten-year-old girl and smiled at her.

"Hello," he said.

The girl sat stiffly in her seat, darting her eyes nervously at Jim.

"Yew shore are purty," Jim said, dropping into his yokel voice.

The girl was embarrassed.

"Yew shore got purty legs," Jim said.

The bus driver looked into his rear-view mirror to see Jim leaning toward the girl and putting his hand on her knee.

The bus jerked to a halt at the curb and the driver spun around. "Out, young man. Get out!"

"Oh, please, kind sir," Jim whined. "It was a compliment offered in innocence. She reminds me of my younger sister at home. I was homesick for a moment, sir."

Finally the driver relented, telling Jim he could remain on the bus if he kept his hands to himself.

All his roommates were on the bus and all pretended not to know him. But he was the first to alight once the bus reached the campus and he turned and called, "Hey, roomies!" and waved.

Automatically they all waved back. Then Jim called, "Fuck you!" and bowed and laughed and strutted away.

He borrowed a Thunderbird belonging to one of his housemates and backed it into a telephone pole. He drank their beers, ate their food, and wore their clothes without asking. He kept careful records of all his actions, and their reactions, writing in his journals as if he were an anthropologist and his housemates were his subjects.

In less than three months' time Jim had the household

frantic. Everyone was living in a constant state of anxiety over what was going to happen next. It all blew up one night in December, near the end of the trimester, when Jim was playing Elvis too loud. They told him he was going to have to straighten up or move out. Jim straightened his back. He said it was their problem, he wasn't doing anything they shouldn't be able to put up with, they weren't putting out any effort, and why should they ask him to change when he wasn't asking them to change? They ended up asking him to move out. Jim said okay and peacefully moved his stuff that night, and the next day he was gone.

He moved into a half-trailer behind a girls' boarding-house three blocks from the campus. For this he paid $50 a month, half the sum his grandparents sent him. His parents sent him money, too, whenever he wrote them a letter.

"He had to write a letter every month to get a check," says his brother Andy. "He wouldn't write about dates or anything. He'd tell a story. About how he was at a movie theater when a fire broke out and everybody panicked and stormed the doors, and he was the only one who remained calm. He got up on the stage, sat at the piano and sang a song, and calmed the audience so that they exited from the theater safely. Another letter was filled with details about how he watched a guy drown in a swamp."

Jim took two influential courses the second trimester. One examined the philosophies of protest, considering those thinkers who were critical or skeptical of and in revolt against philosophic tradition: Montaigne, Rousseau, Hume, Sartre, Heidegger, and Jim's favorite, Nietzsche. The second course was on collective behavior, the psychology of crowds.

Professor James Geschwender was a short, rotund man with dark hair and Jim was one of his best students. "He could draw the professor into amazing discussions," says Bryan Gates, a fellow classmate, "and the rest of us would sit there dumbfounded. Jim seemed to know so much about human nature. He effortlessly coasted through the class. I slogged through the books, but you'd have thought Jim wrote them. The professor deferred to him in class, and told us that Jim's final thesis was the best he had ever seen from a student with Jim's limited educational preparation. In fact, he said it would do any doctoral candidate justice."

While still in high school Jim had read Norman O. Brown's Freudian interpretation of history, *Life Against Death,* and its thesis that mankind must be viewed as largely unaware of its own desires, hostile to life, and unconsciously bent on self-destruction greatly appealed to him. Repression had not only caused individual neurosis, Brown wrote, but social pathology as well. Jim concluded that crowds could have sexual neuroses much like those of individuals, and that these derangements could be quickly and effectively diagnosed and then "treated."

The teacher was enthralled! "The final classes were given over to a discussion of the thesis," says Bryan, "with Geschwender and Jim doing all the talking. They left the rest of us behind. We didn't know what they were talking about."

Eager to test his theory, Jim urged three of his acquaintances to join him in disrupting a campus speaker.

"I can look at a crowd," he said to his friends. "I can just look at it. It's all, uh, very scientific, and I can diagnose the crowd psychologically. Just four of us, properly positioned, can turn the crowd around. We can *cure* it. We can *make love to it.* We can make it *riot.*"

Jim's friends looked at him blankly.

"Hey, man," Jim said, "don't you even want to try?"

His friends went away.

On weekends Jim often hitchhiked the two hundred miles back to Clearwater to see Mary. He remained entranced by her innocence, in awe of her psychological and physical virginity. She sang and danced. She liked to walk barefoot in the rain.

Other than Mary, Jim's only close friend during the second trimester was Bryan Gates, who looked a little like a young Basil Rathbone and, like Jim, had a father who'd spent at least half his life in the military. When Jim harassed Bryan for studying for a career in commerce, Bryan would agree that he was superficial and crass. His good-natured refusal to let Jim get to him cemented their relationship. It was not surprising when Jim asked Bryan if he'd like to accompany him on a hitchhiking journey across the United States when the trimester ended and Bryan graduated in April.

Jim had already established quite a reputation as a hitchhiker. Several times during his travels between Tallahassee and Clearwater he had refused a ride—once after standing for an hour in the rain—merely because the driver looked "uninteresting." Bryan thought it over and said he was agreeable.

Jim and Bryan partied for two weeks in Clearwater, during which time Jim made plans for Mary to join him in California after she graduated from high school in June. Once together in Los Angeles, they planned to get an apartment and jobs and enroll at the University of California. Then, he told Mary, he would realize his lifelong dream of enrolling in the school of cinematography so he could learn to translate his ideas and fantasies into film. Then Jim and Bryan headed west, spending six days on the road that would have made Jack Kerouac proud.

They were rousted by the police in Mobile, Alabama, at 4 A.M., and in New Orleans the following day Jim went roaring into what he called "the fringes" to converse with what he thought was a hermaphroditic bartender, then tried to pick up a lesbian, whose lover pulled a knife and threatened to carve him up. In east Texas they were given a ride by a cousin of Vice President Lyndon Johnson and taken to LBJ's birthplace and then to the LBJ Ranch, where they were fed barbecued beef and introduced to Johnson's aunt. They entered Mexico at Juarez at midnight and Jim talked all night in his high school Spanish with a Mexican prostitute in a boozy native cantina. In Phoenix they were picked up at 6 A.M. by a girl who immediately told them, "I might as well level with you, I need a man and I need one bad," causing Bryan to grab the wheel, forcing the car to the curb.

"Come on, man, let's take her up on it," said Jim.

"At six in the morning she wants to take us to her apartment? No way. You go ahead, I'm gettin' out of here."

Reluctantly, Jim followed his friend.

When they arrived in Coronado the following afternoon, their reception was grim. First, Jim's mother told him he couldn't enter the house until he got a haircut. She also told him she was appalled by his hitchhiking after she'd sent him the plane fare. Later she vociferously disapproved of his regular trips into San Diego where he and Bryan were exploring the poker parlors and rough navy bars. But what really stunned her was Jim's announcement that he was going to Los Angeles to enroll at UCLA.

"Just wait until your father comes home," she said, "you just wait. He'll be home in less than a month and . . ."

But then Jim was gone.

For three weeks Jim and Bryan looked for jobs and partied with Bryan's cousins in East Los Angeles, living in a small house trailer. But there were no jobs and eventually there was no more money for partying; the adventure and fantasy crumbled. Then Jim's mother called to say his father was landing in a few days in Long Beach. "I expect you to be at the docks," she told him.

Jim hung up without promising, but he was there. He told his parents he wanted to remain in Los Angeles but they forbade it. Jim presented a dozen alternatives. All were rejected, and two weeks later he was escorted to a plane bound for Florida, in time to register for an abbreviated summer term.

Jim determinedly moved back into his book-littered trailer on College Avenue and on June 18 signed up for the least number of courses he could get away with. It was an uneventful summer except for a course in medieval European history.

Jim told his professor he wanted to write one long research paper, not the two little assigned essays, and he wanted to choose his own subject.

"It was quite unprecedented, but I was intrigued, so I agreed," the teacher recalls.

Jim wrote about Hieronymus Bosch, the Dutch painter who viewed the world as a hell in which we pass through the devil's digestive system, and about whom almost nothing is known for sure. Jim's theory was that the artist was a member of the Adamite Sect, a group of medieval heretics.

"I was unconvinced," the professor says, "but excited by what Jim wrote."

Jim finished classes on August 27, completed his last exam three days later, and then hitchhiked once more to Clearwater for a round of beach parties, dances, and drunks. On September 5 he was back in Tallahassee, registering for a late Renaissance art history class, which included a further study of Bosch, and several courses in the Speech Department: introduction to the theater, theater history, the essentials of acting, and the principles of scene design.

Jim's plan was to lay a foundation for the classes in cinematography he was determined to take at UCLA beginning in January. To that end, a few days after registering at FSU, Jim officially applied for the transfer, writing his old high school in Virginia to have his grades sent to the UCLA registrar.

For this, his fourth and final trimester at FSU, Jim moved into Room 206 of the Cherokee Hotel, a seedy downtown hostelry many of whose guests in years past had been state legislators visiting the resident prostitutes. "The Cherokee wasn't a whorehouse at the time," says Bryan Gates, "but the reputation lingered on, and for Jim, it was home. He felt genuinely comfortable there."

Jim began to run with a small crowd of older students and with some of the instructors and professors, most of them hard-drinking party types in the art department. Within a few weeks he moved out of the Cherokee and into a four-plex with two of them. Now the emphasis was on good times.

Once Jim got juiced on wine, and while engaging in mock battle with umbrellas en route to a Saturday football game, he stole a cop's helmet from a patrol car. He was arrested and handcuffed, and in the confusion that followed an attempted escape, the helmet disappeared and Jim was charged with petty larceny as well as disturbing the peace, resisting arrest, and public drunkenness.

The next day Jim appeared at the home of Ralph Turner, the history professor for whom he'd written the paper on Bosch. He said he'd spent the night in the drunk tank and was afraid he'd have to move back on campus when the university heard about it. The professor, who hosted many parties, quickly agreed to help.

Monday Turner accompanied Jim to a barber shop, helped him borrow a suit, went to court with him, and later called the dean of men in his behalf. Jim was fined fifty dollars (a sum he had but was unwilling to part with, so he asked his mother to send it to him, not telling her why) and placed on university probation.

The intercession of Ralph Turner and Jim's consistently high grades, as well as the respect of several other professors, were what kept him from harsher campus restrictions. He continued to dazzle his classmates and teachers.

For his class in theater history, Jim wrote a tongue-in-cheek paper interpreting *Waiting for Godot* as a Civil War story because there was a Grant and a Lee and a Slave in the cast. His scenic design professor remembers that one of Jim's proposed sets featured a nude male suspended over the stage as if crucified. Another, for *Cat on a Hot Tin Roof,* called for a tiny spot of light on the rear wall at the start of the play that would grow until it covered the set and was revealed at the end to be a slide of a cancer cell (the play's main character dies of cancer).

Then, with no experience whatever, Jim got one of the two roles in a university production of Harold Pinter's absurdist play *The Dumbwaiter.* In the playbill Jim assumed the stage name Stanislas Boleslawski, created from the names of the great Russian actor and producer Stanislavski, father of the Method, and the stylish Polish director Richard Boleslawski, who had been with Stanislavski's Moscow Art Theatre before emigrating to the United States to make films.

Jim's director, Sam Kilman, introduced him to the writing of Antonin Artaud, who wrote his cry for revolution in the theater from insane asylums during the 1930s and 1940s: "We must recognize that the theater, like the plague, is a delirium and is communicative; that is the secret of its fascination." Jim loved it.

"Jim was interesting to work with," says Keith Carlson, the actor who played opposite him in *The Dumbwaiter*. "Every night waiting for the curtain to go up, I had no idea what he was going to do. He was difficult to key on, because he tended to play the role very differently all the time. He wasn't keying on me, or on dialogue, or on any of the traditional things. He played scenes and delivered lines with an inflection that seemed totally unmotivated, or at least unexpected. There was a constant undercurrent of apprehension, a feeling that things were on the brink of lost control.

"Back in those days [in 1963], everyone was uptight about any obscenity on stage but we had some wonderfully obscene rehearsals. There was no obscenity during any of the performances, but with Jim, we just never knew."

"Your father's a captain now, Jim," his mother said, "the captain of one of the biggest carriers in the world [the *Bon Homme Richard*]. There are three thousand men on that ship and your father has their respect, and he has that respect because he is a fine disciplinarian. How would it look if his son, his very own son, showed up looking like a beatnik?"

On January 8, 1964, shortly before leaving his family in Coronado to begin classes at UCLA, Jim joined his father on maneuvers in the Pacific—his hair freshly cut. Unfortunately, it wasn't cut short enough to please, and when Jim arrived at the "Bonny Dick," as the carrier was called, he was rushed to the

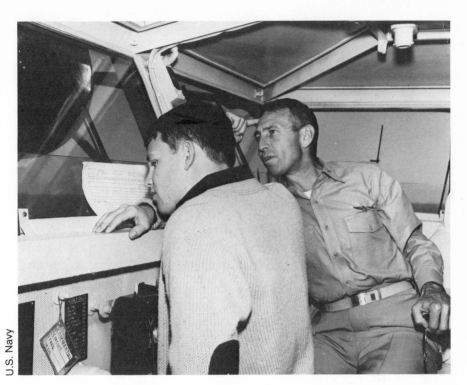

U.S. Navy

Jim and his father (then a captain) on the bridge of the USS Bon
Homme Richard, *January 1964*

ship's barber for another trim, this one exactly like the captain's own: clipper short on the back and sides, just long enough on top to part. Jim was angry, but silent.

The captain was proud but wary. He took Jim to the bridge and introduced him to the officers. Jim shook hands and acknowledged the introductions graciously, without smiling. An official navy photographer took some pictures. Later in the day some humanlike targets were tossed overboard and Jim was given a machine gun and offered the opportunity to shoot at the objects bobbing in the ocean below.

When Jim told the story of this afternoon, he did so with bitterness. He said that when his father returned home from commanding three thousand men with such authority, he felt that at home his mother was in command.

"She told him to take the garbage out," Jim said. "She hollered at him. And my father did it. He took the garbage out."

A week later, with money enough for a small apartment about half a mile from the university, Jim went through the midyear registration process, joining twenty thousand other students on one of California's biggest campuses. Unlike her older sister university in Berkeley, UCLA was virtually apolitical. The students were tanned, athletic, and pleasing to look at, and their attire was casual, classless.

By 1964, when Jim arrived, the film school was entering what the professors now call the Golden Age. The faculty included some of the top directors—Stanley Kramer, Jean Renoir, and Josef von Sternberg among them. The students counted among themselves a score of brilliant and volatile personalities, including the young Francis Ford Coppola. Perhaps most important, the division had an exhilarating, near-anarchic philosophy, which may have inspired Jim to write later, "The good thing about film is that there aren't any experts. There's no authority on film. Any one person can assimilate and contain the whole history of film in himself, which you can't do in other arts. There are no experts, so, theoretically, any student knows almost as much as any professor."

Jim's first six months at UCLA were unremarkable except for his Easter vacation, when he and two of his cinematography classmates—a somber, bearded New York intellectual and an older Irish girl—spent three drunken days in Tijuana.

During the remainder of the spring semester Jim stuck to his leisurely routine—classes in scattered buildings on the huge tree-lined campus; long hours of reading alone in the university libraries or in his tiny apartment; and on Sundays calls to Mary in Florida, using a public telephone, paying only for the first three minutes but usually talking for an hour or more, neglecting to signal when through.

Afternoons and evenings Jim sometimes went to the Lucky U, a Mexican restaurant and bar about a mile from campus, not far from the Veterans Hospital. He enjoyed the place. There were lady bartenders and blind men pushing legless friends in wheelchairs, the legless calling directions. Sometimes the cripples got drunk and fought, battling it out with crutches. It reminded Jim of a Nelson Algren story; he called it a "neat place" to drink.

Weekends Jim went to the Venice beach. Venice had been a mecca for the beat generation in the 1950s and the bohemian tradition clung to it. Poets, painters, and students lived cheaply in big rooms in once-elegant Victorian homes or in cabins beside the crumbling canals.

When summer came, Jim returned to Coronado. He was thin after four months of poor or missed meals, but he soon regained his characteristic chubbiness. Then he was off to Mexico again, this time with his brother and his godfather, a retired navy officer who had served with Steve in the Pacific. Andy remembers it as a drunken trip. "We drove about one hundred miles south to Ensenada. Jim showed me life. I was drinking beers and he was carrying me from bar to bar, arguing with the Mexicans in Spanish when they tried to short-change us, talking to the whores, racing through alleys being chased by dogs. It was great."

Back in the San Diego area, Jim and Andy often went to movie theaters on the post and sometimes Jim would sneak in wine and get drunk. On military bases a film of the flag is routinely shown after the feature and the national anthem is played. Once Jim filled the theater with his voice: "Ohhhhh sayyyyy cannnnn youuuuu seeeeee . . ." He was the only one singing.

Jim didn't have much to do in Coronado and he grew bored and restless. Soon he began to plead to be allowed to return to school early so he could make up his incomplete in history. In early August he left, promising to look for a part-time job. By the end of summer Jim was a student assistant in

the Theater Arts Library, returning books to shelves and posting overdue notices for $1.25 an hour. It was a simple job, but
he failed to keep it. A new librarian arrived and fired Jim in
October, when it became apparent he wasn't interested in reporting to work on time.

Then Mary appeared. She quickly found a job at the
UCLA Medical Center and, much to Jim's dismay, took an
apartment of her own. She said she was going to find an agent
and look for dancing jobs—maybe someday they could make a
film together. Friends say Jim was as pleased as they ever saw
him that fall at UCLA. Even if things weren't precisely as he
had planned them, he and his beloved Mary were together in
California at last.

Jim began to collect a small circle of friends from among
the most enigmatic and explosive students at the film school.
The four who were closest to him were, individually taken,
rather naïve or innocent, but together they came across as sinister, or at the very least, slightly bent.

The oddest was Dennis Jakob, a timid yet often belligerent graduate student of massive intelligence who was privately
called "the Rat" or "the Weasel" because of his scuttling walk
and a back bent from so many hours hunched over an editing
machine. Dennis was a man possessed, the virtual reincarna-
tion of the Soviet director Sergei Eisenstein. Eventually he
would serve as a special assistant to Francis Coppola on *Apocalypse Now.*

One of the reasons Jim was attracted to Dennis was he
had read as many, or more, books than Jim had. It was Nietzsche's works that they discussed most often. By the time they
met, Jim had read most of the German philosopher's writings.
The Genealogy of Morals and *Beyond Good and Evil* he had read
while still in high school. More recently he'd discovered *The
Birth of Tragedy from the Spirit of Music,* a slender volume that
would join Norman O. Brown's *Life Against Death* as a deep influence. The book, Nietzsche's first, is still truly revolutionary
and one of the most relevant statements ever made on trage-

dy. It is concerned with the classic conflict between the Apollonian art of sculpture and the Dionysian art of music. Like Nietzsche, Jim identified with the long-suffering Dionysus who was "without any images, himself pure primordial pain and its primordial re-echoing." But for the suffering there was ample reward. The resolution was not in transcendence of one's individual consciousness, but rather in an ecstatic dissolution of personal consciousness in "the primal nature of the universe"—what Jim, and others, came to call the Universal Mind.

Dennis and Jim would sit discussing Nietzsche for hours, arguing occasionally but generally agreeing ardently, reading long passages from the philosopher's works aloud to each other. One day, talking about Dionysus, and remembering the line from William Blake, "If the doors of perception were cleansed, everything would appear to man as it truly is, infinite," which gave Aldous Huxley the title for his book, *The Doors of Perception,* Jim and Dennis decided to form a band. They told a friend they were going to call themselves The Doors: Open and Closed.

The second student in Jim's group was John DeBella, the vain and lusty son of a Brooklyn policeman who was as proud of the two hundred books he read each year as he was of his well-muscled six-foot-two-inch body. During the week campus legend credited him with visiting bookstores in a long black raincoat with dozens of pockets sewn inside for stealing the books he coveted. Weekends he went to Muscle Beach to look for girls.

John's physical stature and exaggerated but genuine worldliness made him seem the antithesis of Dennis Jakob, but there were similarities. One, of course, was his love of books and doctrinaire philosophies. Another was his age; like Dennis, he was older than Jim, twenty-five. A third was his verbal facility. And both were Catholics. When Dennis or John began to weave an intellectual tapestry, Jim sat fascinated.

"Shamanism," John says. "We were into the shaman: the poet inspired.

"We were all into that. Part of the vague philosophy of the UCLA film students was you blur the distinction between dreams and reality. One of my favorite lines was 'Dreams beget reality.' Phil Oleno was heavy into Jungian psychology and we were picking up a lot of lore from him.

"We had a theory of the True Rumor, that life wasn't as exciting and romantic as it should be, so you tell things that are false because it is better that images be created. It doesn't matter that they aren't true, so long as they are believed."

When they were bored, Jim and John devised amusements. Once Jim and Phil Oleno, a close friend of both, allegedly challenged John to a book-stealing competition at the university bookstore: the one who escaped with the highest retail value in one hour was the winner.

Another time Jim and John decided they'd pick up a stranger, get stoned, and go to the music library where they'd take turns playing their favorite records. Laughing, they talked a girl into it, played the records, started smoking grass, and soon John was making a play for her. She must have thought Jim offered more promise and she went home with him, telling him how her boyfriend had gotten her pregnant, and then she'd contracted a venereal disease, which was followed by a uterine operation that had made her sterile and . . . The details of her life came pouring out, accompanied by choking tears. Jim was reminded of the Dylan Thomas story "The Followers" in which two young boys casually meet and find they both have horror in their lives.

Another time Jim and John got drunk at the Lucky U and Jim insisted on visiting the public library not far away. John reluctantly walked over with him and followed him into the stacks at a leisurely pace, checking out the skirt lengths and pantyhose in the reading room. When he caught up with Jim, he was urinating on the floor between two shelves of books. John grabbed him and began to move him out. A woman approached. "Hey, lady," Jim called, "hey, lady . . ."

With his dark wavy hair, broad pleasant face, and thick

chest, Phil Oleno, the third friend, looked a little like a slightly larger version of Jim. He was twenty-three, two years older than Jim, and was the only one in the circle who lived at home, a circumstance that earned him Jim's and John's periodic harassment.

Phil had read nearly everything written by or about Carl Jung; on a shelf in his room at home were all the books, heavily underlined with a thick black pencil. Jung was not Jim's favorite psychoanalyst, and he and Phil loved to argue after seeing movies how the filmmaker's symbolism might be interpreted along Jungian or, in Jim's case, Ferenczian, lines.

Like Jung, Sandor Ferenczi was an associate of Freud's who cut himself loose, becoming a Freudian deviant in method more than theory. While Freud recommended sexual abstinence for his patients, arguing that this would concentrate the libido on past emotional experiences, Ferenczi took the denial much further, trying to persuade his patients to give up much of their eating, drinking, defecation, and urination as well. Then he swung the opposite way, toward love and permissiveness, believing that neurotics were people who had never been loved or accepted by their parents and what they really needed was affection, warmth, and coddling.

As is generally true when talking about psychoanalysis, the conversations were filled with sexual references, often ranging over a wide assortment of neuroses, fetishes, and abnormalities—from hermaphroditism and necrophilia to masochism, sadism, and homosexuality. So when Jim and Phil made a film together, the subject was not surprising.

They had talked of making several films. One, Phil's idea, was to capture something of the life of Rimbaud and he asked Jim if he'd like to play the leading role. Another, Jim's suggestion, was to show the famous scene from Nietzsche's life where he comes upon a man beating a horse and forcefully stops the beating. The soundtrack for this short film, Jim said, would be applause. Neither of these films was made. The one they did make had no intellectual pretensions, but was a joke.

Jim and Phil were taking only beginning courses in camera, lighting, sound, and editing, but even neophytes at the
film school were expected to use whatever education and
imagination they had to produce a film. It didn't have to be
long, or complicated, or even good; the object was to get the
student familiar with the *tools*. Actually, Phil didn't make a film,
but satisfied the requirement by hiring himself out to some
graduate students in the psychology department who were
making a film under top-secret conditions that was to be kept
thereafter in the department's safe. It was of a man and a
woman, both nude, simulating the positions and actions of
lovemaking. With Phil's assistance, Jim obtained outtakes,
spliced them together in climactic sequence, and used the end
of Ravel's "Bolero" for a soundtrack. At the screening the students were hilariously amused and most of the instructors and
professors were incensed. Jim was told he deserved the worst
grade possible, and he was marked down as a troublemaker, a
designation that would cause him to be assigned to a special
workshop class of "problem students" the following semester.

The student screenings were held twice a year, at the end
of each semester's workshop sessions. Other screenings were
held more regularly, usually on Friday nights. Invited profes-
sionals from the nearby film factories would show one of their
films and then open themselves—or so they thought—to a
friendly question-and-answer session. The program was canceled when the students persisted in harassing the lecturers.

The ringleader at those screenings—the student generally
thought to be the blackest, noisiest, and most cynical—was another of Jim's closest friends, the fourth arch-kook of the
Golden Age, a loquacious, blond Mephistopheles named Felix
Venable. Felix's love of booze and pills and all-night storytelling sessions reminded Jim of the hero of *On the Road,* Dean
Moriarty. Felix was, at thirty-four, the oldest student in the
film school. He had come to UCLA after thirteen years of odd
jobs, including one long period as a bus driver and another as

a boat builder. Most of his jobs had been in the San Francisco area, where he'd attended the University of California at Berkeley from 1948 to 1952, though he had failed to graduate. He was readily accepted at UCLA as a graduate student anyway, perhaps because his grades at Berkeley, one half of them A's, the other half F's, presented such an intriguing record, perhaps because when a man is thirty-four and he wants a degree, he should be given the opportunity to get one.

Like John DeBella, Felix liked to talk about himself, but his tales were generally less boastful, and funnier. Felix was not so intellectual as Jim's other close friends at the film school, but the attachment was no less tight. Stanton Kaye, who used Felix as the major character in one of his films, believed the relationship was based in part on psychological likeness. "I felt that Felix was coming apart as a man, not having any definition or identity, being older and feeling the coercive pressures of society much more because of it. He was helpless almost to the point of impotence. He was in constant anxiety. And so, of course, was Jim. I saw this profound nihilism, a sense of despair that was stronger than my own. Maybe it was anger, maybe that's where the despair came from."

"The voyeur," Jim scrawled in one of his notebooks, "is a dark comedian. He is repulsive in his dark anonymity, in his secret invasion." He went on to describe the threat and power of the silent partnership made with the unsuspecting.

There were hundreds of notes like this. Some of them would be published four years later, first privately, then by Simon and Schuster as *The Lords: Notes on Vision*. While Jim was at UCLA they surfaced as a paper on film aesthetics. He wasn't able to make films yet, so he would think and write about film as art. "The appeal of cinema lies in the fear of death." Pages of his notebooks were filled with film lore, much of it learned from John DeBella.

On other pages Jim struggled—for definition. Images of magic and violence and sex and death ran through his notebooks like a dark river. Kennedy was killed with the sniper's "injurious vision" and Oswald found haven, "devoured in the warm, dark, silent maw of the physical theater." Oedipus made an appearance: "You may look at things but not taste them. You may caress the mother only with the eyes." It seemed the more he saw, the more he experienced, the more he wrote—and the more he wrote, the more he seemed to understand.

Jim bared himself in his notebooks, as he threw open his psyche for examination. "I won't come out," he wrote, "you must come in to me. Into my womb garden where I peer out. Where I can construct a universe within the skull to rival the real."

The end of 1964. After a history-making cruise into the Indian Ocean in a show of strength, and participation in the Gulf of Tonkin incident off Vietnam, Captain Morrison held his final officers' push-up contest on the *Bon Homme Richard* (he always won), turned the carrier over to another man, and began packing for another move, this one to London, where he would serve under the Commander-in-Chief of the U.S. Naval Forces, Europe. But first he would travel to the West Coast to take a brief vacation with his family. Jim spent Christmas at home and then his family left for a jaunt to Florida to visit relatives. It was the last time Jim ever saw his parents.

The January rains receded and the film school students began hanging out at the Gypsy Wagon, a small snack bar on wheels not far from the cinematography bungalows. There, mixing with student musicians and artists, Jim and many of his classmates exhibited what one of Jim's fellow students, Bill Kerby, came to call "the film school bullshit and flash"—gliding through school, expending as little effort as possible, while covering up this inactivity with a thick layer of swagger and buncombe. Jim walked along fences yelling and shouting on the way to class, filled up the walls in the men's room with pungent graffiti, and rolled empty wine bottles down the aisles of the theater where the screenings were held. Then the classic stories began, most having as their focus drugs, nudity, or daredeviltry. One combined all three and had Jim getting drunk and climbing one of the campus towers at midnight to strip and throw his clothes to the ground.

"With an image," he wrote in his notebook, "there is no attendant danger."

Some of the instructors appreciated Jim, making allowances for what one called his "dilettantism," and Jim himself liked several instructors. His favorite was Ed Brokaw, who told his classes outrageous lies to see if anyone was listening. Jim especially liked the fact that Brokaw occasionally disappeared for several days—as Jim himself would in later years. "Brokaw would've been drawn to Jim's destructiveness," says Colin Young, head of the film division. "He would've smelt it and warmed his hands around that fire, because of how often that's connected with real talent." Brokaw was Jim's faculty advisor and it was to him that Jim went to say he was dropping out. Then he went to Colin Young and said the same thing.

Jim's decision to quit came only a week or two before the end of classes, following a two-day screening of student films. This was the main event of the student year, as close to a final examination as anything the film school offered. Although graduation did not depend on whether a student's film was accepted for a subsequent public showing at UCLA's Royce Hall, the competition for acceptance was great.

Most of the forty or so films screened that May had been made in the Project 170 workshop classes in which short silent films with "voice-over" or "sound-over" tracks were made. Filming was normally done on Saturdays and the procedure was for every student to fill all roles—serving as a cameraman one week, an actor the next, a sound man the third, and so on, at some point directing his own film.

Jim did not produce a script for his film, telling John De-Bella, whom he picked as his cameramen, "I'll explain things as we go." What Jim had in mind, as he'd explain later, was "a film that was questioning the film process itself . . . a film about film." It was untitled and took the form of a montage or sequence of abstract and loosely connected events, what De-Bella called at the time "a diffused medley of images about the filmmaker and the filmmaker's eye." It opened with Jim taking a huge pull from a pipeful of grass and throwing his head back. Then the camera cut to the wiggly test pattern used as a title logo on the *Outer Limits* television show. There followed a scene of a woman (DeBella's tall German girlfriend) dressed only in a bra, panties, and garter belt, with the camera panning slowly down from her face to show her spiked heels dancing on top of a television set that had been turned on to reveal Nazi soldiers marching in parade. Then came a scene in an apartment (Jim's) whose walls were covered with *Playboy* nudes that'd been used as targets for darts. Several men got stoned, then seated themselves to watch stag movies, but the film broke and the men jumped up and began to make finger shadows against the white light of the screen. After that there was a closeup of a girl licking DeBella's eyeball (cleansing it of the filth collected from the images it had seen). The final shot was of the television set being turned off, with the picture fading to a white line and then to a dot and then to darkness.

The screening was as chaotic as the film. First, the splices came apart and the film wouldn't go through the projector. Jim was told to resplice it for a later showing that night. When he did, the reaction ranged from confusion to amusement to discontent. Some of the students thought Jim deranged and few had any comment to make, although most howled with delight to see DeBella's girlfriend in her underwear. Even Ed Brokaw, who generally was intrigued by Jim's mind, palpitated an imaginary basketball with his fingers, bouncing his left hand against his right and saying, "Jim . . . I'm terribly disappointed in you." The film was not included in the Royce Hall lineup and Jim was given a "complimentary D."

Jim was hurt by the rejection. Some say he went outside and cried. Whether or not this is true, he clearly was embittered. First he became defensive, then petulant, and finally he announced his imminent departure from UCLA. Colin Young talked him out of it, but in June, when it came time for him to collect his diploma, Jim was walking the Venice beach, smoking dope.

By now, Jim and Mary were drifting apart. She still insisted on including stardom in her destiny—a conviction Jim had humored at first and then tried to discourage. Then she said she might audition as a go-go dancer at the Whiskey a Go Go, a club that had opened on the Sunset Strip in January. Jim told her he didn't want her in a short fringed skirt in a glass cage, shaking her ass for middle-aged drunks. They fought again when she got an agent, who told her not to appear in a film Jim wanted to make because it would be damaging to her career to be in a student film. They fought a third time when Mary appeared unexpectedly at Jim's apartment and caught him with another girl. Jim told Mary she had no right to come to his place unless she was invited. Besides the fights, there were the polite but annoying reminders that, in her opinion, he was taking too many drugs.

Jim saw Ray Manzarek coming across the campus. Ray was a friend of John DeBella's. Jim admired Ray and had secretly applauded his refusal to edit a nude shower scene from a film he'd made of his girlfriend. Jim was additionally attracted to Ray's music and had been to hear him and his band, Rick and the Ravens, at the Turkey Joint West in Santa Monica, a nearby beach community. Once Ray had invited Jim onstage, with several others from the film school, and everyone, full of beer, crashed through a chorus of "Louie, Louie." Now, in June, Ray's band had been hired to back up Sonny and Cher at a high school graduation dance. But when one of the band members quit and Ray called the school to say there'd be five musicians instead of six, he was told that if he didn't produce six musicians, as contracted, they wouldn't be paid.

"Hey, man," said Ray, spotting Jim, "wanna play a gig with us?"

"I don't play anything, Ray."

"That's okay, all you have to do is stand there and hold an electric guitar. We'll just run the cord around behind one of the amps. We won't even plug it in."

Jim said afterward that it was the easiest money he ever made.

The
Arrow
Flies

CHAPTER

3

Do you know what we oughta do?"

Jim was stretched out on the bed, staring at the ceiling. He was using a voice his friends knew well—a perplexing amalgam of boorish jest and vague taunt that left the listener wondering if he was serious or jiving. Sometimes Jim used this voice to disguise his vicious teasing. Other times, as now with his friend from Florida State University, Sam Kilman, who had appeared in L.A. soon after classes ended, he used it to cover his doubts about a suggestion he was going to make. It lessened the risk factor for him.

"No," said Sam, "what?"

"Start a rock group," Jim said, still looking at the ceiling.

"Shit, man, I haven't played drums in seven years . . . and what are *you* gonna do?"

Jim sat up. "I'm gonna sing." He almost hummed the words. "Uhmmmm . . . gonnnna . . . singgggg."

Sam looked at Jim incredulously. "Can you sing?" he asked.

"Fuck no! I can't sing!" Jim barked.

"Well, okay then, Jim, say we got this rock group started, and say you could sing—which you can't—what're we gonna call it?"

"The Doors. There's the known. And there's the unknown. And what separates the two is the door, and that's what I want to be. Ahh wanna be th' dooooorrrrr . . ."

John DeBella and Phil Oleno had gone to Mexico; Dennis Jakob and Felix Venable stayed in Venice; Jim considered moving to New York, but remained in West Los Angeles a few weeks, looking for a job with Sam, and then he, too, moved to Venice. *Escaped* might be a more fitting word for the move was preceded by a crisis that left him shocked. He reported for his army physical on the 14th of July and learned two days afterward that he had passed, meaning he had lost his student deferment and was now classified 1-A.

Jim thought fast. He had lied to the government, saying he was still enrolled at UCLA, but they must have found out. The next day he went to the registrar's office and put his name down for several courses he never intended to take.

Venice was ideal for Jim. The small artistic community was attracting more and more long-hairs, runaways, and artists every day. Bodies covered the beach; tambourines clanged merrily to the dozens of transistor radios; dogs chased Frisbees; cross-legged blue-jeaned circles smoked pot; LSD was sold over the counter at the local headshop. San Francisco had Haight, and Los Angeles had Venice. The time of the hippie was just beginning.

Jim was one of the anonymous drifters in long hair, T-shirt, and jeans. He lived with Dennis Jakob for a while, in a shack on the edge of a polluted canal, and then he moved onto an empty warehouse rooftop. There he had a candle for light, a Bunsen burner to warm his occasional canned meals, and a blanket to keep warm. He rarely slept or ate, except to gobble the good acid that was soaking the beach community, and he began to write, creating in a single flare of enlightenment more material in less time than he ever would again.

"Ya see," he said, "the birth of rock and roll coincided with my adolescence, my coming into awareness. It was a real turn-on, although at the time I could never allow myself to rationally fantasize about ever doing it myself. I guess all that time I was unconsciously accumulating inclination and nerve. My subconscious had prepared the whole thing. I didn't think about it. It was just thought about. I heard a whole concert situation, with a band and singing and an audience, a large audience. Those first five or six songs I wrote, I was just taking notes at a fantastic rock concert that was going on inside my head."

Though what was about to happen to Jim was in no way preconceived, he was conscious of the music ringing in his inner ear, begging to be released.

"Actually, I think the music came to my mind first and then I made up the words to hang on to the melody, some kind of sound. I could hear it, and since I had no way of writing it down musically, the only way I could remember it was to try and get words to put to it. And a lot of times I would end up with just the words and couldn't remember the melody."

> Hello, I love you
> Won't you tell me your name?
> Hello, I love you
> Let me jump in your game

It was 1965, three years before the world would hear "Hello, I Love You," and Jim was sitting in Venice on the beach sand, watching a young, long thin black girl insinuate her way toward him.

> Sidewalk crouches at her feet
> Like a dog that begs for something sweet
> Do you hope to make her see, you fool?
> Do you hope to pluck this dusky jewel?

For "End of the Night" he took his inspiration from a novel by the French Nazi apologist and adamantine pessimist, Louis-Ferdinand Céline, *Journey to the End of the Night:* "Take the highway from the end of the night . . ." A third song, "Soul Kitchen," was dedicated to Olivia's, a small soul food restaurant near the Venice arcade where Jim could get a big plate of short ribs, beans, and cornbread for 85 cents and a steak dinner for $1.25. Still another, "My Eyes Have Seen You," included a description of all the TV antennas Jim saw from the rooftop: "Gazing on a city under television skies . . ."

However obvious the inspiration for these songs, they were not ordinary. Even the simplest of them had an enigmatic and visionary twist, a rhythm or line or image that gave the verses a peculiar strength. As when he inserted the line "Faces look ugly when you're alone" in "People Are Strange." And in the song about Olivia's there was this verse: "Your fingers weave quick minarets/Speaking secret alphabets/I light another cigarette/Learn to forget, learn to forget, learn to forget."

These first song-poems were shot through with the darkness Jim was so attracted to, felt so much a part of. Visions of death and insanity were expressed frighteningly, with compulsion. In one that later became part of a longer work, "The Celebration of the Lizard," Jim wrote, "Once I had a little game/I liked to crawl back in my brain/I think you know the game I mean/I mean the game called go insane." In "Moonlight Drive," an otherwise pleasant love song with abundant imagery so strong it acted on the senses more like a painting than a poem, Jim wrote the surprise ending: "Come on, baby, gonna take a little ride/Down, down to the oceanside/If we go, get real tight/Baby gonna *drown* tonight/Go down, down, down, down . . ."

Once he had written the songs, Jim said, "I had to sing them." In August he got his chance when he encountered Ray Manzarek walking along the Venice Beach.

"Hey, man!"

"Hey, Ray, how ya doin'?"

"Okay. I thought you went to New York."

"No, I stayed here. Living with Dennis on and off. Writin'."

"Writing? What'cha been writing?"

"Oh, not much," Jim said. "Just some songs."

"Songs?" Ray asked. "Let's hear 'em."

Jim squatted down in the sand, Ray kneeled in front of him. Jim balanced himself with a hand to either side, squeezing the sand through his fingers, eyes clamped shut. He chose the first verse from "Moonlight Drive." The words were slow and careful.

> Let's swim to the moon/uh huh
> Let's climb through the tide
> Penetrate the evenin' that the
> City sleeps to hide . . .

When he finished, Ray said, "Those are the greatest fuckin' song lyrics I've ever heard. Let's start a rock 'n' roll band and make a million dollars."

"Exactly," Jim said back. "That's what I had in mind all along."

There was an angularity to Ray, what is commonly called "the rawboned look." He was a half inch over six feet and slim, weighing about 160 pounds. But the shoulders were unusually broad, the jaw was hard and rectangular, the eyeglasses rimless, cold, intellectual. If he had believed in Hollywood casting clichés, he might have cast himself as what he had recently been, a graduate student who takes himself seriously, or perhaps a stern young schoolmaster in a Kansas frontier town. But there was a softness too. The box-like chin line had a dimple in it and his voice was always controlled, gracious, reassuring. Ray liked to think of himself as potentially everyone's big brother: organized, intelligent, mature, wise, capable of great compassion and able to accept great responsibility.

He was four years older than Jim, born in Chicago in

1939, the son of working-class parents. After studying classical piano at the local conservatory and earning a bachelor's degree in economics from DePaul University, Ray enrolled in the UCLA law school. Two weeks later he dropped out to take a management trainee's position at a branch of the Westwood Bank of America, a job he kept for three months before returning to UCLA, this time as a graduate student in the cinematography department. A broken romance ended that in December 1961, when Ray enlisted in the army. Although his duty assignment was a soft one—playing piano in an interservice band in Okinawa and Thailand (where he was turned on to grass)—Ray wanted out, so he told the post psychiatrist he thought he might be turning gay. He was released a year early and returned to the UCLA film school the same time Jim arrived.

Ray began producing films of exceptional quality, all of them autobiographical, all in praise of the sensuality of his Japanese-American girlfriend, Dorothy Fujikawa. In one of these, called *Evergreen,* there was a scene that seemed inspired by the repeated cuts between a boy and a girl running in slow motion toward each other in Alan Resnais' *Hiroshima Mon Amour* and had Ray and Dorothy finally meeting, nude, in a shower. The faculty wanted Ray to edit that scene and he agreed, but when several students criticized him for waffling, he went back on his agreement and distributed a flier at the student screening in December explaining why the film wasn't being shown. (Eventually that film, and all the others Ray made, would be shown, and praised.) In June, when he received his master's degree, Colin Young, the division head, said Ray was one of the few students that year who were ready to go on to feature-length films. Even *Newsweek* Magazine recognized Ray's early accomplishments.

Ray met Jim through John DeBella, and within a short time they became fairly good friends, never truly close but sharing an intellectualism and a naïve Nietzschean philosophy.

Jerry Hopkins

Ray Manzarek

In many ways they were opposites. Ray would never forget to shave and the creases in his chinos were always sharp. Jim was deliberately slovenly, given to sandy T-shirts and jeans, and when it was cool at night he wore a grimy welder's jacket he'd picked up at a surplus store. Ray had familiarized himself with Eastern thought and in 1965 was beginning to study the Maharishi Mahesh Yogi's transcendental meditation, while Jim turned his back on that, believing The Way was paved with drugs and shamanism. Ray was a practicing aesthete, while Jim reveled—sometimes wallowed—in the Dionysian. But still they were mutually attracted, and when they met on the Venice beach, Ray asked Jim to move in with him—he could sleep on the living room couch, and they could work on the songs during the day when Dorothy was at work. Jim moved in immediately and the two began.

Jim's voice was weak, but he and Ray agreed that that was largely a matter of confidence, which would come with practice. They worked on the songs for two weeks solid, Ray at the piano in his small, funky apartment, Jim nervously holding the lyrics for security (although he knew them all), standing stiff and motionless, wishing the moth he was sure was stuck in his throat would go away. Then Ray took Jim to his parents' house where Rick and the Ravens rehearsed.

Jim's lyrics sailed over Ray's brothers' heads. Obviously Rick and Jim Manzarek didn't understand Jim *or* his lyrics, though they agreed to try working with him. Other people didn't understand Jim either. When Ray bumped into two of their former film school buddies and announced he had started a band with Jim, they were shocked. "You're in a band with *Morrison?* For God sake's Ray, why would you want to go and do something like that?" Jim was still regarded as an extravagant albeit intelligent flake. Many classmates didn't give any band Morrison was in one chance in a million to make it.

Ray remained loyal, seeing in Jim something few others did, something Jim himself was only beginning to recognize. The most evident change was physical. Jim had gone from 165

Bobby Klein

Jim in Venice, 1966

to 130 pounds and had lost his characteristic plumpness—now he was lean and sinuous. With the new physique was longer hair, sprouting over the ears and curling past the collar, framing a face that had lost all puffiness and become positively handsome. The transformation was radical.

But the most important difference was in what Jim felt. A delirious, humming confidence, an otherworldly magnetism that seemed to pull everything he needed his way.

Shortly after Jim met Ray's family the brothers Manzarek and he moved their rehearsals into a house behind the Greyhound bus station in Santa Monica where they added a new drummer, John Densmore, whom Ray had found in his meditation class.

John had much in common with Jim. Both had solid middle-class backgrounds; John's father was an architect. Both had a brother and a sister. In high school both had shown an aptitude for a minor sport; for John, it was tennis; Jim had excelled in swimming. With Ray, John shared an excitement for jazz, along with the avidity and dedication of a new convert to the yogic disciplines of the Maharishi.

John told Ray and Jim that he had a fiery temper and hoped the meditation would help him learn to control it. He was twenty and still living at home (which made him an immediate target of Jim's ridicule), though he was aching to break away from his parents, longing for the liberation a working band might bring. In the years to come, Jim and John would work together in the Doors, but never became close as friends.

John had been playing the drums since the age of twelve. He had played tympani snare at University High School in West Los Angeles, then switched to jazz during college, which he had started at Santa Monica City, going next to Los Angeles City, finally dropping out of San Fernando Valley State.

After two weeks of rehearsal Ray and his brothers drove with their new singer and drummer and a pickup bass player (a girl whose name everyone has forgotten) to the World Pacific

Jerry Hopkins

John Densmore

recording studio on Third Street in Los Angeles. Rick and the Ravens had a contract with Aura Records and had cut a couple of songs with Ray singing as Screaming Ray Daniels. After release, the single had sunk without notice and Aura decided to give the boys some free studio time instead of recording more songs. In three hours they cut six songs. "What we got," said Jim years later, "was an acetate demo, and we had three copies pressed."

These were the discs that Jim and Ray and John, and sometimes Dorothy Fujikawa, took from record company to record company, songs Jim had written in Venice that summer, including "Moonlight Drive," "My Eyes Have Seen You" (a song then called "Go Insane"), "End of the Night," and an innocuous little tune with a perennial theme, "Summer's Almost Gone." The songs and the group were rejected by every record company.

About this time Jim met Pamela Courson.

Pamela was a redhead only eighteen years old. She had freckles on the backs of her hands, smeared across her pale, delicate, fawnlike face, sprinkled like cinnamon on a body the length of a rope. She wore her hair parted in the middle, straight and long. Her eyes were a translucent lavender, larger than most, giving her the look of a painting by Walter or Margaret Keane: vulnerable, dependent, adorable.

She was born December 22, 1946, in Weed, California, a few miles from Mount Shasta, considered a holy mountain by the Indians. Her father, like Jim's, had been a navy flyer—but a bombardier, not a pilot—and now was a commander in the U.S. Naval Reserve and principal of a high school in Orange, the town that gave Orange County its name. She told Jim she'd dropped out of her art classes at Los Angeles City College and was looking for something meaningful to do.

Years later Pamela would say it was Jim who told her about life. She called herself "Jim's creation." He taught her about the philosophers, writing out a paragraph about each of

Bobby Klein

Pamela and Jim in Santa Monica

them, from Plato to Nietzsche, introducing her to the great ideas of the Western mind. Jim gave her his journals to read, and immediately she appointed herself custodian of his poetry.

Jim was rereading Aldous Huxley's *The Doors of Perception:* "Most of these modifiers of consciousness cannot now be taken except under doctors' orders, or else illegally and at considerable risk. For unrestricted use the West has permitted only alcohol and tobacco. All the other chemical Doors in the Wall are labeled Dope, and their unauthorized takers are Fiends." Jim was amused at the representation and began to increase both the variety and quantity.

Now Jim was doing everything and anything to blow his mind. Open the doors of perception . . . break on through to the other side . . . take the highway to the end of the night . . . visit weird scenes inside the gold mine . . . ride the snake . . . the striking phrases that he would later scatter through his songs were being written in notebooks on the warm autumnal beach. He was in the rush of discovery of his particular vision and vocabulary.

He gobbled acid tabs like beer nuts—or aspirin, for that's what they now looked like: early Owsley from San Francisco, the original "white lightning," pure and cheap and . . . clunk. And grass, of course—bags and bags of it from Mexico. And then the sugar cubes.

> Break on through to the other side
> Break on through to the other side
> Break on through to the other side

Jim decided it was time to tell his family in London of his plans. He wrote that he had tried to find work after graduation, but people had laughed at his cinematography degree, so now he was in a group and singing—and what did they think of that?

Jim's father was stunned and wrote a letter of strong objection. He reminded Jim of the abandoned piano lessons and his childhood refusal to join his family in Christmas caroling . . . and now he was starting a band? After his father had paid the bills for four years of college?

"Well," said the fast-rising navy staff officer, "I think it's a crock."

Jim never took criticism lightly and he never wrote his parents again.

Sometime in October a picture of Billy James appeared in the trade magazines Jim and Ray now read weekly. Billy, who was thirty-three and a onetime actor, had been doing Bob Dylan's publicity in New York after he signed with Columbia, and in 1963 he had moved to California to do publicity there. For a while he was successful at it, which is to say he satisfied all the usual corporate demands, but then he began to adopt the lifestyle of the musicians, eventually changing so radically that he could no longer communicate with his East Coast friends and nearly all his superiors at Columbia. So Billy was given a new title—manager of talent acquisition and development—vague enough to cut across conventional corporate charts. So far as he was concerned, the title was the go-ahead to sniff out the stuff that appealed to him.

Ray and Jim looked at the photograph. Billy wore a beard.

"Maybe he's hip," said Ray.

When Billy returned from lunch he found Jim, Ray, Dorothy, and John standing in the hallway next to the water cooler outside his office. He nodded absently, told the boys to come in, accepted their acetate graciously, and listened to their rap, which he instantly knew had been delivered many times. He promised them he would call, probably in a day or so. Two days later Billy's secretary got Jim on the phone. She said Billy wanted to see them in his office as soon as it was convenient.

"I told them I could produce their records if I wanted to, but that though I felt the talent was there, I was not at all sure I could bring it out in the studio," Billy recalls. "So I knew I would have to interest another Columbia producer in them. Because I anticipated that that might be a problem, the contract I offered was for five and a half years, with six months as the initial term, during which the company agreed to produce a minimum of four sides and release a minimum of two. I didn't want them to be hung up under contract to us beyond six months with nothing going on."

Jim couldn't believe it. Columbia. Dylan's label.

Despite this encouragement, the band began to fall apart, as one of Ray's brothers quit and the other was replaced. The replacement was Robby Krieger, a guitarist who was in John and Ray's meditation class.

At nineteen, Robby was the youngest of the four. He was also the least imposing. He had frizzy toast-brown hair and vague green eyes that gave him a dazed look, which some thought was caused by either drugs or ill-fitting contact lenses. The eccentric image was fostered by the way he talked—hesitantly, as if he were falling asleep, the ends of his sentences drifting up into a question mark or disappearing into a whisper. But appearances can be deceiving. Behind that dazed child's look there was a quick mind and a subtle sense of humor, both inherited from his father, a modestly wealthy man who advised government agencies and businesses on planning and finance.

Like John, Robby was a native of California—born January 8, 1946, in Los Angeles, one of nonidentical twins—and he had gone to "Uni" High. But Robby had also attended high schools in Pacific Palisades, a rich Los Angeles beach suburb, and in Menlo Park, a toney suburb near San Francisco. He had spent a year at the University of California at Santa Barbara, and then a stretch at UCLA, where he had changed his major for the third time and was studying physics when John asked him to meet some guys who were calling themselves the Doors.

"The Doors?" Robby said, grinning vacantly. "Far out!"

Robby and John had played together in a group called the

Jerry Hopkins

Robby Krieger

Psychedelic Rangers. Until now he'd thought that was an unusual name.

Robby told Jim he had begun playing the guitar at fifteen,
and at eighteen was an aspiring Montoya or Segovia. But he
changed musical styles as often as he changed schools, moving
quickly from flamenco to folk to blues to rock. He especially
liked the folk people, he told Jim, recalling the time he went to
see Joan Baez at Stanford University. Jim, of course, started
talking about Dylan. Then Robby plugged in his guitar and casually played some bottleneck. Jim had heard bottleneck on
records, but this was the first time he had seen it done. For a
while he wanted Robby to play bottleneck on every song.

The shop talk and rehearsals continued and the four grew
closer, meeting every day—at Ray's, at Robby's house where
his parents had a piano in a side room, or at a friend's house in
Venice. Five days a week, all afternoon, they rehearsed. They
worked an occasional gig on weekends—mostly bar mitzvahs,
weddings, and fraternity parties—leaning heavily on a few easily recognized songs such as "Louie, Louie" and "Gloria," occasionally playing one of their own compositions. Jim, still too
shy and insecure to face an audience, no matter how small,
turned his back to the dance floor, or when he faced it, closed
his eyes and held on to the microphone as if it were all that
was keeping him from sinking through the stage. In fact, on
most of the Doors' earliest dates it was Ray who sang most of
the songs, with Jim punctuating the verses by honking on a
harmonica or grunting "Yeah!" and "Drive on!"

Phil Oleno had a job as night manager of a supermarket,
and on those rare afternoons when Jim wasn't rehearsing, they
often killed some time smoking dope and hanging out on the
UCLA campus, talking to girls in the art department. One was
Katie Miller, who was a year or two younger than Jim and
looked something like the young Tuesday Weld: innocent,
blond, ethereal.

Katie was a sensitive girl, insecure about her capabilities,
always prefacing her remarks with apologies. But it was her
generosity that gave her the most pain. It was as if she were

trying to be a mother to the strays she met at school. She invited Jim to stay at her apartment any time he wanted and cooked sumptuous meals, urging him to take her car when he needed transportation. Sometimes Jim would disappear with her car for days, leaving Katie to walk and wonder. Other times he stayed at her apartment for days, making a terrible mess and abusing her viciously, castigating her with a satanic tongue, boasting drunkenly of the other women in his life, threatening to take a knife to the huge paintings she'd done in school and hung on her apartment walls. He also reassured her: she was fine, he said, she was beautiful.

"You really ought to meet Jim," she told her friend Rosanna White, another art student. Rosanna had heard some of Katie's stories and was repelled, but when she finally met Jim, he fascinated her. Often he went without a shirt, and with his hair grown out and the way he turned his head sideways, bunching up the muscles in his neck, Rosanna thought he looked like a Greek statue come to life. She was equally gripped by his voice, which never in the six months she saw him off and on rose above a whisper. Rosanna admitted to being afraid of Jim, but still she offered him her black couch in her apartment, giving him a second place to crash when he didn't make it back to the beach.

Rosanna's apartment was as severe as Katie's was lush. She lived on natural foods, so there was never much to eat, and because she never smoked marijuana there was none of the trash food that grass smokers liked. She seldom even drank wine, so Jim had to bring his own. She did have an organic shampoo he liked, however, and often when Rosanna returned from class she found him in the bathroom in his jeans and the ratty pajama top he wore, posing in front of the mirror, sucking in his cheeks like a fashion model with the haunting, hungry *Vogue* magazine look, preening his still-damp uncombed hair.

"Jim," she said, "why don't you brush your hair?"

Jim gave his hair a final pat and looked at Rosanna in almost a caricature of sexiness. "Because I want it to look like a bird's wing." Then he caressed himself, folding his arms across his chest to rub his biceps sensually through the thin flannel covering, staring at her petulantly.

One night not long after she met Jim he appeared at her apartment with John Densmore and Katie, both of whom soon left, leaving her and Jim alone. Rosanna, who had been increasingly annoyed by Jim's preening and whispering, decided to get things off her chest. "What is this bullshit!" she said when Jim began to whisper at her. "You don't *really* talk that way. Now stop it."

Jim turned his whisper into a greasy proposition, telling Rosanna what she really wanted was to go to bed with him. "Oh, come on, Jim," she said, sounding disgusted. "Don't be such a goddamned phony. You're stoned all the time, I can't relate to you. I can't even talk to you now because I think you're stoned and you're phony. Jim, you're putting on an act."

Jim rushed into the kitchen and in seconds returned with Rosanna's curved carbon-steel carving knife. Standing in front of her, he grabbed her right wrist and bent her arm behind her in a hammerlock. Her blouse came unbuttoned in the movement, and Jim put the blade to the flesh of her soft stomach.

"You can't say that to me," he whispered. "I'm gonna cut you and see if you bleed." He sounded serious.

Someone entered the apartment. Jim spun around, saw John Densmore, returning unexpectedly. He looked back at Rosanna and then down at the knife he held. He laughed. "Hey now, what's this? A knife? Now where did that come from?"

Afterward Rosanna apologized and then Jim apologized, asking if he could sleep on her couch that night. She said yes.

Sometime in November Jim called Ray. It was 8 A.M. and Jim was peaking on acid. He wanted to get together to rehearse. Ray said it was too early. Jim insisted, said if Ray didn't come over right away, that was it, to hell with the Doors, he was quitting. Ray told Jim he'd see him later.

Several hours passed and Jim was at Phil Oleno's house with Felix Venable, coming down from the effects of the drug. They were talking about some pictures they'd seen of spider webs spun under the influence of LSD and mescaline. Oleno produced the book—he'd taken it from the UCLA library—and opened it to the photographs. The webs spun by spiders that had been given acid were geometrical, and the mescaline webs were arbitrary, chaotic, illogical, perhaps (said Jim) insane. They decided they must go sample some mescaline in its purest form, the peyote cactus. That meant driving into the desert, to Arizona.

The three headed east in Phil's dilapidated red Chevy convertible, which had no first or reverse gears. While driving through Hawthorne, scarcely out of Los Angeles, Jim ordered the car to a noisy halt, leaped out, ran over and kissed a young girl, dashing back to the car just as a police cruiser nosed in front of the Chevy. Jim's whimsical flight had not gone unnoticed. The police asked him for identification, talked to the girl, and learned she was only fourteen.

"C'mon," called Jim, "why'n't-cha shoot me? C'mon, muthafucker, chickenshit asshole, shoot me."

Mysteriously, the police let them go with a warning. The journey to the east resumed.

Two days later when Jim and Felix returned without Phil and covered with bruises and cuts the stories began. Jim told some people that they had driven to Arizona, met some Indians, gone into the desert with them to shoot a circle of arrows around the peyote cactus, because if you can draw the bow and shoot the arrow (Jim explained), it meant you were strong enough to have a good trip. Then they had chewed the peyote and afterward Phil had decided to head for Mexico.

Others were given another version, which explained the bruises. In this one Jim and Phil and Felix never found any Indians, never found any peyote, but found, instead, some Chicano low-riders who lived near the Colorado River and liked to stomp men with long hair.

Elektra Records

The earliest group publicity photo—never used. 1966

Nothing was happening at Columbia. The contract had been signed and there had been a celebration dinner at Robby's house, but after that, nothing. Billy James was finding it impossible to get the attention of Columbia's staff producers. The Doors continued to rehearse, play an occasional party, and audition wherever they could.

In December, at a UCLA film school screening that included one of Ray's classroom exercises of the previous year, the Doors appeared onstage—in their first truly public appearance—improvising a soundtrack with acoustical instruments. Then they auditioned at a club in Westchester, home base for the Turtles, a then-popular Los Angeles band, and were rejected. They similarly were turned away from Bido Lito's, the tiny but very hip club in Hollywood where Love had been the house band for so long. The trouble, they were told, was the lack of a sufficient bass sound.

They began inviting bass players to their rehearsals, but the sound was too full, like that of the Rolling Stones (they played many of the same songs) or that of any electric blues band. They were still trying to decide if they wanted to change their sound that much, still auditioning at clubs without a bassist, when, in early January, they were offered a job as house band at the London Fog, a small club on the Sunset Strip less than fifty yards from the Whiskey a Go Go, whose owner bore the unlikely name Jesse James. The Doors watched the banner go up outside: "Doors—Band from Venice," and they were ecstatic. The first night they played, not a single person entered the club.

The owner's terms were so stingy that it seemed he was trying to get even with them for filling the house with friends from UCLA the night they auditioned. Since the Fog was a nonunion club, like Bido Lito's, the musicians hired didn't have to belong to the musicians' union, and the club didn't have to pay union minimums. The Doors played from nine to two, five sets a night, with a fifteen-minute break each hour, six nights a week. For this they were paid $5 each on weeknights and $10 each on Fridays and Saturdays. In cash at the end of the evening—if the owner had it.

The proximity of the Whiskey did nothing for the size or makeup of the Doors' early audiences. Despite its trendy name the London Fog was frequented mostly by sailors, deviates, pimps, hookers, and black-suited mafiosi types, with the odd, puzzled tourist thrown in. All were looking for action that clearly was somewhere else.

Between sets the Doors would take turns walking down the street to the Whiskey, where they'd be allowed to stand in the entrance way and watch the headliners, hoping one day to be, as Jim later put it, "as big as Love," then the most popular "underground" band in Los Angeles.

Still, the job encouraged them and gave them the chance to build confidence while they polished their original material. At first Jim continued to interject himself in the instrumental breaks on harmonica, or picked up the claves, while Ray played flute. But as he began to concentrate more on his visual performance, he stopped trying to play an instrument. Ray discovered the Fender keyboard bass, an instrument he could play with his left hand while continuing to strike chords and solo with his right hand on the Vox organ that Columbia Records had bought for him. The bass dilemma was resolved.

By February the band had no less than forty songs in its repertoire, about twenty-five of them originals, including "The End," which in early 1966 was no more than a nicely written song about faded love:

> This is the end, beautiful friend.
> This is the end, my only friend. The end
> of our elaborate plans. The end,
> of everything that stands, the end.
> No safety or surprise, the end.
> I'll never look into your eyes again.

With the exception of "Alabama Song," taken from a Brecht-Weill musical about the glory and degradation of prewar Nazi Germany, *The Rise and Fall of Mohagonny,* the songs the band played were old blues classics or recognized rock hits such as "Money," "Back Door Man," "Gloria," and "Louie, Louie." Jim was now singing nearly all of them.

As the weeks passed, Jim gained self-assurance. He didn't think he had much of a voice—"I don't sing, I shout," he told people—but he knew he was getting much better. While the band loosened up, he would do a dramatic turn with a black handkerchief, draping it over the microphone and rubbing it sensually around his face.

Most important to the Doors was their growing sense of "oneness." After rehearsing every day, and now playing together publicly, the three musicians and singer knew one another's music intimately and they were getting very good. Ray's assertive, vaguely churchy Flash Gordon organ; John's jazzy drumming, punctuating Jim's lyrics perfectly; Robby's subtle, seemingly off-handed blues and flamenco finger-picking; Jim's slightly hoarse, uneven, but sensual tenor/baritone—all came together in a style that had only been hinted at on the demo disc. Much of the time Jim still stood with his back to the audience, facing the others, assuming the stance he took in rehearsals, when, according to Ray, they turned inward to "direct our energies toward each other." With the help of LSD, Ray says, the Doors developed their "communal mind." Most musicians who play together for a time, and who respect each other's musicianship, feel a closeness nonmusicians and nonsingers cannot comprehend. "Yeah," says Ray, "there was that. But there was also an unusual *intensity.*"

They had an unusual partnership agreement whereby everything was to be shared equally. Jim was writing nearly all the songs, but when they recorded, he said, the Doors would be listed as composer, and royalties and all other income would be divided equally four ways. All creative decisions would be made not by majority rule but by unanimous vote.

Jim began to bring his drugs on stage, sometimes internally: eyes dilated, sensory perception alternately distorted and intensified, ego fragmented; other times in his pockets: whipping out an amy just as Ray was beginning an organ solo and popping it under his nose. Once he popped amies for everyone as they began "Little Red Rooster" and when they got to the lyric "the dogs began to bark and the hounds began to howl," Ray began barking, John began howling, and Jim fell off the stage. Another night, fucked up on booze, Jim reverted to an odd sort of teenage grossness, improvising new lyrics for "Gloria," adding, "and then she come on my floor/She come on my bed/She come in my mouth . . ."

Jim was still without a mailing address, moving from couch to bed to couch. Pamela was his number one girl, but he was not a monogamist. They talked about getting an apartment in Laurel Canyon, but at the time he was spending his nights all over West Los Angeles. He still didn't have a car and depended on Ray's ancient yellow Volkswagen or John's Singer Gazelle. When hungry, the Doors would all go to John's house, John's mother being the softest touch among the three Doors mothers available.

By April the Doors were in a funk. They remained broke. Forty dollars apiece wasn't enough to live on, and often they didn't get that. John had been offered a spot in another band. John and Robby were arrested for possession of marijuana and Jim, who had gotten a student's deferment illegally the preceding summer, was reclassified 1-A and told to report for a new physical in May. Then Columbia put them on the "drop list."

One of Columbia's staff producers, Larry Marks, came into the London Fog one night and introduced himself as their producer, but they'd never see him again. Nor had they heard anything from Billy James. It was John who noticed the Doors' name on the "drop list" on Billy's desk. They asked for an immediate release.

"Stick it out," said Billy. "You get a thousand bucks if you finish the six months and they haven't cut the songs." They shook their heads. Billy sighed and called someone in the legal department. The Doors were legally free.

A few days later the owner of the London Fog fully liberated the Doors. He fired them.

The group's luck changed in May.

First, Jim tampered with his blood pressure, blood sugar, heartbeat, respiration, vision, and speech with a wide and plentiful assortment of drugs, marched into the army induction center for his physical, told the doctors he was a homosexual and if they took him they'd be the sorriest motherfuckers on the face of the earth. He was refused for service. Then, on the band's final night at the London Fog, the talent booker for the Whiskey a Go Go appeared to ask them if they were available to fill in on Monday night. One night only, the pretty brunette named Ronnie Haran said, but the owners would be watching.

"I've really talked you up," she told Jim, "and we've been kind of looking for a house band." If it worked into a regular job, she said, it would mean two sets a night—compared to the four and five at the Fog—for union scale, $499.50 for the four of them. Jim and the others were casual in their response, but inside they were exploding with relief.

"Yeah," said Jim, "I think we can make it. Monday, huh? Hey, that's tomorrow. That's not much notice, y'know."

The man who made the decisions and was part owner of both PJ's (a lizard lounge just off the Strip) and the Whiskey a Go Go was a middle-thirtyish ex-vice cop from Chicago with the Runyonesque name of Elmer Valentine. Ronnie Haran, who had met Elmer when she was a starlet hanging out nights at PJ's, was handling the publicity for both clubs and scouting new acts. She also did publicity for the Scottish singer Donovan in 1966, and when she was looking for a photographer, someone had suggested Paul Ferrara, who had gone to UCLA with Jim and told Ronnie she ought to see the band at the Fog. He was not the first nor the last to tell her about the Doors, and as she relied heavily on what she heard on the street—rather than listen to "managers"—she finally paid the Fog a visit.

Elmer admits Ronnie Haran begged him to book the Doors a second time, because the first time he thoroughly hated them. He told her he thought Jim was an amateur without potential who affected a far-out pose to cover his lack of talent. He also thought Jim had a filthy mouth. But Elmer liked Ronnie, so he agreed to put the Doors back in for another two days.

The Doors remained at the Whiskey from mid-May until mid-July, during which time they were fired at least once a week for infuriating the owners. Although the Doors wanted to favorably impress the headliners at the club—the Rascals, the Paul Butterfield Blues Band, the Animals, the Beau Brummels, Them, Buffalo Springfield, Captain Beefheart—they also wanted to "blow them off the stage," causing Elmer's partner Phil Tanzini to scream at them, "Too loud! Too loud! I'm gonna throw you out in front of everybody. Turn down, turn down!" In revenge, every time the band played "Unhappy Girl" Ray would lean on the highest note until the organ, and Tanzini, screeched. Jim's antics aggravated the situation. He would sometimes get so wiped out on booze or drugs that he failed to show up. Worse, he would sometimes jump onstage between sets, screaming, "Fuck Elmer! Fuck the Whiskey! Fuck Phil!"

Whenever the Doors were fired, Ronnie Haran called a fourteen-year-old girl in Beverly Hills, who by now was one of the Doors' biggest fans—she was allowed to stand by the box office but was not permitted inside—who would get on the phone and call all her girlfriends, all of whom called the Whiskey to ask when the Doors would be back. Elmer was in the habit of taking a lot of the calls at the club, using them the same way Ronnie used street talk, to keep in touch.

"It was always the same thing," says Elmer, who still doesn't know he was at least partially conned. "The chicks, the chicks, the chicks, all asking, 'Is that horny motherfucker in the black pants there tonight?' Now, my mother didn't raise any idiot kids, so I kept putting 'em in as the second group."

On the street the word was: "You've got to go see the Doors at the Whiskey, the singer is *crazy.*"

The Doors' image was blatantly sexual—a skinny singer rubbing his crotch against a microphone stand—but it was also intellectual. The gallery of grotesques in Jim's lyrics fascinated the band's mid-sixties constituency. Songs like "When the Music's Over" were by turns mournful, outraged, consoling, demanding, pleading, and above all, frustrated.

The Doors' set was fluid. Often they'd spend five minutes between songs trying to decide what to play next. "How about 'Crystal Ship'?" Jim would ask. "Nah, don't think so," Ray would say, "don't feel like it." John would suggest a song that gave Robby a long solo and Robby would shake his head. " 'When the Music's Over'?" said Jim. Ray looked contemplative, widened his mouth into a Henry Fonda no-teeth-showing grin, and nodded. John said okay and Robby said sure. It was unanimous. Doors policy.

"When the Music's Over" was an improvisational number that ran eleven minutes or more, depending on the length of the instrumental breaks and the scraps of poetry Jim threw in. In many ways it was the classic Doors song: delivered in a highly dramatic style that insisted the band be regarded in theatrical as well as musical terms.

The song began with a bouncy organ riff and Jim urging, almost under his breath, "Yay . . . c'moan." Then John Densmore began exaggeratedly wheeling his arms, adding a loud metronomic drumbeat, and suddenly, startling everyone, Jim leaped straight into the air with his hand mike and screamed, "Yeeeaahhhh!" The organ carried the melody line, Robby adding accents, and Jim crooned a fatalistic lament:

> When the music's over
> When the music's over

When the music's over
Turn out the lights
Turn out the lights
Turn out the lights

Then, more forcefully:

For the music is your special friend

And still more assertively, almost a shout:

Dance on fire as it intends

Then, a consolation (and warning):

Music is your only friend

The drums rattled.

Until the end
Until the end
Until the end

Here Robby provided feedback/freakout/"psychedelic" guitar, John slammed away on the cymbals, Ray sustained piercing organ notes, and in the midst of this cacophony Jim writhed on the floor, clutching the microphone to his chest, pumping his legs, alternately assuming a fetal position and then going perfectly rigid. The music slowed, the musicians composed themselves. Jim was back on his feet.

Cancel my subscription to the Resurrection
Send my credentials to the house of detention
I got some friends inside
The face in the mirror won't stop
The girl in the window won't drop
A feast of friends alive she cried
Waiting for me
Outside

The last word was another scream. The music turned hypnotic:

> Before I sink into the big sleep
> I want to hear
> I want to hear
> The scream of the butterfly
>
> Come back baby
> Back into my arms

A note of impatience entered Jim's voice, implied violence:

> We're gettin' tired of hangin' around
> Waitin' around with our heads to the ground

The voice left violence behind, became as hypnotic as the music:

> I hear a very gentle sound
> Very near yet very far;
> Very soft, yeah, very clear;
> Come today, come today.

A mood of sadness was created, turning to anger:

> What have they done to the earth?
> What have they done to our fair sister?
>
> Ravaged and plundered and ripped her and bit
>   her,
> Stuck her with knives in the side of the dawn,
> And tied her with fences and dragged her down.

There was only the rhythmic heartbeat of Ray's organ: two notes, bum-*bump*, with the apocalyptic intrusion of drums. Bum-*bump*. Bum-*bump*.

> I hear a very gentle sound
> With your ear . . . down to the ground.

Jim's face was next to the microphone, held almost lovingly in his left hand, while his right hand covered his ear. His right leg was pushed forward, bent at the knee, his foot holding the microphone stand. The left leg was rigid, poised.

> We want the world and we want it . . .
> We want the world and we want it . . .

A drum roll. And:

> Now
> Now?

The drum roll ended. He leaped. He screamed:

> Now-wowwwwwwoooooooo-
> ooooooooowwwwwwwww!

The organ returned, full frenzy:

> Persian night;
> See the light,
> Save us, Jesus, save us!
>
> So when the music's over,
> Turn out the lights.
>
> The music is your special friend
> Dance on fire as it intends
> Music is your only friend
> Until the end
> Until the end
> Until
> THE END!

Even the go-go dancers, who'd seen everybody do everything twice, sat mesmerized.

CHAPTER

4

When it became apparent the Doors were to remain at the Whiskey for a while—they had stopped taking the firings seriously after the first two weeks—all four of them moved. John and Robby finally left their parents to share a small place in Laurel Canyon and to try to find other jobs for the band. Ray and Dorothy took a beachfront apartment that had but one room, sixty feet long, perfect for rehearsing. Jim moved into Ronnie Haran's place, a small $75-a-month apartment a few blocks from the Whiskey, and it was here that she began talking with Jim about drawing up a contract for what she called "promotional management." She also began calling record companies, inviting representatives to come see what she called "America's Rolling Stones." A few actually came. The Beach Boys' producer Nick Venet didn't like them at all. Lou Adler, who already had the Mamas and Papas, was as unmoved as he had been when Jim and Ray took him their demo nine months earlier. Some of the Rolling Stones came in when they were in town; they weren't impressed either. Nor was Jac Holzman, the thirty-six-year-old electronics freak and folk music producer who was founder and president of Elektra Records. Elektra was then a small company making its first inroads into the rock market with Love. As he left the Whiskey that first night in middle June, Jac pronounced, "This group doesn't have it."

Holzman was urged to see the Doors once more, by Ronnie, of course, but also by Arthur Lee, the leader of Love. So he returned and decided there *was* something appealing in Ray's organ playing. By the fourth visit he found himself making his pitch, offering the Doors a contract. He wanted them for one year, he said, with options for two more, or until they'd delivered six albums, whichever was longer. In exchange, the Doors were to get $2,500 as an advance against future royalties of 5 percent of the records' wholesale price.

Jac's pitch emphasized Elektra's two most obvious characteristics: its sincerity and its size. Jac wanted it understood that Elektra was an intimate business operation whose small, but tidy, organization was always accessible. Elektra's artists, he said, had easy and immediate access to anyone in the company ... and with so few artists signed (compared to Columbia, say), the staff could apply themselves more directly to promoting all the acts.

It sounded good. There had been a time when the Doors had wanted only to be as big as Love. Now they wanted more, and maybe a small company could do it. Besides, it was the only firm offer they'd had. They were cautious about contracts after their experience with Columbia, but also eager to record. They told Jac they'd like to think about it, and Jac flew back to New York.

The first person they showed the contract to was Billy James, their friend from Columbia. He said he wasn't in a position to evaluate it fairly because he was about to leave Columbia to open a West Coast office for Elektra. If they elected to go with Elektra, Billy promised to do all he could to get them everything they wanted. And then he told them to find themselves a lawyer who could give them advice that meant something.

When they went to Ronnie Haran with the contract, she took them to her lawyer, Al Schlesinger, who promised to represent them with the caveat that in the event of a conflict with Ronnie, he'd have to take Ronnie's side. That made them nervous, so Robby talked to his father, who'd been serving as their interim business adviser, and he sent them to his attorney, a dapper white-haired Beverly Hills counselor with another wonderfully Runyonesque name, Max Fink.

During the time Max negotiated with Holzman Jim seemed unusually tense. He had gone through two weeks of heavy drinking when the British band Them had headlined at the Whiskey, for that group's singer-songwriter had not only the same surname as Jim, but also many of the same habits. Jim and Van were convinced they were related and they drank to it.

That was followed by a period of heavier-than-usual drug taking. Nearly every day Ronnie watched him swallow acid and once, she swears, he smoked six ounces of grass in one day, which he managed to do by staying up half the night and chain smoking bombers as thick as his index finger. The tiny apartment was littered everywhere with seeds and stems and Ronnie was furious. Jim ignored her, saying that ever since Robby and John had been busted, they were paranoid about drugs and were on his ass to get him to cut down. "Just because those guys are into meditation . . ." He left the sentence unfinished. Jim wasn't ready for meditation, but he went to one of the Maharishi's lectures to look into his eyes to see if he was happy. Jim decided he was and dedicated a song to him, "Take It As It Comes": "Go real slow/You'll like it more and more/Take it as it comes/Specialize in havin' fun." But he wasn't about to take up the discipline of meditation.

By now the Doors were packing the Whiskey with their own devoted fans. One night Jim didn't show up for the first set, so Ray and Robbie and John played without him, with Ray singing all the vocals. Robby went back to the dressing room afterward and John and Ray hurried over to the Tropicana, where they hoped they'd find Jim.

During the ten-minute ride Ray and John talked about Jim and drugs. John was visibly upset, verging on anger. Ray was calmer. "It just *looks* like Jim is taking a lot of drugs, because you've cut down so much," he said.

"Yeah? Well, I never took acid more than once a week," said John, "and Jim's on it every other day, at least."

They parked the car near Jim's room.

John admits he never really understood Jim. "He really wanted to get out of himself, totally go to the ends, as far as you can go, every time. Find out! I never understood, because I came from the Indian side of metaphysics, the bright side, whatever. He was always into Nietzsche and what-does-it-all-mean and existential exploration."

Ray sighed as he crossed the parking lot, heading for Jim's $8-a-day room. He muttered a line from a song: "Break on through to the other side . . ."

John and Ray reached Jim's door. They knocked. There was no answer but they thought they heard a movement. "Jim? C'mon, it's Ray and John." Finally Jim opened the door.

Jim gazed at the two. "Ten thousand mikes," was all he said.

Ray laughed. He didn't believe it was possible. A normal LSD hit was 350 to 500. "C'mon, let's see what happens. You've already missed the first set. Let's give Tanzini something to remember."

Jim scuttered back into his room, shaking his head. "No, man, no. Here . . ." He opened a drawer in the dresser. "Here, take these." Jim scooped up two handfuls of LSD in little purple vials, offering them to John and Ray. Ray noticed there was a brick of grass in the drawer, too. A full kilo.

The second set was a shambles, but by the time the Doors were to go on for the final forty minutes, Jim was reasonably coherent. "We'll do 'The End' this set," he said, nodding as if preoccupied.

"The End" was the Doors' most memorable work—or would be after this performance. It embodied the concept of rock theater even more than "When the Music's Over." Starting as a simple two-verse farewell song, it had recently been running twelve minutes in length, with Jim inserting and removing new bits of poetry nearly every time they performed it. Tonight Jim had a new surprise.

In dark chino pants and T-shirt, hair curling to his collarbone, an unshaven Botticelli face, he lurked around the kinetic flash and shadow of the Whiskey a Go Go dance floor. He stopped, stood watching the girls in the glass cages. On the floor were Vito and his music-crazed harlequins in see-through lace who were known for picking the top new bands. They found the Byrds at Ciro's, then Love at Bido Lito's, became members of Frank Zappa's Mothers' Auxiliary. Vito and his entourage were admitted to the Whiskey on week nights free, for where Vito went, the paying customers soon followed.

Jim slouched toward the stage, eyes lidded, head low on one shoulder. He watched John and Robby and Ray get into position, then joined them, moving to one side near Ray's organ. There were the discordant sounds of warming up, followed by silence, Jim and the musicians remaining in darkness.

The dance floor stilled.

Jim hung on the microphone stand like a shirt, his head tilted back, eyes closed, one hand cupping the mike, the other covering one ear. He planted one booted foot on the base of the mike stand and began a mournful recitation.

> This is the end, beautiful friend
> This is the end, my only friend, the end
> of our elaborate plans. The end,
> of everything that stands, the end,
> No safety or surprise the end.
> I'll never look into your eyes again.

Can you picture what will be,
So limitless and free
desperately in need
of some stranger's hand
in a desperate land.

The musical accompaniment was as hypnotic as Jim's plaintive, threatening voice. There were heartbeats from Ray's organ, sudden ejaculations from John's drums, sitarlike excursions from Robby's guitar.

Lost in a Roman wilderness of pain,
and all the children are insane;
waiting for the summer rain—*yahyyyyyyeh*

Jim's enunciation was careful. He paused between syllables, as he did when speaking, as if choosing words and phrases as carefully as a surgeon handling a scalpel. There was in his delivery and in the music a sense of holding back, a warning, anticipation, fear.

There's danger on the edge of town
Ride the King's highway, bay-beh
Weird scenes inside the gold mine;
Ride the highway west, bay-beh.

The Whiskey dance floor was motionless, packed with bodies holding on, staring at Jim, who hadn't moved since the song began. Even the bar was still. Nowhere in the club was there any talking. Even the waitresses were mesmerized by the figure on the stage.

Ride the snake.
Ride the snake, to the lake,
The ancient lake
The snake is looooooong . . . seven miles;
Ride the snake.

He's old . . . and his skin is cold.
The west is the best.
The west is the bessssssssss-tttttttt.
Get here and we'll do the rest
The blue buuuuuus . . . is calling us
The blooooooooooe buuuuuuuus . . . is calling
    us
Driver where you takin' us?

Jim squinted as if peeking at the audience, then shut his eyes again as the haunting sounds from the other three Doors formed a mysterious backdrop.

Jim's eyes opened. He eased the microphone from the stand and glared at the audience, legs braced, reciting the twelve lines that complete the song in its final version, and in less time than it takes to tell the story, propelled Jim into contemporary pop mythology.

The killer awoke before dawn,
He put his boots on,
He took a face from the ancient gallery,
And he walked on down the hallllll.

He went into the room where his sister lived
    annnd . . .
Then he paid a visit to his brother,
And then he . . . walked on down the halllllll.

And he came to a dooooooor,
And he looked insidddde,
"Father?"
"Yes, son?"
"I want to kill you. Mother . . . I want to
FFFUUUUCKKK YOOOOO!"

Jim's voice rose in a primal scream, making the sound of silk yardage being torn by broken fingernails. Behind him the instruments bellowed and shrieked. Neither John nor Robby nor Ray had heard these words before, but they were not so startled that they didn't continue their improvised instrumental fill.

When he heard Jim say something about fucking his mother, all the blood in Phil Tanzini's face rushed to his heart, which began racing. "That," he growled, "is the last time. Never, *ever,* will the Doors enter the Whiskey again. Not even if they're *paying* their way in."

Jim was still singing, his eyes closed.

> Come on, bay-beh, take a chance with us,
> Come on, bay-beh, take a chance with us
> And meet me at the back of the blue bus
> Come on, yayehhhh

The band began a rapid chugging rush to the shuddering, primal finish, with Jim grunting sensually. Then, returning to the same mysterioso opening, Jim sang what originally had been the song's second verse.

> This is the end, bewwwww-ti-fulllll friend
> This is the end, my only friend,
> It hurts to set you free, but you'll never follow
>   me,
> The end of laughter and soft lies,
> This is the end, bewwwwww-tee-fulll friend
> This is the end, my only friend,
> It hurts to set you free, but you'll never follow
>   me,
> The end of laughter and soft lies,
> The end of nights we tried to die
> This
> is
> the
> ehhhhhhhhhhh-ennnnnnnnnnd.

Slowly those on the dance floor moved back to their tables or to the bar, the waitresses began to take orders for drinks, and people resumed talking.

Phil Tanzini was waiting upstairs in the artists' lounge as the Doors entered.

"You," he shouted at Jim as he slouched into the room, "are one foul-mouthed son of a bitch and you are fired! All of you! Out! And don't bother to come back."

The Doors knew he meant it this time.

"Fuck the mother, kill the father, fuck the mother, kill the father, fuck the mother, kill the father . . ."

Like a mantra the words filled the dimly lit recording studio. There were other sounds—the tuning of instruments, the scrape and thunk of microphones being adjusted, the voice from the control room on the PA calling instructions—but all ears heard the soft, repetitious, annoying chant of Jim Morrison, who lay on his back near the drum kit.

"Fuck the mother, kill the father, fuck the mother . . ."

The inspiration came from Nietzsche's *The Birth of Tragedy*: "Oedipus, murderer of his father, husband of his mother, solver of the riddle of the Sphinx!" Jim said, "You can really get into your head just repeating the slogan over and over."

"Fuck the mother, kill the father, fuck the mother . . ."

Sophocles had a romantic notion about Oedipus, one that Nietzsche wrote about. He called Oedipus the "most sorrowful figure of the Greek stage . . . the type of noble man who despite his wisdom is fatal to error and misery, but who nevertheless, through his extraordinary sufferings, ultimately exerts a magical, healing effect on all around him, which continues even after his death."

Jim liked that.

"Fuck the mother, kill the father, fuck the mother . . ."

"Okay, I think we're ready now," Paul Rothchild's voice came from the control room. When Jim didn't stop, he called again, "Jim, I think we're ready now."

Paul was the producer Elektra had assigned them. He was stocky and little, about three inches shorter than Jim, and his kinky blond hair was short because he had recently spent eight months in jail for smuggling marijuana. Paul was the thirty-year-old son of an opera singer and a literate British business-man and had grown up in Greenwich Village's liberal, kooky mold. Jac Holzman flew him to Los Angeles to hear the Doors at the Whiskey in July, and recording began after Labor Day.

Rothchild and the Doors picked the songs that worked best in performance, to make what Paul called an "aural docu-mentary." A studio bass player was brought in on two songs, and on a third the Doors stood up and stamped their feet to provide a rhythm track, but virtually everything else was done as if the funky Sunset Sound studio were a nightclub. Despite their unfamiliarity with studios and recording techniques, the Doors felt comfortable, and the first songs were laid down in only two or three takes apiece. Then came the song that would fill up more than half of one side of the album, the Oedipal epic drama, "The End."

"Fuck the mother, kill the father, fuck the mother . . ."

Paul was getting impatient. "Jim . . ."

Jim was stoned, and as he lumbered to his feet—his Oedi-pal chant dying out at last—his eyes fell on the small television set he'd brought in. He looked at Johnny Carson, whose lips were moving silently, then he picked up the set and threw it to-ward the control room, causing Paul and the engineer to duck. The set bounced off the thick soundproof glass separating them and came back to rest on the floor. Jim looked puzzled.

Paul halted the session, suggested the girl with Jim take him home.

"Nahhhhh," said Jim, disagreeing. "Let's go hang out, man."

Paul shook his head no and eased Jim into the girl's car. She moved into traffic on Sunset. Jim was mumbling.

"Fuh th muh, kih th fah, fuh th muh . . ."

Then he clearly said, "Gotta get back to the studio," threw open the car door, and leaped out.

He ran back, climbed the eight-foot-high wooden gate, somehow got through an outside door and a second door leading back into the studio. He was breathing heavily as he peeled off his shoes and jeans and shirt.

"Fuh th muh, kih th fah, fuh th muh . . ."

Naked, he grabbed one of the large sand ashtrays and heaved it wildly. Then he pulled a fire extinguisher from a wall and sprayed the chemical foam all over the control board, the walls, and the instruments, ruining one of Robby's guitars and a rented harpsichord.

Jim put the fire extinguisher down. He heard a voice.

"Jim? Jim? Are you here?"

It was Paul Rothchild, summoned by Billie Winters, the girl Jim had abandoned in the middle of the Sunset Strip. They were peering through the gate. Jim ran outside.

"Hi, man, it's goooooood to see you! C'mon in, man, let's cut . . . let's cut some songs."

"Wait a minute, man," said Paul. "I mean, we gotta get outta here, let's go have a party someplace else. We'll get busted here, man. What a dumb way to fall."

Jim was talked into leaving, but he forgot his shoes and the following morning the studio owner called Paul. He'd found these shoes in the middle of all the destruction. Did Paul want him to find out who the shoes belonged to? Paul said send the bill to Elektra, and when the Doors entered the studio that afternoon, it was perfectly clean and the damage wasn't mentioned.

"Okay," said Paul, "today we cut 'The End' and I think we can get it in one take."

They got it in two.

Later, when Ray, John, and Robby kidded Jim about the "fire" he'd put out in the studio (Paul had eventually told them about it), Jim denied the story. The ashtray, they prodded him, the chemical foam.

"No," said Jim. "Really?"

Publicity photo for first album

The band's second group publicity shot

Ray was the first to appear onstage, lighting a stick of incense. Then came Robby and John, and finally, Jim, in a sinewy street-punk slouch.

They were in a chic new disco called Ondine, near Manhattan's Fifty-ninth Street Bridge. This was one of those proper clubs designed for the Uptown Bohemian, a Brechtian cabaret where apocalyptic celebration was as thick as the marijuana smoke. This was the group's first out-of-town date. New York City!

Jim's eyes were lidded, his head was tipped back insolently. He planted one boot on the base of the mike stand, pushing his crotch up against the shaft, casually shook his mane of curly dark hair. Behind him, Robby began the hypnotic first notes of "Back Door Man."

There was a scream, the bark of a cougar at night, and

then Jim sang, "Oh ahm a back door man/The men don't know, but the little girls unnerstan . . ."

The word went out, hitting the street and spreading like a shipment of good cheap Mexican weed. On the second night all the top groupies came. "You've got to see this group," one of them told all her friends. "The singer is really ripe."

In the weeks that followed, Jim wandered the streets of lower Manhattan, drinking beer on the Bowery, looking inside the small boutiques that were opening on the Lower East Side, exploring the used bookstores on Fourth Avenue. There were meetings with Elektra—to sign the publishing agreement with Nipper Music, one of Jac Holzman's companies, named for Holzman's ten-year-old son; to approve the album cover photography; to agree, reluctantly, to edit "Break On Through" so that the line "She gets high/She gets high/She gets high" would be heard as "She get/She get/She get." This was to be the Doors' first single and Holzman was afraid the word "high" would discourage air play. Because the Doors had very little money, they spent many afternoons in their rooms in the Henry Hudson Hotel, watching soap operas on television, smoking dope; occasionally, when he got bored, Jim would hang by his hands from a hotel window ledge.

The band returned to Los Angeles the end of November and Jim moved in with Pamela Courson. They'd been seeing each other off and on for about a year and now she had a small place in Laurel Canyon. If Pamela hadn't fully accepted Jim's irresponsibility, by now she'd come to expect it. To begin with, "moving in" for Jim meant little more than that he was sleeping there, because he owned almost nothing and had nothing to move in. More important—and frustrating—to Pamela was the fact that just because Jim spent Tuesday through Friday nights in her bed, it didn't mean he'd be there Saturday and Sunday, or the following Wednesday or Thursday nights.

In fact, it worked both ways. When the Doors were in New York Pamela had called their hotel three times a day trying to

[No One Here Gets Out Alive]

Doors autograph

find Jim in his room, then gave up and began seeing a young actor named Tom Baker. When Jim returned (and Pamela returned to Jim), the two men became friends, learning they shared a love for the theater and poetry and a nomadic military background.

In the following weeks the band had little to do, so they hung out at the tiny Elektra offices, helping prepare their record release.

"Hi, guys," said their old friend Billy James. "You ready?"

"We've been thinking," said Ray, "and we're not sure we want a bio. We think where we came from and what our favorite colors are is irrelevant to our music."

"You're right, of course," Billy agreed. "Still, sooner or later you're gonna be asked what you're trying to do. It might be a good idea to lay that much out right away and be done with it."

The five young men discussed the subject of publicity for nearly an hour. They appreciated the value of a successful image, but all the bios for other artists they'd seen—even those on the Elektra list—were so boring.

Billy walked to a window, where he stared at the smog for a while and then said, "Well . . . how about we write it now? You guys can say anything you want and that's what we'll send to New York."

The office manager, Sue Helms, took everything down in shorthand and then typed it up for their approval. It filled thirty pages and the part that was eventually released included some of Jim's most imaginative catch phrases, lines that would appear in print, defining—and limiting—the Jim Morrison image long afterward.

> On stage the Doors look like they're in their own world. The songs are space-like & ancient. It sounds like carnival music. When it ends, there is a second of silence. Something new has come into the room.
>
> You could say it's an accident that I was ideally suited for the work I am doing; it's the feeling of a

bow string being pulled back for 22 years and suddenly let go. I am primarily an American; second, a Californian; third, a Los Angeles resident. I've always been attracted to ideas that were about revolt against authority—when you make your peace with authority you become an authority. I like ideas about the breaking away or overthrowing of established order—I am interested in anything about revolt, disorder, chaos, especially activity that seems to have no meaning.

The fact sheet that accompanied this studied blurb was more traditional. Here, Jim said his favorite vocal groups were the Beach Boys, the Kinks, and Love. He said he admired Frank Sinatra and Elvis Presley, and in acting, Jack Palance and Sarah Miles. He also said he had no family, that his parents were dead.

"Jim!" said Sue Helms. "That's not nice. What'll your parents think?"

Jim insisted. If anyone asked, his parents were dead. And that's what it said in the biography.

In the first week of January 1967 the album, titled *The Doors,* and the single, "Break On Through," were both released. A billboard showing their faces and the message "THE DOORS: Break On Through with an Electrifying Album" became the first rock signboard on the Sunset Strip, and the band went into Bill Graham's Fillmore Auditorium in San Francisco, third-billed to the Young Rascals and the Sopwith Camel. The pay, $350, was minimal, but the venue was America's best.

They went to San Francisco early, in time for the Human Be-In on Wednesday, a catalytic and spiritually orgasmic event that entered pop mythology even before the day was over. All the Doors were immensely impressed by the gathering in Golden Gate Park. The Haight-Ashbury era was formalized that week in San Francisco and the Doors, to a man, felt a part of it.

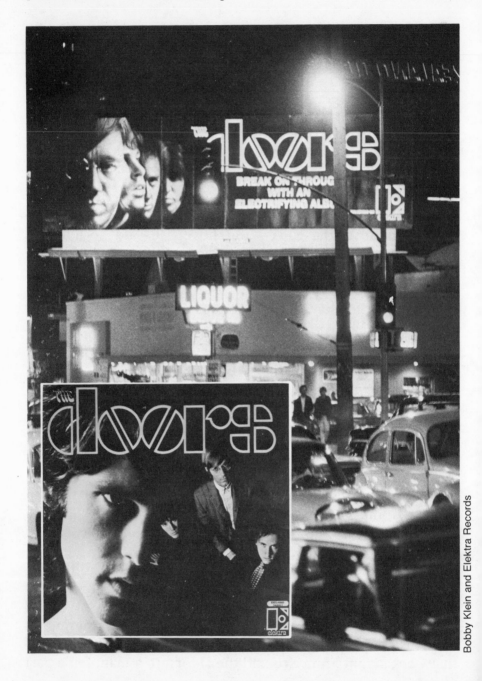

The Doors' Sunset Strip billboard. The First of an era—1966–67
The Doors' first album cover (inset)

They opened their set at the Fillmore with their single, "Break on Through," and then they played the song Jim had dedicated to the Maharishi, "Take It As It Comes," both of them songs of contemporary existential advice. Usually the band at the bottom of the bill gets little attention at such concerts, but by the third song, the Young Rascals and Sopwith Camel and Fillmore fans began to push toward the stage to look, to listen more intently. The band played "Light My Fire."

> You know that it would be untrue
> You know that I would be a liar
> If I was to say to you
> Girl, we couldn't get much higher

This was, essentially, Robby's song. He had written the melody and nearly all the words, with only a small assist from Jim. But Ray had invented a carnivalesque opening organ run that soon came to be regarded as a kind of definition of the Doors' sound. More significantly, the song was seven or eight minutes long, most of it an instrumental interlude that made it clear the Doors were more than Jim Morrison. The band claimed they never played this song twice the same way, but used it as an aural loom on which to weave intricate and jazzy improvisation, building to a dizzying climax.

> The time to hesitate is through
> No time to wallow in the mire
> Try now we can only lose
> And our love become a funeral pyre.
>
> Come on baby, light my fire
> Come on baby, light my fire
> Try to set the night on fi-yer
> Try to set the night on fi-yerrrrrrrr!

The Fillmore audience stood hypnotized.
In the second set the Doors performed "The End" and

Jim, trying to grab the mike, went tumbling into the drums, hurting his back. Coming as it did, after he screamed "Mother? *I want to fuckkkkk youuuu!,*" the audience thought the tumble part of the strange choreography. By the following night the word was out in another city: Go to the Fillmore to see the opening act.

The Doors returned to San Francisco three weeks later for another series of performances at the Fillmore, third-billed this time to the Grateful Dead and Junior Wells Chicago Blues Band. And, as at the Whiskey, they "blew the headliners off the stage."

For the next two months, until the middle of March, the band remained in California, nudging their single up the charts by calling the leading rock radio station to request the song until it was number eleven in Los Angeles.

They were picking up momentum. They did a benefit concert for KPFK-FM, the listener-supported Pacifica station. Then they played the old Moulin Rouge, now called the Hullabaloo, and worked for a week at Gazzarri's on the Sunset Strip, where they were given a small but encouraging review in the *Los Angeles Times.* The same week, in late February, another *Times* critic (John Mendelsohn) called Jim "somewhat overmannered, murky and dull" and said "The End" was an "exploration of how bored he can sound as he recites singularly simple, overelaborated psychedelic non sequiturs and fallacies." Nearly a year later Jim met this critic in an elevator, and once the elevator was in motion and the critic could not escape, Jim smiled and said, "Singularly simple, overelaborated psychedelic non sequiturs and fallacies, huh?"

Then the Doors went to San Francisco for their first appearance at the Avalon Ballroom, the funkier and "hipper" of the city's two large dance halls. There they were headliners, performing after sets by the Sparrow and Country Joe and the Fish.

By now Jim and Pamela had a new apartment in Laurel Canyon, on Rothdell Trail. The place was sparsely furnished

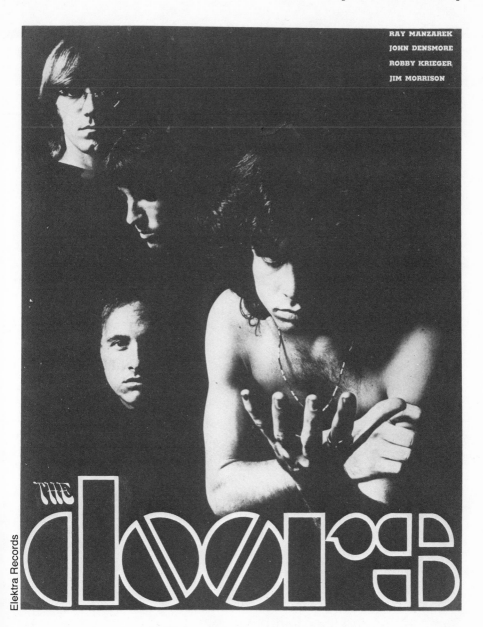

RAY MANZAREK
JOHN DENSMORE
ROBBY KRIEGER
JIM MORRISON

Elektra Records

Publicity photo for the first album

and in the background was the constant burr and rattle of traffic on Laurel Canyon Boulevard. Often Jim sat on the balcony with beer, watching the people enter and leave the Country Store, a small grocery only fifty yards away. In a garage apartment just two doors away lived the friendly neighborhood dealer, an ex-disc jockey named Ted. It was to him that Pamela went for heroin, a drug she seldom used, but one she kept a secret from Jim. "Oh, please don't tell Jim," she'd plead, "don't ever, ever tell Jim. He'd absolutely kill me."

Pamela was at Gazzarri's every night the Doors were there, and when the Doors weren't working, she was on the Strip with Jim, sitting nearby as he drank himself into a frenzy and then joined whatever band was playing in whatever place they were, to sing for as long as they'd put up with him. Then they walked home. They'd be tired and drugged and boozed and spent and it would be late, after 2 A.M., and their apartment was a twenty-minute walk uphill.

"Please, Jim, please let's hitch a ride tonight."

Jim would always say no and night after night they walked. Pamela would hang her arm behind Jim's back, holding on to him, her head against his right shoulder, bobbing and dozing. She'd stumble and wake up.

"Please, Jim, let me hitch . . ."

"C'mon, honey, it's just a little further. It's only a few more steps . . ."

Later Jim wrote a song about their place on Rothdell Trail called "Love Street." Like all his other songs about or dedicated to Pamela, there was a hesitancy, a refusal to make a final commitment, a biting sting at the end:

> She lives on Love Street
> Lingers long on Love Street
> She has a house and garden
> I would like to see what happens
>
> She has robes and she has monkeys
> Lazy diamond studded flunkies

She has wisdom and knows what to do
She had me and she has you

I see you live on Love Street
there's the store where the creatures meet
Wonder what they do in there
Summer Sunday and a year
I guess I like it fine . . . so far.

But he was still sleeping wherever unconsciousness
caught him. He ricocheted along the Sunset Strip, singing with
instantly forgettable bands, getting falling-down drunk with
pickup friends. One night he raced intoxicated through a Hollywood cemetery looking for Valentino's grave; another he
played matador with fast-moving cars; on a third he incinerat-
ed a number of his notebooks and poems in a girlfriend's
kitchen.

"Tandy Martin! Well I'll be dipped."
Jim was surprised to see his high school sweetheart in
New York. It was mid-March and the Doors were there again
for another week at Ondine. Tandy told Jim she was married
to a painter who was the poetry editor of the *East Village Other,*
a successful underground newspaper. Jim invited her to Jac
Holzman's apartment as his dinner date and made it clear as
he introduced her that she was an old friend, not another of
his pickups.
"Robby, this is Tandy Martin, I went to school with her
. . . Jac, this is Tandy, she was my friend in high school . . ."
After dinner Jim got drunk.
"Do you always drink this much, Jim?"
"Not always. Uh . . . sometimes I drink more." He
laughed.
Tandy looked at Jim blankly.
"I've been drinking," Jim said finally, "but I'm getting
good at it. I can tell now, I can, uh, gauge everything so that I

stay in one place. Every sip is another chance. Another flash-
ing chance at bliss."

Jim's rap came rolling out like molasses, one phrase poetic, the next incoherent. They were seated in Jac's big living
room, near a window. He stared out at the lower Manhattan
night, not looking at Tandy as he talked.

"We're supposed to be getting songs together for the second album. We have enough, but I've, uh, been trying to write
some more."

"Do you still have those journals you used to let me
read?"

Jim looked at Tandy, frightened by what he was about to
say. "Some of them. But I can't find a lot of them and I stupid-
ly burned some in L.A. when I was on acid. Do you think if I
took sodium pentathol I could remember what I wrote in
them?"

Tandy sat quietly, hands folded on her lap, looking at Jim
intently, sadly. They both were oblivious of the others in the
room.

Jim began rummaging around in his pockets, extracting
thick wads of napkins, matchbook covers, and business cards.

"Somebody gave me the name of a shrink," he said, finally holding a torn envelope aloft. "A *lady* shrink." He dropped
into his stupid, walking-through-quicksand voice. "Uhhhh,
whatta ya think ah that?"

"I think it might help. Maybe not, but what've you got to
lose? It can't hurt."

Jim sat silent for a moment, then said, "Oh, I don't need a
shrink, I don't have to do that, I don't have a drinking problem." Then he asked her to come hear him at Ondine.

"Hey, Jim!" Ray was calling from across the room. "Time
to go to the club. You ready?"

When Tandy arrived at Ondine, Jim had forgotten to put
her name on the list at the door and she was refused entrance.
Then Jim arrived. Tandy was irate. "Jim! Goddamn you, Jim!
That man just treated me like trash. Now you tell him you for-

got to leave my name. Tell him, he just made me look like a fool."

Jim said to the man at the door, "Uhhh, I was, uhhh, supposed to leave her name." He turned back to Tandy. "Is that okay?" he asked sweetly. Then he told her to go to his dressing room, he'd see her later, and he went to the bar, where dozens of New York's trendiest faces were eager to buy him drinks.

Much of the adulation was due to the critical acceptance the Doors, and especially Jim, were getting from Richard Goldstein, who at twenty-five was one of the two or three most important rock music critics in the country. He had missed the Doors their first time at Ondine, but on a visit to Los Angeles he had heard them at Gazzarri's and now he was in their corner, calling their Ondine return a "stunning success" in *The Village Voice,* and describing the album as a "cogent, tense and powerful excursion." Of "The End," he argued that "anyone who disputes the concept of rock literature had better listen long and hard to this song." It was, Goldstein said, no less than "Joycean pop." He called Jim a "street punk gone to heaven and reincarnated as a choir boy."

"Man, you shoulda seen the letters," John said to the others a week later back in Los Angeles. "Dave Diamond took me and Robby to his house and the mail was stacked this high."

"Everybody wants to hear 'Light My Fire,' " Robby added. "Dave says we're nuts if we don't make it our next single."

Dave Diamond's Diamond Mine was one of the top rock radio shows in Los Angeles and it was one of several on which the song was being played. But how to release it? On the album it was nearly seven minutes long, and the average single ran less than half that.

Someone told Jim to put the song on two sides of a 45, in the tradition of the Part 1 and Part 2 songs of the past. Others told him not to compromise, to release the song unedited—hadn't Dylan had a hit with the six-minute "Like a Rolling

Stone"? Jac Holzman, however, held out for a shorter version, asking the Doors to return to the studio and record the song again. They tried that, but in the end asked their producer Paul Rothchild to take a piece out of the instrumental break.

A few days later the Doors were at Ciro's on the Sunset Strip, the onetime glamour club for film stars, more recently the launch pad for the Byrds. Jim had worked hard to prepare for this date. Onstage he did a shaman's dance, whirling and leaping and swinging the microphone, then heaving the microphone stand and falling on it, to rise and retrieve it and throw it again. A tall black woman with a shaved head joined him in his dance. David Thompson, an old film school pal who was running the club's light show, was so gripped by the performance that he shut off his equipment and stood through the remainder of the set, staring. A young man came out of the audience as if thrown by a giant spring, embraced Jim, offered him communion from his cup. Jim drank. Afterward Jim and the others talked excitedly. They had gotten high on stage, and they had gotten the audience high.

A week later the Doors did it again, playing to ten thousand—their first really big audience—at a high school stadium in the San Fernando Valley, where they opened the show for San Francisco's Jefferson Airplane. It was a Doors audience. After the Doors played, a third of the stadium walked out.

Until now the Doors' business and bookings had been handled largely by Elektra and Robby's father, or by the boys themselves. But when "Light My Fire" appeared on the national sales charts, they concluded it was time to get some professional managers.

The move was not prompted entirely by anticipated success. As Robby recalled, "Jim was freaking, giving us trouble. We had to try hard in those days just to get a gig, and then we'd have to try hard to get Jim there on time. So we said, why should we do this? We ought to get a manager to babysit."

Of course they had the usual reasons for seeking a manager—to get them a booking agency and hire a publicist; to organize their lives and operate the business efficiently; to serve as a protective wall between them and the promoters, club owners, press, and public; and, as Ray put it, "to answer the goddamned telephone."

After a few weeks of looking around and discussing the few offers they had, the Doors finally signed with Asher Dann, a prosperous realtor who sold homes to stars and now wanted a bigger slice of the glamour pie, and his new partner, Sal Bonafede, who had directed a successful East Coast group called Dion and the Belmonts and currently managed a busty, middle-of-the-road belter named Lainie Kazan.

Like Jim, Asher was a shy charmer and he was handsome in the California tennis style. Since he was also a heavy drinker, he was regarded as Jim's number one babysitter. Sal was slick, talked fast, and in no way appealed to Jim, who thought he looked like a Mafia don—all he lacked was a mustache.

Sal and Ash—who were taking 15 percent of the Doors' earnings, plus expenses, a standard contract—quickly steered the group to a booking agency and publicity firm. Todd Schiffman was a trim twenty-five-year-old agent who wore checkered suits and wide ties. The first thing he did was drive the band's concert price up. At the time they were getting $750 to $1,000 a night in Los Angeles, but in New York, where they had three weeks coming up, they were to do three shows a night for $750 a week. Todd thought those prices were far too low, so he went to work on a small-time talent buyer for Denver schools who had called requesting the Airplane for two nights in September. By the time Todd got through fast-talking and bluffing him, the promoter had agreed to take the Doors instead, for $7,000. As it happened, when September came, the Doors were worth more than that, but in April, before "Light My Fire," the deal established a price the agent would continue to use to the band's advantage.

One exception was made. That was the May 7 performance at the Valley Music Theater in suburban Los Angeles for $750, a thank-you to Dave Diamond, who promoted the

Paul Ferrara

In San Francisco at the Botanical Gardens

show—and grossed over $10,000 on it—for helping to build their local following.

Mike Gershman, a smooth New Yorker recently transplanted to Beverly Hills to start the rock department of Rogers, Cowan, and Brenner, the General Motors of Hollywood publicity, learned about the rock scene by going to a store and asking for "a dozen records by bands with freaky names." What he found out was enough to make him bombard *Time* and *Newsweek* with pitch letters for the Doors.

The Doors team was complete. They had a lawyer in his fifties whose specialty was criminal law but who also enjoyed legal work associated with show business. They had managers drawn not to their music but to Jim's star potential. They had a youthful agent and publicist, who both were starting new departments and were thus eager to prove their worth. It was a casual assortment, but not unusual.

Summer of '67. June was good. On the 3rd the edited version of "Light My Fire" made its first appearance on all the national charts, and then the Doors went to San Francisco to headline for the first time at the Fillmore, playing with the Jim Kweskin Jug Band. On the 11th they flew to New York, where they were met by Elektra's new publicity director, Danny Fields, and whisked by rented limousine to the Village Theater on the Lower East Side, where radio station WOR-FM was celebrating its first anniversary. Other bands had already performed when the Doors arrived and a bunch of local jazzers posing as rock and rollers were finishing a noisy set. The compère, one of WOR-FM's disc jockeys, made some reference to "lighting up" and introduced the Doors. The curtain went up and Jim went with it, holding on with both hands. The applause was prolonged.

A day later the Doors started what would be their last nightclub date, three weeks in another of New York's modish discothèques, this one run by a charming self-promoter and scene maker named Steve Paul and called, appropriately, the Scene. Like Ondine, the Scene was a mecca for the pop cognoscenti; a late-night spa that attracted fickle uptown happeners in crushed velvet jeans and gear imported from Carnaby Street. Others came from the East and West Village—the stoned-out music freaks wearing feathers and fringe, peace symbols, and oddball theatrical costumes.

As it happened, many of these New Yorkers had gone to California the same week to attend the Monterey Pop Festival. The Doors had been overlooked until it was too late, according to festival director John Simon, and that bothered them, especially when the Scene was closed for the three days and the Doors shuttled off to do shows on Long Island and in Philadelphia.

Jim was moody and drinking excessively. He went for long solitary walks that stretched from the time he awoke, usually in the afternoon, until he had to go to the club. Once, on a Monday night, he accompanied Danny Fields and Paul Rothchild to Max's Kansas City on the East Side and refused to speak to anyone all night. At the Long Island show during the pop festival weekend he startled the other Doors by attempting to take off his clothes on stage.

Still, the shows were good and Jim's mood improved when Richard Goldstein again turned over a large portion of his *Village Voice* column to the band, calling Jim a "sexual shaman," saying "the Doors begin where the Rolling Stones leave off." Lillian Roxon, another respected rock critic, said, "The Doors are unendurable pleasure prolonged."

Then Pamela came to New York to be with Jim. Now he wandered the city with her, running into an old friend from Los Angeles, Trina Robbins, who had a boutique where Pamela bought several pair of velvet bellbottoms. Back at the hotel, Tom Baker called. Pamela said Jim was closing that night, could he come? Tom said yes, and he'd bring friends with whom he intended to make a movie, Andy Warhol and Paul Morrissey.

Tom sidled up to Jim at the post-concert party. "How's it goin'?"

"Purty good, purty good."

Ray joined them. "That's right. The Beatles bought ten copies of the album."

Jim added, "Yeah, we must be doing okay, 'cause Pamela's looking for a house."

In the week that followed, the Doors played two other dates, second-billed to Simon and Garfunkel at Forest Hills, New York, and top-billed in the Greenwich, Connecticut, high school auditorium. At Forest Hills they faced a Simon and Garfunkel audience totally disinterested in Jim's pyrotechnics, not even caring much for rock.

"How'd it go?" Danny Fields asked when Jim appeared at Elektra's offices the following Monday.

"They laughed at me."

Danny's voice dropped. "What do you mean?"

"They opened the curtains and there I was and they laughed. Those fuckers hated me. And I hated them. I wanted to kill them. I never hated anybody so much before. The rest of the show I couldn't get off, I hated them so much."

At the same time, "Light My Fire" was moving fast, its popularity sweeping from West to East much as the Doors themselves had. The third week of June it entered the hallowed Top 10 and there it hung for a solid month, inching upward. Finally on July 25 Sal and Ash got a call from Elektra.

"Would you please tell the boys," the voice said, "that in next week's issue of *Billboard,* the Doors are number one."

They'd made it! Number one. True stardom was at hand.

CHAPTER

5

To celebrate, Jim went out and bought a suit—a custom black leather outfit that clung so tightly that when he slipped into the pants and stepped in front of the full-length mirror, he looked like a naked body dipped in India ink.

He stood in front of the mirror a long while, striking poses, taking off and putting on his leather coat. He tossed the coat aside finally, and flexed his lithe but muscular arms and chest, marbling the muscles of his stomach, bunching those of his neck. With his wavy dark hair and sunken cheeks he looked like David come to Hollywood, a fist in a glove of black kid.

"That June," said Danny Fields, "when I saw Jim surrounded by groupies backstage at the Fillmore, I decided that if I'm going to be in charge of this person's image, if I do nothing else, I'm going to elevate his taste in women."

In July Danny introduced Jim by telephone to Gloria Stavers, the editor of *16* magazine. Then, when he discovered that some of the Andy Warholians were staying at the Castle,

Elektra Records

"Light My Fire" is number one. Billboard *Award presentation, 1967.*
(Left to right): *Steve Harris, John Densmore, Jim Morrison,*
Ray Manzarek, Billboard *presenter, Jac Holzman, Robby Krieger*

the often vacant home of actor Phillip Law, he saw that Jim
met one of the Warhol girls.

Nico was ageless, elusive, charismatic. She had been a
cover girl in her native Germany, in 1958 had appeared in Fel-
lini's *La Dolce Vita,* once was the mistress of French actor Alain
Delon, was an intimate of Bob Dylan and Brian Jones, and was
one of the stars of Warhol's *Chelsea Girls.* Now she was a vocalist with Warhol's kinky contribution to rock, the Exploding
Plastic Inevitable. She was fully as tall as Jim, and no matter
how weird he got, she bested him. She also loved to drink. To
Jim she was irresistible.

It was like an Ingmar Bergman film, as written by Ber-
tolt Brecht and staged by Ionesco. Jim was drinking wine
when he discovered Danny had a quarter ounce of hash, and
he smoked it up. Then he remembered he had some acid and
he gulped it down with vodka.

From a photo session, 1968. Jim with leathers and haircut

Danny was talking shop. "You must understand how important *16* magazine is. It is *the* key to the under-twelves."

Jim looked at Danny distractedly. "Got any Tuinal?" he asked.

"It's important to project the proper image, Jim."

"Are you sure we finished the hash?"

Jim and Nico positioned themselves in arches and doorways to stare at the floor between them.

Late that night screams came from the Castle courtyard, where Jim had Nico by the hair. Finally she broke free and minutes later Jim was naked and walking around the Castle parapets in the white glow of the filling moon.

The next day Jim plowed through the water of the Castle pool. Length after length of the pool he swam, an aggressive, one-man aquacade.

"Jim isss crazy," said Nico in her deep Wagnerian voice. "He isss totally crazy." It was obvious she adored him.

The following day Jim returned to Pamela. Nico, along with several others, would reappear over the years, but it was Pamela he thought of as his "cosmic mate," an expression he used for her alone. The Nicos in Jim's life—the dozens of women who passed in the Hollywood night—were the appetizers, desserts, and apéritifs: Pamela was his sustenance.

In many ways Pamela was like Jim. She was bright, physically attractive, and the indoors type, not given to athletics, avoiding sunlight, preferring the anonymity of dusk. She was a willing drug experimenter—although unlike Jim she favored tranquilizers over psychedelics, and an occasional noseful of heroin—and she wasn't opposed to outside dates or settling in for a night with a pickup. She considered traditional morality irrelevant: life in the sixties was more existential than that, more hedonistic, less uptight.

In some ways Pamela was also like Jim's mother. Jim told friends that she was a "nest builder," a good cook. But she also nagged, she felt alienated from the other Doors, and she told Jim incessantly that she didn't like his choice of career, that he was better suited to poetry. She also told him he drank too much. Sometimes it got to Jim and he turned on her. She said the rejections showed themselves most brutally verbally. Like the time they were going to the Cheetah in Los Angeles for a Doors homecoming concert.

Jim was in his leathers, checking his shampooed hair in the bathroom mirror. He sucked in his cheeks and muscled his neck, patting his hips and thighs with his hands, striking a cheeky, androgynous pose. "It's going to be a good concert," he said to Pamela, who was dressing in the adjacent bedroom. "I can feel it. The Cheetah's actually in Venice, y'know."

"Oh Jim," she said, "are you going to wear the same leather pants again? You never change your clothes. You're beginning to smell, did you know that?"

Jim said nothing. They heard a car horn below—the limousine come to take them to the strip of Los Angeles beach where almost exactly two years earlier Jim had met Ray and sung "Moonlight Drive." They ran down the steps, and as Pamela went to enter the limo, Jim stepped in front of her.

"Jim?" she said. "What's . . ."

"I've changed my mind. I don't want you to come. You'd just do something to bum me out."

Jim got into the car and ordered the driver to go, leaving Pamela standing there.

"Light My Fire" remained in the number one position through the middle of August, so it was with great confidence that the Doors began recording their second album, *Strange Days*. A year had passed since they had recorded their first album, and in that time Studio Number One at Sunset Sound had doubled· the number of tracks available to eight. The Doors took full advantage of this opportunity for expanded creativity.

Behind Jim's high school poem, "Horse Latitudes," Paul and engineer Bruce Botnick created a backdrop of *musique concrète.* On one track Bruce took the white noise of a tape recorder, varied the speed by hand-winding it, and got something that sounded like wind. Jim, John, Robby, and Ray all played musical instruments in unusual ways—plucking the strings of a piano, for instance—and the organic sounds were tampered with electronically to create different times and effects. They even dropped a Coke bottle into a metal trashcan, beat coconut shells on a tile floor, and had some friends wail their lungs raw. Against this background, and barely over it, Jim shouted the lines of his poem:

When the still sea conspires an armour . . .

On the title song, "Strange Days," Ray recorded one of the earliest uses of the Moog synthesizer in rock. On a third, "Unhappy Girl," he had to play the entire song backward, and John played backward high-hat, providing a soft-suck rhythm sound.

There were other kinds of experiments. Paul tried to create a special studio atmosphere for the recording of certain songs. For one of the ballads, "I Can't See Your Face in My Mind," Paul told the boys in a sultry whisper to pretend they were in Japan and "off in the distance there is the sound of a koto." The Doors responded with a noisy obscenity. Then Paul suggested that Jim get some girl to go down on him while he was singing "You're Lost Little Girl," a ballad they hoped Frank Sinatra would record for Mia Farrow. Paul liked the idea so much, he said he'd even pay for a hooker. But Pamela liked the idea, too, and she stripped right where she stood in the control room and padded softly into the vocal booth to Jim. Paul waited for a slow count of sixty, then said, "Uhhhhh . . . you let me know when, uhh, you're ready, Jim." About twenty minutes later Jim entered the control room and Paul shrugged his shoulders. "Well," he said, "you can't win 'em all."

Jim's lyric intensity was undiminished. There was his fascination with sacrificial death in the drowning of Spanish stallions in "Horse Latitudes." "Moonlight Drive" had its shocker

Live at Cal State, L.A., 1967, shortly before Strange Days *was released*

ending: And there was the honest, painful insecurity of "People Are Strange." The eleven-minute stretch of "When the Music's Over" contained an angry protest, "We want the world and we want it now!" as well as Jim's continuing preoccupation with his own death ("Before I sink into the big sleep/I want to hear/The scream of the butterfly"). And finally, there were Jim's putdowns of women in "Unhappy Girl" ("You are locked in a prison/of your own devise") and in the title of "You're Lost Little Girl." The second album was not quite so strange a catalogue of psychic jolts and pains as the first, but still it was an amazing array of woes for 1967, when everyone else seemed to be singing about incense and peppermints and marmalade skies. The album also had a most unusual cover: a strong man, a cornetist, two acrobats, a juggler, and two midgets cavorted in a mews, with the only mention of the band a small poster on the alley wall. Elektra had wanted a group photo featuring Jim, but the band, especially Jim, was adamant—no photo on the cover. The compromise was a shadowy photograph on the inside of the dust jacket, facing the lyrics.

In the late summer of 1967 the Doors kept crisscrossing the country. One week they appeared before nine thousand people at the Anaheim Convention Center in southern California, where Jim wore a paint-smeared, sleeveless gray gym sweatshirt over his black leather pants. He threw lighted cigarettes into the audience and the audience in turn began striking matches when the group played "Light My Fire." Then they went east for a week of shows in Philadelphia, Boston, and New Hampshire, returning to Los Angeles to appear once more with the Jefferson Airplane at the Cheetah. "Light My Fire" remained lodged in the number one spot for three weeks, then gave way to the Beatles' "All You Need Is Love" the same week that Elektra issued the following press release:

Elektra Records has requested the Record Industry Association of America (RIAA) to certify that the Doors' album and single both qualify as Gold Records. As of this week (August 30), announced Elektra President Jac Holzman, the album *The Doors* has accounted for sales substantially in excess of a million dollars wholesale, and a million copies of the Doors' single "Light My Fire" have gone to market.

Elektra Sales Manager Mel Posner claimed that the separate running sales tallies on the LP and the 45 crossed the million mark within an hour of each other.

This double display of commercial power establishes the Doors as the strongest group to appear upon the pop music scene since the year began. The Doors now have the distinction of being the only group this year to strike gold with their first LP; furthermore, of all the groups making their recording debuts in 1967, only the Doors have had a million-selling single. . . .

There were other firsts in late August. The Cheetah concert was the first time they topped the bill over their San Francisco rivals, Jefferson Airplane. And it was the first time Jim included a sort of tightrope walk in his act, teetering along the edge of the ten-foot-high stage, then toppling into the audience. It looked like an accident and it was shockingly sensational. The crowd was ecstatic.

By now the Doors had polished and perfected what might be called the pregnant pause in their music and performance. Sometimes they would drop a moment of silence into the middle of a song, or Jim would similarly pause between syllables. Owsley, the legendary acid manufacturer and friend to San Francisco rock bands, told the Doors the silences drove him nuts. Occasionally, individuals in an audience laughed. When that happened once in Berkeley, Jim was offended and said,

*Jim getting through an East
Coast concert, August 1968*

"When you laugh at a performance, you're really only laughing at yourselves." Later, he explained, "The only time I really
open up is onstage. The mask of performing gives it to me, a
place where I hide myself then I can reveal myself. It's because
I see it as more than performing, like going on and doing
some songs and leaving. I take everything really personally. I
don't feel I've really done a complete thing unless we've gotten everyone in the theater on kind of a common ground.
Sometimes I just stop the song and just let out a long silence,

Eric Rudolph

let out all the latent hostilities and uneasiness and tensions before we get everyone together."

Shortly after trying the pregnant pause in Berkeley Jim
used it at a university in New York. He stopped in the middle
of "The End" for four minutes, but this time there was no
heckling. Instead, the effect in the gymnasium was like that inside a pressure cooker. As the pressure built, so did the temperature, and then just as the audience was ready to blow, Jim
signaled the band and they slipped back into the song.

[133]

"It's like watching a mural," he said later. "There's movement and then it's frozen. I like to see how long they can stand it, and just when they're about to crack, I let 'em go."

"But what would you do if they went berserk and rushed the stage," someone once asked him, "not out of adoration, but like they were going to kill you?"

Jim remembered Norman O. Brown and his own theory about the sexual neuroses of crowds. He seemed confident. "I always know exactly when to do it," he said. "That excites people. You know what happens? They get frightened, and fear is very exciting. People like to get scared. It's exactly like the moment before you have an orgasm. Everybody wants that. It's a peaking experience."

Unknown to Jim, while "Light My Fire" was number one, his father reached the top of his own chart, becoming, at age forty-seven, the youngest admiral in the U.S. Navy. He was attached to the Pentagon and the Morrisons—Andy was now eighteen and Anne twenty—moved to Arlington, Virginia.

One day a friend of Andy's came to the house with a copy of the Doors' first album. "Look at this," he said. "Isn't this Jim?"

Andy says he'd been listening to "Light My Fire" for weeks and hadn't known his brother's voice. He borrowed his friend's record and that night he played it with his parents in the room. Clara put down the book she was reading but the admiral continued to read his newspaper. When the Oedipal section of "The End" rolled around, the paper began to shake, slowly at first but then more violently as it became clear what the song was about. To this day the admiral has never commented on his son's work.

The following morning Jim's mother called Elektra Records in New York and told them she was trying to locate her son. After providing convincing detail about Jim, she was given the number of the Manhattan hotel and the name of the Doors' road manager. She hung up and dialed New York again.

U.S. Navy

Rear Admiral George S. Morrison

"Hello? This is Mrs. Morrison, is Jim there?"

"Jim who?"

"Jim. Jim Morrison. I'm his mother."

"Yeah?" The man sounded bored.

Another voice came on the line. "Hello?"

"Jim? Oh, Jim . . ."

"Yes, Mother . . ."

She nervously told him how good it was to hear his voice, asked about his health, admonished him for not writing, told him she was so worried she had wanted to hire a private detective but the admiral had stubbornly refused to let her. After the flood of relief came pique. Jim's replies to her questions and charges were grunts.

"Jim . . ."

"Yes, Mother . . ." He groaned.

"Please come home for an old-fashioned Thanksgiving dinner. Andy and Anne . . ."

"Uh . . . I think I'll be pretty busy then," Jim said.

"Please try, Jim. Please."

Jim finally said he might be in Washington for a concert soon and maybe she could come to it.

"One thing, Jim. Will you do your mother a big favor? You know how your father is, will you get a haircut before you come home?"

Jim said goodbye and turned to the others in the room, who'd been standing there silently listening.

"I don't want to talk to her ever again."

The concert was in the ballroom of Washington's Hilton Hotel and Mrs. Morrison arrived with Andy early in the afternoon, waiting in the lobby until she heard someone at the desk mention the Doors' name. It was Todd Schiffman, the band's agent, and Clara quickly introduced herself and informed him she wanted to see her son. Todd sent a friend to the ballroom where the Doors were setting up for that night. When the friend returned, he told Todd quietly, "Jim says, 'No way.' "

Edmund Teske

Jim, Bronson Caves, Hollywood hills, California

So for the next four hours Todd kept Clara and Andy away from Jim, took them to dinner and made excuses, said Jim would see them that night.

"We all did the same," says Ray. "We all took turns, kind of diverting her."

"Oh, didn't we all!" says Bill Siddons, who was then a handsome nineteen-year-old surfer and the Doors' road manager.

Ray reenacted the incident. "Yes, ma'am, he's over here, I saw him walk by here . . ."

"No, I saw him go outside," Siddons added, continuing the deception.

Clara arrived early for the concert and heard Bill remark, "There's something wrong with the PA."

Clara didn't know what a PA was but said, "What do you mean there's something wrong? Where's Jim? What's wrong with my son's PA?"

Clara and Andy stood to one side of the stage that night with Todd Schiffman, who assured them they'd see Jim immediately after the show. Clara was stunned and Andy embarrassed by Jim's rendition of "The End" that night. After screaming, "Mother? I want to . . . *FUCK YOU!*" he gave his mother a vacant stare, and then he screamed again, this time showing his teeth.

After the concert Todd shepherded Clara and Andy to a hotel room where they were told Jim was waiting to see them, but once there, he confessed that Jim had already left for New York to appear on *The Ed Sullivan Show.*

It was bedlam each Sunday backstage at the Ed Sullivan Theater on Fifty-fourth Street. Sometimes there were more than a hundred guests and the logistics of the show were complicated. The hallways and dressing rooms reverberated with the sounds of jugglers and drill teams and sopranos and tap dancers, as production personnel carrying clipboards tried to organize the unruly crowd.

The Doors met Bob Precht in their dressing room. He was Ed Sullivan's son-in-law as well as the show's director.

"We have the tiniest little problem," Precht said, holding the finger and thumb of his right hand close together. "Nothing very important, but . . ."

The four Doors exchanged puzzled glances.

"It's about your song 'Light My Fire,' which I think is just wonderful."

The Doors remained silent.

"Uh, the network, that is, we, I mean, on CBS you cannot say the word 'higher.' I know it's silly"—he shrugged dramatically, gestured with his hands—"but we'll have to change the song." He pulled a scrap of paper from his jacket pocket and read, "The line is, 'Girl we couldn't get much higher.' "

Jim and the others were not surprised. Hadn't their own record company edited the word "high" from a song on their first album? Jim was also aware that a week earlier Pete Seeger had been censored on another CBS program, the popular *Smothers Brothers Show*, and that Precht had personally censored Bob Dylan's appearance on the Sullivan show.

"Sure," said Jim, "I think we can come up with another line."

Precht grinned broadly, told the Doors they were super sports, loped to the dressing room door, and called in his father-in-law. Precht called him "Mr. Sullivan."

"You boys look great when you smile," Sullivan said. "Don't be so serious."

Jim looked at the television impresario from under drooping lids and said, "Well, uh, we're kind of a sullen group."

When Precht and Sullivan left the room, Jim and the others exchanged looks. Right. They'd sing a new line in rehearsal and then, on the show, they'd sing the original.

In the control room when it happened, Bob Precht began to scream in anger. "You can't do that!" he shouted at the tiny images on the television monitors in front of him. "You guys are dead on this show! You'll never do this show again!" After the show he went up to the boys, whining, "You promised me, boys, you promised . . ."

"Gee," said Jim, shrugging, "I guess we just forgot in all the excitement."

The same week there was a party in the wine cellar of Delmonico's, an expensive restaurant on Park Avenue. All the important writers and editors turned out, radio programmers were there, so were Steve Paul (owner of the Scene) and Andy Warhol. Danny Fields sat sipping wine with Gloria Stavers. The best and the worst groupies came and stayed and drank. Jim got drunk and threw ice cubes at the girls. Danny suggested the bar be closed. Jim objected. He knew well whose party it was and opened a bottle of champagne by smashing the neck on the edge of a table. He followed this by pulling bottles of vintage wine from the racks, breaking them, heaving them, and distributing them to fellow drinkers.

The behavior was unchanged after the party. Andy Warhol gave Jim an ivory and gold French telephone. Soon Jim was sitting in the back seat of a limousine with Steve Paul, Gloria, and Andy. As the limo rounded the corner of Park Avenue and Fifty-third Street, Jim leaned out the window and tossed the French phone into a trash can and yelled at the passing cars.

It was nearly 3 A.M. by now and Jim decided to get even with Jac Holzman for not showing at the party. Jac had seen no reason to put in an appearance as everything was going great for his clients—the party, in fact, was to celebrate the success of "Light My Fire" and to serve as the Doors' official introduction-to-stardom press party. Clearly Jac had done his job well, so why flatter himself by attending? A serious misjudgment he was soon to learn.

In a loud whiskey-slurred voice Jim ordered the limo driver to the Holzmans' elegant Chelsea address. Gloria shivered, Danny questioned Jim's judgment, and Steve begged to be let out to catch a cab. Jim ignored them.

Paul Ferrara

Publicity photo, in snakeskin suit

At Jac's house Jim insisted everyone accompany him to the door of Holzmans' ten-room luxury apartment. He tried the downstairs buzzer, and when no response came from Jac's apartment, he rang all the other apartments until one foolhardy neighbor buzzed the group through the security doors.

At Jac's front door Jim's performance graduated from persistent ringing to slamming into the steel door with his sweat-drunk body. After beating himself to the floor and still receiving no response, Jim ripped up half the hallway carpet and then noisily led his party down the eight flights of stairs to the marble lobby, where he carefully and methodically threw up all over the entrance.

And then the Doors went west again.

In the publicity business the "A" list is the list of writers and editors whose attention the publicist would most like to attract to his client. These are the people at *Time, Newsweek,* and *The New York Times,* and in 1967, at the *Saturday Evening Post* and *Life* and *Look.* The "A" list for the Doors was broader than it was for most bands because they had potential appeal to a broader audience. This meant their list stretched from the *Times* to the underground press, from *Vogue* to *16* magazine.

"He made good copy," says Danny Fields, the Elektra promotion man. "He was so smart. He gave such great interviews and such fabulous quotes. He just threw them out. And the writers got off writing about him. That was the true secret. He made the writers *enjoy* writing about him. So they didn't laugh at him. They took him perfectly seriously."

Jim and the other Doors *wanted* to be taken seriously. So their interviews sounded rather like college bull sessions. The interview with *Newsweek*'s man in Los Angeles in October when they returned from New York was a good example. "There are things that you know about," said Ray, quoting Jim, "and things you don't, the known and the unknown, and in between are the doors—that's us." Later this line would be attributed to William Blake.

"It's a search," Jim said, "an opening of one door after another. As yet there's no consistent philosophy or politics. Sensuousness and evil is an attractive image to us now, but think of it as a snakeskin that will be shed sometime. Our work, our performing, is a striving for metamorphosis. Right now I'm more interested in the dark side of life, the evil thing, the dark side of the moon, the nighttime. But in our music it appears to me that we're seeking, striving, trying to break through to some cleaner, freer realm.

"It's like a purification ritual in the alchemical sense. First you have to have the period of disorder, chaos, returning to a primeval disaster region. Out of that you purify the elements and find a new seed of life, which transforms all life and all matter and the personality until finally, hopefully, you emerge and marry all those dualisms and opposites. Then you're not talking about evil and good anymore but something unified and pure. Our music and personalities as seen in the performance are still in a state of chaos and disorder with maybe an incipient element of purity kind of starting. Lately, when we've appeared in person, it's started to merge together."

Then he delivered his best slogan yet: "Think of us as erotic politicians."

To the *Time* magazine writer Jim was pleased to talk about the concept of rock theater, mixing music with "the structure of a poetic drama." About Los Angeles he said, "This city is looking for a ritual to join its fragments. The Doors are looking for such a ritual, too—a sort of electric wedding." And then: "We hide ourselves in the music to reveal ourselves."

At all times Jim was aware of image and press. Before each concert he asked one of Elektra's publicists which writers were in the audience and who read the publications they wrote for. He worked closely with Gloria Stavers on the stories she printed in *16,* going over each one until he was satisfied.

The way Jim worked with photographers was revealing, too. During the Doors' stay in New York in September there were three important photography sessions and it was for these that he went to Jay Sebring, Hollywood's most fashionable hair stylist, before he left Los Angeles.

"What do you want it to look like?" Jay asked.

"Like this," Jim said, producing a page torn from a history book showing a picture of a statue. "Like Alexander the Great."

Jim with new leather at Gloria Stavers'

Gloria Stavers

Modeling Gloria's fur coat just before a concert in New York City, 1967

Gloria Stavers

Circa 1967, New York City

"Now, Jim," said Gloria Stavers, "you must listen to me." Gloria had Jim in her East Side apartment and was shooting some pictures for *16.* "I want you to look at the camera, not at me. Imagine the camera to be whatever or whomever you want it to be—a woman you want to seduce, a man you want to kill, a mother you want to upset, a boy you want to seduce, whatever you want it to be, it is. Remember that."

The other Doors had left. Jim began to prowl through the spacious flat, looking into closets and opening drawers, pulling out coats and jewelry. Gloria followed him, watching intently. He went to a mirror and rearranged his hair, leaving it in precise disarray. When Gloria wanted to comb it, he snapped at her, "Get that comb away from me!" She returned to her silent role as photographer. Jim pulled her three-quarter-length fur coat over his embroidered Nehru shirt, stood against a wall with his hands crossed at his crotch, his skinny leather-clad legs widespread. He looked at her from under lidded eyes as the camera began to click. Then he took off the coat and shirt and began trying on her necklaces.

The following day the Doors reported to the studio of Joel Brodsky, Elektra's photographer. Jim was still wearing his low-slung leather pants and was shirtless again. Around his neck was a single strand of tiny colored beads borrowed from Gloria the night before. The other Doors were given black ponchos and positioned against a black background so only Jim's figure and three heads would appear in the photographs. For an hour Joel had John, Ray, and Robby move only slightly, but allowed Jim to strike whatever pose he wanted. He grimaced and glowered, pointed his finger accusingly and held out his hand for help, flexed and contorted his supple physique. He began to drink, gulping the whiskey between poses: throwing his head back to bunch up the stallionlike muscles of his neck, duplicating a Mick Jagger pout, then a curled-lip Elvis sneer, snarling, spitting, hissing, sticking out his tongue. Never smiling, never laughing.

"Most groups, when you take their picture in a studio," says Brodsky, "kid each other, make jokes, try to break each other up. The Doors never did that. They were serious about what they were doing at all times. And Jim was the most serious of the four."

Gloria had taken only one roll of film. As soon as she saw the proof sheet, she sent it, and the Doors' first album, to a friend at *Vogue*. Less than a week later Jim entered a *Vogue* studio and went directly to a hat rack hung with costumes from an earlier shooting. He began trying them on and leaping about.

"Ahhhhh," said the photographer, "I have a live one."

In October the Doors performed for nearly fifty thousand people and another thirty-five thousand marched on the Pentagon. Elektra announced it had orders for five hundred thousand copies of the second album. Five U.S. marines were killed and thirty wounded in Vietnam when they were bombed accidentally by U.S. planes. John Wayne started making a movie about the Green Berets. A parade was held in San Francisco marking the "Death of the Hippie and the Birth of Free Man" and Joan Baez, Mimi Fariña, and their mother were arrested for demonstrating at the Oakland army induction center. "People Are Strange" went into the national Top 20 and on another record a middle-aged advertising executive named Victor Lundberg read "An Open Letter to My Teenage Son" to a background of "The Battle Hymn of the Republic." The final lines:

> If you are not grateful to a country that gave your father the opportunity to work for his family, to give you the things you've had, and you do not feel pride enough to fight to continue in this manner, then I assume the blame for your failure to recognize the true value of our birth right. And I would remind you that your mother will love you no matter what you do because she is a woman. And I love you, too, son, but I also love our country and the principles for which we stand. And if you decide to burn your draft card, then burn your birth certificate at the same time. From that moment on I have no son.

The lines were clearly drawn. In 1967 it was Us vs. Them. In October Jim began writing his most militant songs.

The first of these took its name from a revered national monument, "The Unknown Soldier," and was worked out on the road in much the same way the Doors had created their earlier songs in concert at the Whiskey a Go Go and Ondine. Over a period of two or three months it developed into one of the band's most successful theater pieces.

> Wait until the war is over
> and we're both a little older.
> The unknown soldier

Suddenly the dirge became a celebration. John and Robby

joined Ray in a rhythm that was both military (metronomic) and carnivalesque.

Breakfast where the news is read
television children fed
unborn living, living, dead,
bullet strikes the helmet's head.

And it's all over for the unknown soldier,
It's all over for the unknown soldier.

There was the sound of marching feet as Jim, Ray, and Robby began stomping in unison and John provided appropriate marching rhythm on the snare drum. Ray counted cadence.

Hut
Hut
Hut ho hee up
Hut
Hut
Hut ho hee up
Hut
Hut
Hut ho hee up
Comp'nee
Halt

The stomping stopped and Jim adopted the tortured stance of a prisoner about to be executed by firing squad. There was a second of silence as all eyes focused on him, his arms held taut behind his back, head held high, his chest thrust forward proudly.

Preeee-zent!
Arms!

There was a long drum roll and then John usually broke a drumstick slamming the rim of his drum, simulating a shot. Simultaneously Jim violently folded in the middle as if hinged and fell to the floor in a heap. Another, longer silence, and then Ray's mysterioso organ resumed and a solemn voice came from the still-crumpled form on the stage floor.

Make a grave for the unknown soldier
nestled in your hollow shoulder
The unknown soldier

The celebration was revisited. Jim was up dancing joyously as he shouted:

It's all over!
The war is over!
It's all over
The war is over!

The second of Jim's militant songs written in this period—and what at first appears to be his most militant ever—was misunderstood by nearly everyone because they listened only to the first two verses.

Five to one, baby
One in five
No one here gets out alive
You get yours, baby
I'll get mine
Gonna make it, baby
If we try

The old get old
And the young get stronger
May take a week
And it may take longer

They got the guns
But we got the numbers
Gonna win, yeah
We're takin' over
Come on!

The song took its title from the first line, "Five to One," a statistic that went unexplained by Jim. Paul Rothchild's theory is that, "Five to one is the same as one in six, the approximate ratio of blacks to whites in the U.S., and one in five I remember was being reported as the dope-smoking ratio in Los Angeles." But whenever he was asked, Jim would only say that he didn't consider the song political.

Listened to in its entirety, the song seems to be a parody of all the naïve revolutionary rhetoric heard on the streets and read in the underground press in the late sixties. This interpretation is strongly supported by the final verse, the verse Jim's audience paid little attention to. In it Jim addressed some of the young people in his constituency, the "hippie/ flower child" hordes he saw in growing numbers, panhandling on the city sidewalks outside every concert hall.

Your ballroom days are over baby
Night is drawing near
Shadows of the evening crawl across the years
You walk across the floor with a flower in your
    hand
Trying to tell me no one understands
Trade in your hours for a handful of dimes

This is not to say that Jim had turned his back entirely on the "love generation" from which the band evolved. "We all really believed it," Ray says. "When we were playing at the Whiskey a Go Go, we believed that, hey, man, we are fucking taking over the country, we are gonna turn it around, we are gonna make the perfect society."

Jim himself said in 1969, "From a historical vantage point it probably will look like the troubadour period of France. I'm sure it will look incredibly romantic. I think we're going to look very good to future people, because so many changes are taking place and we're really handling it with a flair." It was, he said, a spiritual and cultural renaissance, "like what happened at the end of the plague in Europe that decimated half the population. People danced, they wore colorful clothing. It was a kind of incredible springtime."

As much as Jim empathized with his young fans, however, he remained different in many basic ways. Unlike the prototypal "hippy," Jim thought astrology was a pseudoscience, rejected the concept of the totally integrated personality, and expressed a distaste for vegetarianism because of the religious fervor often attached to the diet. It was, he said, dogma, and he had no use for that.

Jim's education, intelligence, and background further separated him from many of his fans. A college graduate instead of a dropout, a voracious reader with a highly catholic taste, he was hardly Marshall McLuhan's nonlinear, postliteral, tribal man. Whether he liked it or not, he was the obvious product of a Southern upper-middle-class family: charming, goal-oriented, and in many ways politically conservative. For instance, he looked down on most welfare recipients with the same contempt he felt for the long-haired panhandlers he criticized in "Five to One."

Another wedge between Jim and his audience was his move from psychedelics to alcohol. The binges were by now acquiring near mythic proportions.

Asher Dann had a theory: If he and Jim went out and got drunk the night before an important concert, Jim would get the urge out of his system and be relatively sober at showtime. It was a useless theory the November night the Doors performed for Bill Graham at Winterland in San Francisco. Jim drank with Ash at the hotel bar from three until eight: maybe ten or twelve drinks. Then they were joined by Todd Schiffman, who bought another round before urging them into a car for a rush down Fillmore Avenue, during which Jim sprayed the night with obscenities.

"Do you think he can go on?" Todd asked.

"Of course," said Asher Dann. "When he's drunk like this, he puts on a better show."

Only part true: when he was drunk he often gave his best shows; when he was drunk he also gave some of his worst shows.

The limousine came to a stop. Bill Graham appeared. *"Where the fuck've you been?"* he screamed.

"We're here, Bill," said Asher, obviously as drunk as Jim. "We're not late for the show."

Graham made his face into a mask and shouted, *"The contract reads the band was supposed to be here an hour ago: that means all four members of the band! Including Jim Morrison!"* Graham thrust a finger in Jim's direction. *"He's drunk, right?"*

From the moment Jim mounted the stage it was chaos. The crowd was ecstatic, adoring, stoned. Jim ran around, driving the spotlight man in the balcony crazy. He pitched himself at the edge of the tall stage, teetering above the light-show equipment in the pit, whirling the microphone like a lariat, sending it whistling over the heads of the audience. Bodies were getting crushed in front of the stage.

Bill Graham came rushing into the ballroom from his upstairs office, struggling through the crowd. He waved his arms, bidding for Jim's attention. Jim continued to whirl the microphone. His eyes were shut, the music pounding. Finally he let it go, whereupon it sped at Graham like a bullet, hit him in the forehead, and knocked him down.

Afterward in the dressing room Jim dared Asher to hit him and Asher did, sending Jim sprawling to the floor.

In November the Doors hit the newstands with the cream of the "A" list: *Newsweek, Time, The New York Times,* and *Vogue.* These were not just mentions or complimentary record re-

Paul Ferrara

In a favorite floppy leather hat and a rare smile

views—the press hierarchy were investigating and trying to *define* the Doors.

On November 6 *Newsweek* said, "The swinging Doors open up: Chill steel, weird twangs, a Halloween world and forbidden fruit." On the 15th *Vogue* used Jim's picture—barechested, wearing his silver Indian concho belt around his neck—to illustrate an article by a professor of art history, who told middle America that Jim "gets people. His songs are eerie, loaded with somewhat Freudian symbolism, poetic but not pretty, filled with suggestions of sex, death, transcendence . . . Jim Morrison writes as if Edgar Allan Poe had blown back as a hippie." On the 20th *Time* used Jim's quote from the Elektra biography: "I'm interested in anything about revolt, disorder, chaos," and then described the music as a search that "takes the Doors not only past such familiar landmarks of the youth odyssey as alienation and sex, but into symbolic realms of the unconscious—eerie night worlds filled with throbbing rhythms, shivery metallic tones, unsettling images." The photograph, taken backstage, showed Jim in black leather, slumped as if drugged, his face the only one hidden from the camera.

"There really hasn't been a major male sex symbol since James Dean died and Marlon Brando got a paunch," wrote Howard Smith, *The Village Voice*'s purveyor of the hip. "Dylan is more of a cerebral heart throb and the Beatles have always been too cute to be deeply sexy. Now along comes Jim Morrison of the Doors. If my antenna are right, he could be the biggest thing to grab the mass libido in a long time."

With this prognostication Smith published one of the Joel Brodsky photographs, what became known as the "Young Lion picture" at Elektra—a bust shot showing Jim's naked chest and one shoulder, a single strand of Gloria Staver's beads around his muscled neck, a Steve Canyon chin line, lips parted sensually, a look of searing intensity in his eyes, sideburns emphasizing the high cheekbones, hair sculpted à la Alexander the Great.

Even the more cynical critics admitted that Jim Morrison was a cultural superman, larger than life, capable of moving little girls, and many men, to sexual delight and intellectuals to profundity. The egghead New York critic Albert Goldman called him a "surf-born Dionysus" and a "hippie Adonis," while Digby Diehl, soon to become book editor of the *Los Angeles Times*, described him by referring to Norman O. Brown's "polymorphous perverse infantile sexuality."

On the Doors' next visit to New York Jim appeared wild-eyed and drunk at midnight at the boutique on the Lower East Side where he and Pamela had had an old friend make some bellbottoms on a previous East Coast visit. Trina Robbins was living in a back room, and when he rattled the window, she

Gloria Stavers

For a 16 magazine layout

woke up and let him in. "He didn't say a word. He walked in, took off his clothes, and just stood still, naked. And he was so beautiful, you know. He seemed a little shy but he asked me if I was going to take mine off or not."

Jim often saw Gloria Stavers, the understanding thirtyish ex-model with a brittle façade and soft candy center who edited the teenybopper magazine, *16.* Ray and John and Robby warned Gloria about Jim shortly after they first met, telling her about the night he hosed down the recording studio with a fire extinguisher. "Be careful," said Robby, when Gloria told Jim to stand against a wall for a photograph, "he'll do what you say and do what you say and do what you say, but then one day he'll do something very strange and violent." It was as if Robby were talking about a beloved brother who had fits. The warning was gentle and sincere.

The communal mind was still in operation. When Gloria told Jim she wanted to write about and photograph him rather than the group, Jim was concerned that the other Doors would feel slighted and went to some lengths to see that the whole thing was handled gracefully. When their managers told Jim he could be a bigger star without the other three, and richer if he merely had salaried musicians on the payroll instead of equal partners, Jim said he would think about it, then promptly told Ray and Robby and John, and together they began to talk of getting new managers. Jim told Gloria, "I can just look at Ray and know when I've gone too far." When Gloria told that to Ray, Ray said, "Well, I love him a lot."

In performance the communal mind was at its peak. "You see," says Ray, "when the Siberian shaman gets ready to go into his trance, all the villagers get together and shake rattles and blow whistles and play whatever instruments they have to send him off. There is a constant pounding, pounding, pounding. And those sessions last for hours and hours. It was the same way with the Doors when we played in concert. The sets didn't last that long, but I think that our drug experiences let

Gloria Stavers

Jim in Gloria Stavers' apartment, New York, 1967

us to get into it that much quicker. We knew the symptoms of the state, so that we could try to approximate it. It was like Jim was an electric shaman and we were the electric shaman's band, pounding away behind him. Sometimes he wouldn't feel like getting into the state, but the band would keep on pounding and pounding, and little by little it would take him over. God, I could send an electric shock through him with the organ. John could do it with his drumbeats. You could see every once in a while—twitch!—I could hit a chord and make him twitch. And he'd be off again. Sometimes he was just incredible. Just amazing. And the audience felt it, too!"

The police also felt it on December 9, 1968. One day past Jim's twenty-fourth birthday the Doors were in New Haven, Connecticut. Jim was backstage talking with a girl in a miniskirt. Cops were lounging against the hallway wall. Equipment managers were moving amplifiers. Hangers-on, like the girl, were everywhere. It was thirty minutes before the Doors were due to go on.

"We can't talk here," Jim told the girl. "Let's find someplace quieter."

The girl nodded mutely and followed Jim as he pushed open a door to a shower room, peered in, and then entered.

A few minutes later Jim and the girl were necking.

A cop walked in. "Hey, you kids! Get outta here! Nobody allowed backstage!"

Jim looked at the cop. "Who says?"

"I said get outta here. Come on now, move!"

"Eat it." Jim slapped his crotch with a cupped hand.

The cop reached for the can of mace that was hooked on his belt. "Last warning," he said. "Last chance."

"Last chance to eat it," Jim taunted.

The girl ran as the cop stepped forward and Jim caught the chemical spray in his face.

Jim propelled himself forward past the cop, then blindly threw himself into the hallway, bellowing, "*I've been maced! The fucking pig!*" A crowd gathered, and by the solicitous way Jim

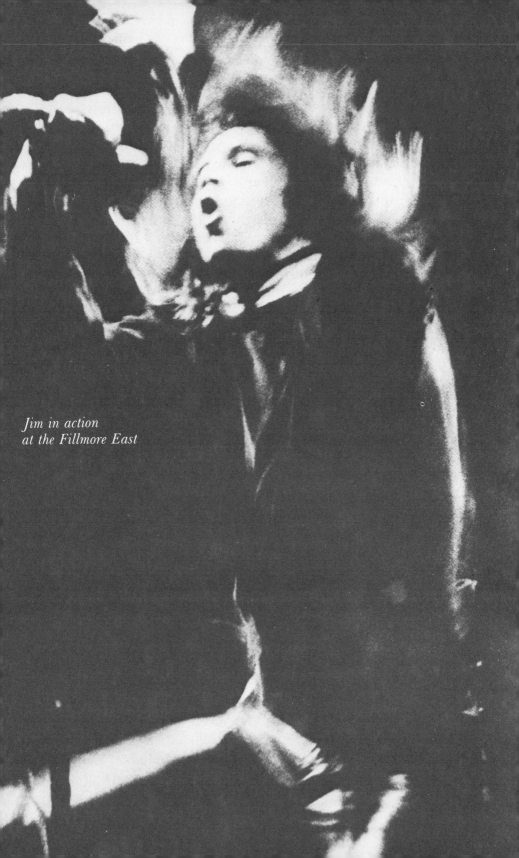

*Jim in action
at the Fillmore East*

was being treated, the cop realized he'd made a mistake.

Bill Siddons, the Doors' roadie, came rushing up and with the cop's assistance took Jim to a washbasin, where they doused his eyes with water. The cop apologized, and a few minutes later the show began.

During the show, the students applauded frequently and many of them joined Jim when he shouted, "We want the world and we want it . . . *now!*" When he spat at the audience contemptuously and threw his microphone stand, they hurled back adoration. Then during the instrumental break of "Back Door Man" Jim began to talk.

"I want to tell you about something that happened a few minutes ago right here in New Haven. This is New Haven, isn't it? New Haven, Connecticut, United States of America?"

The audience grew still as Jim recounted the details of his recent arrival: dinner and drinks, a conversation about religion with a waitress, an encounter with a girl in the dressing room. He and the girl began talking, he said. Against the rhythms of "Back Door Man" the spontaneous rap became hypnotic. "And we wanted some privacy. . . . And so we went into this shower room. We weren't doing anything, you know. Just standing there and talking. . . . And then this little man came in there, this little man in a little blue suit and a little blue cap. . . ."

A row of policemen stood along the front of the stage, facing the audience as cops at rock concerts traditionally do, to keep the teenyboppers armed with Instamatics at bay. But as Jim told his story, a few turned around.

" 'Whatcha doing' there?' " Jim was quoting the cop in the shower room.

" 'Nothin'.' "

"But he didn't go 'way. He stood there, and then he reached 'round behind him and he brought out this little black can of somethin'. Looked like shaving cream. And then he sprayed it in my eyes."

Nearly every cop was facing Jim now. He had been using a "dumb Southerner's" voice in telling the story, using it to ridicule the little man in the little blue suit. There was laughter from the audience, laughter directed at the cops.

"The whole world hates me!" Jim cried. "The fucking world . . . nobody loves me. The whole fucking world hates me." The audience sat rapt.

Jim gave the band a signal and crashed into the final chorus of the song: "Oh, Ahm a back door man . . ."

Suddenly the lights went on and Robby came forward to whisper in Jim's ear, "I think the cops are pissed."

Jim asked the audience if it wanted more music, and when the answer came back a noisy "Yes," Jim screamed, "Well, then turn off the lights! *Turn off the lights!*" The lights remained on and a police lieutenant who was head of the New Haven Police Department's Youth Division walked onstage and told Jim he was under arrest.

Jim whirled to face the cop, leather-clad legs braced in defiance, long wavy hair in damp disarray. He thrust his microphone under the cop's nose.

"Okay, pig," he said in a mix of schoolboy bravado and grown-up abhorrence of authority, "come on, say your thing, man!"

A second cop appeared and each took Jim by an arm and led him offstage through the curtains. They dragged him down a flight of stairs, wrestled him across a parking lot, stood him next to a patrol car and photographed him, knocked him down, kicked him, and threw him into the car for a ride to the station house where he was charged with performing an "indecent and immoral exhibition," breach of the peace, and resisting arrest.

The cops also arrested a writer for *The Village Voice* and a *Life* magazine photographer, unintentionally guaranteeing Jim maximum publicity.

A few days later Jim sat on the floor of the Doors' office amid collapsing piles of fan letters, two weeks' worth of newspapers and magazines, and the latest bundles of clippings from the Doors' publicist. Jim unfolded an article written by the film critic of the *Los Angeles Free Press*.

"Hey," he said after a minute, "any of you guys read what Gene Youngblood says about us?"

The others in the room looked up. Jim was smirking.

"He says, and I quote, 'The Beatles and the Stones are for blowing your mind; the Doors are for afterwards, when your mind is already gone.' "

Jim sat up straighter, as if reading from tablets. "Listen to what he says about the music. 'The Doors' music is the music of outrage. It is not sham. It probes the secrets of truth. It is avant-garde in content if not technique: it speaks of madness that dwells within us all, of depravity and dreams, but it speaks of them in relatively conventional musical terms. That is its strength and its beauty—a beauty that terrifies.

" 'The music of the Doors is more surreal than psychedelic. It is more anguish than acid. More than rock, it is ritual— the ritual of psychic-sexual exorcism. The Doors are the warlocks of pop culture. Morrison is an angel; an exterminating angel.' "

John Densmore took the clipping from Jim's hands and looked at it. "Hey," he said, "in the first paragraph he says he was fucking and just as he came we were playing 'Horse Latitudes.' "

Everyone gathered around, reaching for the clip.

"Lookit that," Bill Siddons said. "It says, 'Doors can provide instant enlightenment through sex.' "

There was laughter and for ten minutes jokes were made. For months afterward Jim said Youngblood was the first to really see where his head was at.

Then, just before Christmas, the afternoon before they played their first date at the Shrine, Ray and Dorothy asked Jim and Pamela to be best man and bridesmaid at their wedding.

"Far out! When, Ray?"

"This afternoon . . . at City Hall."

That night Jim had to be dragged off the stage because he wanted to sing ballads to the newlyweds all night.

CHAPTER

6

Jim was living in a $10-a-night
room in the Alta Cienega Motel, an anonymous two-story
structure of virtually identical rooms built against a hillside
that was a short steep walk to the Sunset Strip. In the years to
follow, this motel became the center of Jim Morrison's universe.

It was suited for when Jim had no car, or his license had
been taken away for drunkenness. Everything was within walking distance, even by L.A. standards. Elektra's new offices and
recording studio were less than a hundred yards down La
Cienega Boulevard, a broad avenue known as Restaurant Row
where Jim ate hundreds of meals. Even closer were the Doors'
own offices and Jim's three favorite bars.

Jim was in Room 32 on the second floor, sprawled across
the green chenille spread that covered the lumpy double bed.
A thin girl of seventeen or eighteen stood near the small television set, her back to the tiny bathroom.

Jim drained a beer and threw the can at a plastic trash bas-

Jerry Hopkins

Alta Cienega Motel, West Hollywood. Jim lived here off and on (1969)

ket next to the blond dresser. He missed, knocking a book to the floor: *The Origins and History of Consciousness.*

"Fuck it." Jim belched. He looked at the girl. He moved his chin upward, signaling her to come to the bed. She was a pickup from the night before; he got her whole life story, then he "butt-fucked" her, and now he was bored.

"Let me see your hands," he said.

The girl held out her hands. Jim took one hand by the wrist and began pulling the rings off her fingers. He was rough. She cried in pain.

"Give me your other hand," he ordered before releasing the first.

She hesitated. He squeezed her wrist and repeated his order. She complied and he pulled off all her other rings, tearing the skin.

Then he released her. He held the rings in one hand, and leaning across the bed, pulled another can of beer from a paper bag and ordered the girl to open it. She complied.

There was a sudden knocking at the door.

"Yeah?" said Jim irritably. "Who is it?"

"It's a secret," came a woman's teasing voice.

Jim obviously knew the voice. "Whyn't you come back later, I don't have any clothes on," he said.

"Jim, I came all the way down here and now you won't even let me in."

"Now, Pam sweetheart, I'm busy."

"Jim, I know there's someone in there. I know there is! I can't believe you're doing this again. You're really disgusting!"

Jim was silent.

"Jim, I've got this wonderful leg of lamb in the oven for supper and my new apartment is—"

Jim interrupted. "Well, you see, there's this crazy girl in here, Pam, she's just lying on the bed with her legs open and I don't know what to do."

"You're disgusting, Jim Morrison, and I'm leaving!"

"But, Pam sweetheart, she's your sister, Judy. You shouldn't be mad."

Jim turned to the girl in the room and apologized for there being no back door for her to escape through. "And you can't go out the window; it's twenty feet to the sidewalk." He looked around. "Maybe you should go stand in the shower."

Pamela called out, "I want to see her, Jim."

The maid arrived outside and began arguing with Pamela, telling her she was making too much noise, she had to leave. Jim pulled on a shirt and pants and left the room.

"Now, Pam sweetheart," he said, putting his arm around her shoulder, "I was just kidding you, I didn't have your sister in there with me." Jim held out his hand, showing her the rings. "Look," he said, "these are for you. One of my fans gave them to me."

Pamela took a turquoise ring, slipped it onto a finger, and pocketed the others. They walked to Pamela's car and got in.

The scene was typical. Jim was capable of tenderness and cruelty in the space of only a few minutes. To some, he appeared to be a "cuddly teddy bear." To all, he pledged love, the moment's truth. But to many, including Pamela, the pledge tested credibility.

To make amends, Jim told Pamela he was taking her to Las Vegas with Bob Gover and his girlfriend. Gover was the randy fortyish author of *$100 Misunderstanding,* a funny novel about a naïve white college male and an incredulous but very hip black whore. He had an assignment from the *New York Times Magazine* to write a story depicting Jim as the product of Machiavellian Hollywood puppeteers. When he insisted that Jim was his own creation, he was taken off the story, but by then the two had become pals, sharing a love of books, women, and alcohol. Gover had once lived in Vegas and said he wanted to show Jim the side of town the tourists don't see. Predictably, Jim and Pamela fought, so Jim went to Vegas without her.

Jim alighted with several others from Gover's car, stood in the dry, desert evening heat, and stared for a moment at the nightclub marquee: Pussy Cat a Go Go Presents *Stark Naked and the Car Thieves.* Jim laughed and swaggered forward through the parking lot. He had been drinking since noon and it was now about ten. He glanced behind him at the others in his party and, throwing his fingers to his lips, sucked noisily on an imaginary joint.

"Wanna hit?" he asked.

The guard stepped back as if repulsed, then leaped forward, drawing his billy club in the same motion. "Hey, wait a minute." One of Jim's companions stepped in front of Jim to protest.

The guard brought the club down on the nearest skull, then turned and clobbered Jim. Jim looked more surprised

Paul Ferrara

Age twenty-four

than hurt, although blood was running down the side of the his face, and the guard hit him again.

Soon after that the police arrived, putting Jim and Gover—the two with the longest hair—in the rear of their black-and-white.

"Chickenshit." Jim spoke in a whisper and sat quiet again.

"*Chickenshit.*" He raised his voice, then was silent.

"Pig," he said.

"*Pig.*" Again.

"Chickenshit pig."

The cops in the front seat ignored Jim's taunting and it was Gover who tried to silence him. "Cool it, man, these guys can shake our brains if they want, they're allowed to do that."

"No, man," said Jim, "it's a test of courage."

Bob was booked for public drunkenness, Jim for the same, plus vagrancy and failure to identify himself. As usual, he carried nothing in his pockets except a credit card.

"Hey, whatcha got there," one of the cops at the jailhouse said when Jim and Bob were ushered in, "a couple of girls?"

"Yay, boy, lookit that hair. Haw haw."

"Think those beautiful creatures oughta strip so's we know for sure what sex they are, whatcha say?"

Bob and Jim were made to strip and after booking were told to get dressed and then put in the jail's holding tank. The bars of the tank reached to a twenty-foot-high ceiling, and when the door was locked, Jim scrambled to the top of the cage like a monkey to look down over the adjacent room of desks and cops.

"*Hey, Bob,*" he called, "*ain't they the ugliest motherfuckers you ever saw?*"

Jim began to laugh. "Ah-hee-hee-hee-hee-hee . . ."

One of the cops approached and looked up at him. "I get off at midnight and that's when we got a date. Just you and me in a room. See ya later . . . sweetie."

At five minutes to midnight Jim escaped a certain beating

when Bob's friends bailed them out, and Jim resumed his partying.

This, too, was a typical scene. In the first months of 1968 Jim's drinking accelerated at a pace that had the other Doors alarmed. In the Dylan Thomas and Brendan Behan tradition, Jim was becoming not just a Mythic Drunk, but an Everyday One.

At a party at singer John Davidson's house Jim and Janis Joplin got drunk together. Paul Rothchild remembers them with their arms draped over each other's shoulders: "Mr. and Mrs. Rock 'n' Roll." But then Jim turned mean and grabbed Janis by the hair, pulling her head into his crotch and holding it there. Finally she broke free, fleeing to the bathroom in tears. Jim was wrestled into a car. Janis came running after him. She reached inside the car and began hitting Jim on the head with a bottle of Southern Comfort. Jim was laughing as they pulled away.

In New York, at the Scene, Jim stumbled and emptied a table of drinks in Janis's lap, then, moved by the music, lurched to the stage where he fell on his knees, gripping Jimi Hendrix's legs in a fervent, sodden embrace.

Back in Los Angeles at Barney's Beanery he got into an argument with his pal, Tom Baker. In a film he'd made with Andy Warhol Tom appeared nude, and now he called Jim a "prick-tease."

"At least I let it all hang out, man," he said.

Jim was drunk and he reached for his zipper. "Well, I can do that," he bragged. "I can do that. That's nothin'. That's not art."

In a Midwestern airport, drunk again, Jim insisted someone push him around in a wheelchair, from which he fell periodically, jerking violently as if in the grip of a massive seizure. Finally he fell out and didn't move. He had passed out under a bench, and Bill Siddons politely blocked him in with carry-on luggage and guitar cases.

Jim welcomed his success in the to-the-victor-go-the-spoils rock and roll tradition. Besides acquiring increasing numbers of girls, he started spending money furiously—not on houses and cars but on huge bar bills and custom clothing including a lizard skin coat and a $2,200 suit of unborn pony hide. The latter was carelessly tossed in an airport trash can after one person too many had taken it for seal skin. He had picked up a small crowd of sycophants who accompanied him everywhere, basking in the peculiar glow pop stardom cast in the sixties. They drove Jim wherever he wished to go, competed to light his occasional filter cigarettes, ran errands to the liquor store, kept the vocal booth in the studio stocked with whacked-out groupie types.

Jim also began assembling his first coterie of serious drinkers, including Tom Baker, the actor; and the then virtually unknown singer Alice Cooper and a member of Alice's band, Glen Buxton. Jim was, by now, very serious about his drinking, no matter how casual he seemed. He spent his days in the bars that practically surrounded his motel. He never entered the studio without a bottle.

Alcohol was Jim's panacea, the magic potion that answered his needs, solved his problems, and seemed to him historically the thing to do. Its consumption was in character with the Dionysian image he identified with and liked to project. It was also firmly embedded in the American cultural tradition.

Almost as soon as the third album started, it got crazy. First in the rehearsal room and then the studio it was wall-to-wall hangers-on. Bruce Botnick recalls the night the fat girl passed out in the vocal booth with her dress hiked up above her waist, no panties on, and everybody who wanted to had a poke.

Then came the night that John threw down his drumsticks and quit. Once before he had done this, when Jim was too drunk to sing for the University of Michigan's homecoming dance. But now there was a finality. "That's it!" John spat.

Paul Ferrara

Publicity photo, 1968

"I've had it, no more, I quit! I've had it this time, I quit!" And he was gone.

Ray and Robby looked at each other and then down at Jim, who was collapsed on the studio floor, lying in a spreading stain of urine. Ray slowly stood and walked into the control room. He shrugged his big shoulders and said, "I don't know . . ." The next day it was business as usual with all four Doors present.

Discreetly, John and Robby and Ray began asking around about who might be hired to exert a little friendly control. Paul Rothchild suggested Bobby Neuwirth, a friend then living in New York. The Doors said, yeah, they'd heard of him. "Wasn't he Dylan's roadie?"

"More than that," said Paul. Neuwirth was a catalyst, a scene maker, a smooth, take-charge personality with a happy-go-lucky façade. He also knew everybody there was to know— "Who do you wanna meet—Brando?" Joan Baez said Neuwirth was Dylan's inspiration for "Like a Rolling Stone." "And," Rothchild told the three Doors, "he can outhit Jim Morrison forever. He can entertain him, and deal with him intellectually, out-boogie him, and drink more, run harder, sleep less, and get him to the show on time."

The three told Paul he sounded right and Paul called Jac Holzman in New York to report that the situation had deteriorated so shockingly they weren't sure there would be a third album unless somebody did something about Jim. Jac said Elektra would pay half of Neuwirth's salary.

Because Neuwirth is what he calls a "hang-out artist," he had met Jim in New York, so they weren't strangers, but to make his role seem natural, Paul brought him along when he joined the Doors on tour in March. A plan developed whereby Bobby would start making a film of the Doors—a miniature documentary that could be used to promote one of the upcoming singles, much like the films made for "Break On Through" and "The Unknown Soldier."

Of course Jim realized what was going on. "Do not say the Doors did it behind his back," says Neuwirth, "because nobody *ever* did anything behind *that* cat's back, man, because if you knew him at *all*, you knew he wasn't that dumb. He was hip to it—*instantly*. I was supposed to be a sort of nondirecting director, right? But it didn't work out like that. The cat was hip to *every* move that was being made." So, Neuwirth says, they settled into a comfortable relationship. First he tried to teach Jim how to play the guitar, but Jim said no, it would take too long. Then they just did what Bobby knew best: they hung out.

"It was not awkward at *all*, man. Potentially volatile, because I like cold beers, too, man . . . and tequila. Let's face it, there wasn't no way to talk Jim outta havin' a drink. You just ended up having one with him."

Jac Holzman visited one of the recording sessions shortly after Neuwirth was hired and was pulled conspiratorially into a vocal booth. "I have to ask you a favor," Robby said.

"Sure, Robby."

Robby told Jac they wanted an advance on the royalties they'd earned, but which weren't due to be paid for a few months.

"How much you need?"

"I don't know, we want to buy our way out of our contract with Sal and Ash."

The Doors had been discussing the move for months. Dann and Bonafede had gotten them a good agent and an efficient publicity firm, but they had also tried to break up the group by enticing Jim to go it alone, and they were providing Jim with too many backstage bottles. So they talked to Robby's father and then to their lawyer, Max Fink.

Jac Holzman had never liked the Doors' managers because he thought they had driven a wedge between him and the group when they had insisted the boys change their telephone numbers and keep the new ones from the people at

Elektra. So he gladly advanced the Doors $250,000, a portion of what the record sales warranted. Dann and Bonafede settled for a fifth of that.

The Doors decided to ask their old road manager, Bill Siddons, to take over. He had left them the first of the year to return to school to avoid the draft, but with the $1,500 a month the Doors promised him—rather than a percentage—he figured he could afford to drop his student deferment and hire a good draft attorney (who later also got Robby an exemption). Bill, just nineteen, was a Canadian citizen with the status of resident alien, but he was the perfect southern Californian: a tall, blond, and well-shaped individual obsessed by surfboards, motorcycles, dope, and pretty girls.

It wasn't unusual in those days for someone of Bill's youth and naïveté to become a successful rock band's manager. The bands often turned to their roadies for help when they were in trouble. Besides, it was understood that the Doors would actually be managing themselves, making all the creative decisions while Bill ran the office and served as a liaison between them and their lawyer, agent, accountant, and publicists.

Jim's mood and behavior improved and a series of four shows at the new Fillmore East in New York topped all others in recent memory. Bill Graham objected strongly to showing the violent impressionistic film the Doors had made for "The Unknown Soldier"—in it Jim was tied to a post on the Venice beach, shot, and blood gushed from his mouth—but finally he agreed.

The teenyboppers, now in full bloom, accepted the black-white Irish Morrison as no less a figure than God. In *Crawdaddy* writer Kris Weintraub described Jim this way in the summer of 1968:

> He stepped to the microphone, grabbed the top with his right hand and the stand with his left fingertips, and looked up so the light hit his face. The world began at that moment. There isn't another face like that in the world. It's so beautiful and not even handsome

David Sygall

Fillmore East, New York

in the ordinary way. I think it's because you can tell
by looking at him that he *is* God. When he offers to
die on the cross for us it's OK because he *is* Christ.

Another, calmer writer for the same magazine recalled:

> After his symbolic death, the whole world cele-
> brates wildly, while Morrison sings hysterically on the
> soundtrack: "It's all over, baby! The war is over!"
> When the film played at the Fillmore East, a
> young audience brimming with anti-war frustration
> broke into pandemonium. "The war is over!" cried
> teenyboppers in the aisles. "The Doors ended the
> fucking war!" The Doors' little passion play had
> grabbed the audience. Jimmy and the boys had done
> it again.

As "Unknown Soldier" went onto the record charts, another crisis occurred. This was in Los Angeles when the Doors
went back into the studio. Ray walked up to the group's equipment manager of four months, Vince Treanor, and asked for
some change for the Coke machine.

"Speaking of change," Vince said, "don't you think it's
time you had a new manager?" He was, of course, recom-
mending himself. Ray was stunned.

It was Vince's opinion that Bill was doing the group great
harm, and he offered it to all four Doors individually. Then
the four Doors and Paul Rothchild went into the control room
and some time later were joined by Bill, who stalked past
Vince with little more than a nod. The Doors decided to stick
with Bill. They agreed that Vince was an electronic genius (in
an emergency situation one night he had disassembled, re-
paired, and rebuilt Robby's guitar amp in the dark onstage).
They further agreed that it would be impossible to find anyone more loyal to the Doors than the somber organ builder
from Massachusetts. But they felt he didn't have the right personality. He had a bad temper and was one of those true ec-
centrics whose manner kept many at arm's length. At the same

time, they decided that Vince should be given a promotion and a raise, from equipment manager to road manager, from $400 to $500 a month, plus $100 a performance.

This small stress past, the Doors turned their attention once more to a major stress, completion of the album.

It wasn't going smoothly. A long composition called "Celebration of the Lizard" was scrapped except for a short piece that appeared as "Not to Touch the Earth." Jim took the song's first lines—"Not to touch the earth/Not to see the sun"—from the table of contents of *The Golden Bough*. "Lizard" in its rough form had run twenty-four minutes and its retirement—after many hours in the studio—left half the album unplanned.

So the Doors dipped into what little remained of their early repertoire and recorded songs Jim wrote in Venice, including what was to be their next big hit, "Hello, I Love You," remembered from the original demo tape by Jac Holzman's young son, Adam. Arrangements for other songs were created in the studio, which ate up expensive studio time. For one, "My Wild Love," the Doors gave up on the music and turned it into work song by getting everyone present including Mark James, Billy's young son, to clap their hands, stamp their feet, and chant in unison.

More time was consumed by the perfectionism of Paul Rothchild. Nearly every song on the album required at least twenty takes—admittedly a lot of the blown takes were Jim's fault—while "The Unknown Soldier," recorded in two parts, required a total of 130 starts. The album was finally finished in May.

Jim staggered through it with determination, but more and more he showed his frustration and boredom by neglecting his music to commit his time to an increasing number of nonmusical activities. One of these was film.

When the French director Jean-Luc Godard appeared for the American premiere of *La Chinoise* at the University of Southern California, Jim took a seat in the front row. His novelist friend Bob Gover was writing a screenplay and they talked about getting Jim involved. Joan Didion, who wrote a flattering piece about Jim for the *Saturday Evening Post,* and her writer-husband, John Gregory Dunne, optioned the film rights for a book called *Needle Park* and wanted Jim and his friend Tom Baker for leading roles. And Bobby Neuwirth's short black-and-white documentary, *Not to Touch the Earth,* was edited as a sort of prototype for other Doors-produced promotional films.

"The idea was," says Bobby, "the Doors would never have to do the *Dick Clark Show,* or some of the other shows. They would just send over the latest film. That way nobody'd have to move any amps, and nobody'd have to be sober."

Bobby's film was never used. The Doors decided not to release "Not to Touch the Earth" as a single and Bobby was dropped from the team.

With Bobby's departure came a decision to make a feature-length documentary. The four Doors eagerly agreed to share the cost; all believed the film would be an investment with a large potential return. If it went into feature release and was as popular as, say, Dylan's *Don't Look Back,* they could show a large profit. Even a television sale would put the project in the black. Either way, the film was expected to enhance the group's creative status while promoting its financial worth. Film was an eminently acceptable thing for rock bands to get into in 1968, and the Doors were among the earliest to get interested.

Twenty thousand dollars were spent on cameras, lights, tape recording and editing equipment, and three full-time "employees" were hired. Two were former film school classmates of Jim's and Ray's. The first was Paul Ferrara, a good-looking smoothie who had been on the early Venice scene and was now into photography. The second was Frank Lisciandro, a soft-spoken and somewhat kooky zen student who with his wife Kathy (later a Doors secretary) had served two years in the Peace Corps in Africa. The third was Babe Hill, one of

Paul Ferrara's old high school friends from the flatlands suburb of Inglewood, where until recently Babe had been married
with two children.

For the next three months these three men followed the
Doors all over southern California—from Disneyland to Catalina—and then all over America, to capture them at work and
play. Like everyone else who entered the Doors' orbit, all
three were drawn by the force of Jim's personality and the
depth of his generosity. In time they became his closest
friends, especially the childlike Babe, whose open and ready
acceptance of everything and everybody entranced Jim. "I
don't know if that cat's stupid or a genius, but he sure knows
how to have fun," Jim once said.

At the same time Jim was wrestling again with his poetry.
Although the other Doors thought of "Celebration of the Lizard" as a kind of albatross around their necks before it was finally discarded from the third album, Jim was happy with the
words, and viewed the piece as "pure drama." It reiterated
many of his favorite themes, including prison, insanity,
dreams, and death. (Unfortunately, only two of the 133 lines
in the poem would be remembered: "I am the Lizard King/I
can do anything.") He also enjoyed digging out some of his
early writings from UCLA for *Eye* magazine—a scattershot essay on vision that was poetic and insightful, but so esoteric the
editors felt impelled to add a slew of footnotes to explain his
arcane references.

Pamela gave Jim a tooled leather satchel to hold the poems that he so neatly and laboriously typed and arranged a
meeting with the San Francisco poet Michael McClure. Jim
said he wanted to see McClure's controversial new play, *The
Beard,* and Pamela called one of her sister's old friends, who
was McClure's literary agent. He got them tickets to the Los
Angeles production and after that Jim met the beat generation
poet who had been one of his high school heroes. The meeting was a disappointment to them both. Michael McClure
hadn't read any of Jim's poetry and Jim's shyness caused him

Griffith Observatory

to get impossibly drunk. But Jim whirled away from this meeting elated. An agent, Michael Hamilburg, said he wanted to read Jim's poetry and agreed that it had to be marketed without reference to Jim's image as a rock star.

Meanwhile, Jim's boredom with rock stardom began to grow. Originally, he and Ray had conceived of the Doors as an intelligent, volatile fusion of theater, poetry, and well-executed, explorative music. It was obvious to Jim that this concept was becoming lost on his audience, the largest part of which was drawn by the sensationalism, the sex-idol hype.

But now he began to show contempt for and turn against his fans. For months he'd been spitting at them (or at their image of him) and getting so drunk that the performances often suffered. In the early summer of 1968 Jim got blatantly contemptuous as a means of denying himself the mindless misguided approval he was being offered.

It was May 10 and the Doors were in Chicago. Jim strode from the trailer dressing room to the stage, protected by a phalanx of Chicago cops, possibly reflecting on the paper he wrote at Florida State on the sexual neuroses of crowds. Certainly what followed was deliberate. Jim admitted it afterward. It was becoming fashionable for bands to get their fans to rush the stage and he wanted to see if he could take it one step further—he wanted to see if he could provoke a riot.

The other Doors were already in place, providing a haunting, typically Doors-ian musical intro. Jim threw out his chest, touched his long hair casually, and mounted the steps. He took six big steps to center stage, gripped the microphone, and growled.

A Hitlerian eruption fifteen thousand strong greeted him and in retort he directed the band through all the "inflammatory" songs, beginning with "Unknown Soldier." Antiwar sentiment was rising like a yeast in 1968, and this song had been virtually banned from airplay, while the violent film the Doors had made to promote it on television had been totally censored. Still the record reached the Top 40, becoming a battle song for what was then so hopefully called The Revolution.

"Break On Through" was next, and then came "Five to One." When Jim shouted, "We want the world and we want it now!" in "When the Music's Over," the whole crowd voiced the same demand.

Jim gave this show his all, using every trick he knew: falling and leaping, writhing in mock agony, throwing himself against the stage floor with such force that he hurt his side, sticking the maracas into the front of his tight leather pants, then tossing them to the girls in the first rows, unbuttoning his shirt and throwing it after the maracas.

There were two encores and then Bill Siddons announced, "The Doors have gone, they have left the building."

It was the same sort of announcement that was made at the end of a Beatles or a Rolling Stones concert.

The crowd was stamping and calling as one: "More more more more more more more . . ."

Someone stood on the railing of the balcony, poised to swan-dive eighteen feet into the crowd rushing about on the concrete floor below. There was a rippling murmur and a sudden hush as everyone in the coliseum turned to face the nameless teenager, who left the railing, arms held out from his shoulders as wings.

The crowd parted to allow for his bulk and he landed with a sticky smack. No one breathed. Then the teenager rose to his feet and broke the silence: "Wow! What a turn-on!"

The crowd erupted. It charged the stage. It swept over the lip and gained the first ten feet, was beaten back, then came in another wave over the instruments.

Finally the Doors' road crew and Mayor Daley's cops, kicking and clubbing the teenagers with billy clubs, John Densmore's abandoned drumsticks, and Jim's microphone stands, drove the last of the Doors' fans back. Jim Morrison had seen the proof of his theory.

To the hundreds of thousands, perhaps millions, in his audience, Jim was a welcome rebel, a fantasy partner in sex, the Lizard King; romantically crazy. To Middle America he was a public threat, obscene and arrogant. That was the apocalyptic side of him.

In private, with his friends, he displayed an original innocence, complemented by a genuinely shy manner and a soft voice. But he was by his own admission attracted to extremes: "I think the highest and the lowest points are the important ones. All the points in between are, well, in between. I want freedom to try everything—I guess to experience everything at least once." He could be extremely civil, polite, even erudite; yet on other occasions he could be gross, or as he preferred, "primitive."

More than anything, Jim Morrison was charismatic.

With his friends he could be soothingly genteel; almost deferential. Jac Holzman says, "He would not, as a rule, try to displease someone he liked by something he said. I think he was trying to search for a way to agree with you—like the Japanese will not say no, they will say, 'Yes, but . . .' " Regularly in interviews Jim reacted to statements he disagreed with by saying, "I see what you mean, but maybe . . ." Similarly he showed a compassion for some of his fans. In Philadelphia, for example, he saw that two teenagers who had been stranded by friends had a hotel room for the night, and in New York after a concert he talked soothingly to another teenager who had been injured. He once gave the jacket off his back to a shivering teenager caught outside on a street corner during a rainstorm. Jac says that "More of Jim's breeding showed than I think he would have liked people to suspect." He had excellent manners, when he wanted, and was a remarkable conversationalist.

He could be incredibly compassionate as well. An example of this involved a young teenager to whom Jim was both a hero and a big brother figure, the latter in particular a role Jim seemed to enjoy. Denny Sullivan had met the Doors through one of their roadies and was so won over after seeing them in concert, he managed to push his way into the Doors West Hollywood offices. Perhaps because he was only thirteen years old, and small, no one bothered to stop him. It wasn't long before everyone in the Doors family knew who he was. It also wasn't long before Bill Siddons decided he was hanging out too much, interfering with office procedure. When Siddons told Denny to minimize his appearances, Denny was crushed. But then Jim made Bill's objection meaningless by putting Denny in charge of the fan mail, which by this time was arriving by the bagful. Denny was paid ten cents for each letter he answered.

Jim did not regard his fans lightly, and he truly believed Denny would handle the job with sensitivity, unlike the commercial service the Doors had been considering. Thus, Denny *increased* his visits to the office, ditching school in favor of being near the people to whom he felt most drawn.

One Friday afternoon, several weeks later, Jim offhandedly asked Denny why he kept his hair so short. Denny told Jim that his parents made him get it cut.

"They make you?" Jim frowned. "Well, they won't make you cut it anymore."

"Why not?"

"Because I said so," Jim stated. "Because I won't let them. From now on you don't have to do anything you don't want to do. You don't have to cut your hair when you don't want to, got that?" Jim poked his finger into Denny's chest. Jim knew his attention made all the difference in the world to Denny. "Next time they hassle you, you tell me, and I'll tell you how to handle them."

His heavy drinking was continuing unabated. As with other aspects of his behavior, it couldn't be stopped. Besides, many reasoned, Jim bore most of the pressure in the group, so he was entitled to drink if he needed or wanted to. In fact, Jim was in a position to do anything he wanted to, regardless of how much it displeased those around him, and he did. It wasn't intentional, but it was self-destructive.

He grew flaccid, bloated. His hair was already showing a

Paul Ferrara

Atop the Griffith Observatory, 1968

few strands of gray. A small roll of flesh now fell over the top of his low-cut leather jeans and he started wearing his shirts outside his pants to hide it. When a fan he met on the street told him he was getting fat, he enrolled in the Beverly Hills Health Club, a membership he then ignored.

Worse, Paul Rothchild told him he was losing his voice. Paul had never been convinced that Jim was much of a singer, although he sometimes said he was the "first real *crooner* to come along since Frank Sinatra." But Jim "didn't have a singer's head. He thought in theatrical rather than vocal terms. And he was ravaging what voice he had with drink."

Still, there was the acclaim. In the early months of 1968 *Village Voice* readers voted Jim Vocalist of the Year. (The Doors ran away with the Newcomer of the Year award, Ray Manzarek was voted third best Musician of the Year after Eric Clapton and Ravi Shankar, and the group's first album was second only to *Sergeant Pepper.*) A seven-page spread in *Life* magazine made a case for the Doors' validity and literacy and reported Jim's New Haven arrest sympathetically. The band also appeared in *Who's Who in America,* an honor rare in their field.

But as the critic Diana Trilling wrote about Marilyn Monroe, fame has a way of dealing a bad hand to stars sooner or later; she called it the Law of Negative Compensation. Jim showed his hand in June, at a scheduled Doors meeting.

He parked his car, a Shelby GT 500 Cobra (he never drove anything but American cars), in the lot of the topless bar next to the Doors' West Hollywood offices. He noticed that the downstairs rehearsal room was empty, so he slowly mounted the outside steps and pushed open the upstairs door.

In the first room there were three or four ordinary desks, a cheap couch, a phonograph, a coffee machine, and the general disarray of fan mail, magazines, newspapers, and record albums. In one corner was a tiny bathroom with a shower stall. On the walls of the office were the Doors' gold records, now numbering four.

Jim crossed silently to his desk in the back corner, saying

Paul Ferrara

At the Griffith Observatory, 1968

nothing to the others present: a secretary, Bill Siddons, the other Doors. He glanced at the day's strangest and most interesting fan mail—put aside daily at his request—then pulled a cold hamburger from a paper sack and bit into it. He chewed slowly, just as he talked slowly and moved slowly. After a minute or two he looked up at the others and said he was quitting.

"What!" Every head turned.

"I'm—uh—quitting," Jim said.

Everyone began talking at once. Finally there was silence and Bill asked, "Why?"

"It's not what I want to do anymore. It was once, but it's not anymore."

The Doors had a long-standing policy: if they didn't all agree on something—a concert, a song, whatever—then nobody did it; unanimity ruled. Jim had only one vote in four, but he couldn't be outvoted.

The other Doors and Siddons chattered about how the band was rolling now, there was no telling where they could go—they had the power to do anything.

"It's not what I want to do," Jim said again. He began pawing through the fan mail in front of him, took another bite of meat and bun.

Ray stepped forward and said earnestly, an edge of panic in his voice, "Six more months. Let's give it six more months."

It's never easy to exit a fast-moving train, so Jim failed to carry through on his threat. Already the Doors were in rehearsal for their most prestigious concert yet, a July 5 extravaganza at the Hollywood Bowl. After that came the enormous Singer Bowl in New York. With a European tour coming up and the simultaneous July release of their third album and a new single, both of which became instant hits, a momentum of sufficient force was created to carry a band for a decade and more.

At the same time, the Doors appeared to be trying to top themselves. For the Hollywood Bowl concert they hired three more cameramen, making it five in all, and for the sound they stretched fifty-two amplifiers ninety-six feet across the stage, producing sixty thousand watts of power on the vocal PA alone, which was sufficient to push Jim's voice far into the Hollywood hills behind the Bowl.

There was no halting the roar to success. Headlining at the Hollywood Bowl had put the Doors in a league with the Beatles, had made them "America's Rolling Stones." Elektra had advance orders of nearly half a million copies for the new album, and within ten weeks 750,000 copies were sold, pushing it to the top of the album charts. "Hello, I Love You" went to first place in the singles charts, becoming the group's second million-selling 45.

The album title was changed several times during the LP's five-month-long gestation, from *American Nights* (Jim's early choice) to *The Celebration of the Lizard* (when Jim wanted the album cover done in an imitation lizard skin), and finally to *Waiting for the Sun,* which was the title of a song that was left out. At one time Jim had wanted to recite small poems between the songs, but in the end it was decided to print the text of the poem that thus far had refused to be wedded to music, "The Celebration of the Lizard," inside the album sleeve.

Jim explained his fascination with reptiles. "We must not forget," he said, "that the lizard and the snake are identified with the unconscious and with the forces of evil. There's something deep in human memory that responds strongly to snakes. Even if you've never seen one. I think that a snake just embodies everything that we fear." His long poem, he said, was "kind of an invitation to dark forces," but the Lizard King image he projected was not. "It's all done tongue-in-cheek," he insisted. "I don't think people realize that. It's not to be taken seriously. It's like if you play the villain in a western it doesn't mean that that's you. That's just an aspect that you keep for show. I don't really take that seriously. That's supposed to be ironic."

Paul Ferrara, Elektra Records

Publicity photo from Waiting for the Sun *album-cover photo session*

The Doors went back on the road, moving in July from the Hollywood Bowl to Dallas and Houston, to Honolulu, and then to New York. The biggest and most memorable of these concerts was August 2 at the Singer Bowl at the old World's Fair grounds in New York. Bill Graham had wanted the Doors for a return date at the Fillmore East, but the outdoor venue in Queens was five times larger and offered them billing with the Who, the British band that had just announced plans to do a rock opera. The Doors were confident of an artistic and exciting evening.

"Morrison Morrison Morrison Morrison . . ."

Jim left the black limousine, his documentary camera crew alternately backing up in front of him and trailing in his leather street-stud wake. His expression was relaxed as he moved slowly through a large throng of girls, then entered the backstage area, where he was wrapped in a cloak of New York cops.

"Morrison Morrison Morrison . . ."

His name was a mantra the audience chanted across the fair grounds. His expression was solemn as he climbed the stairs to the stage. The cops took up positions in front of the stage, and the cameramen (Paul and Babe) scrambled onto the stage behind him. Except for the buttons of light from the am-

Elektra Records

Scenes from Feast of Friends, *Singer Bowl, New York*

plifiers and the glow of burning incense on Ray's organ, the stage was in darkness.

"Morrison Morrison Morrison . . ."

The other Doors were playing the intro to "Back Door Man." Jim arrived at the microphone, a spot went on, the audience exploded, and Jim filled the world with a long, pained ear-piercing scream. For a moment he stood motionless, then dropped to the ground, contorting and kicking.

In the hour that followed, Jim was a vision in a Mexican peon shirt and black leather whirling on one boot, collapsing in primal pain, to rise again and grab his crotch with cupped hands, hopping forward, eyes closed, lips pursed in ecstasy. The kids in the audience began coming at the stage like bugs smashing into a radiator grill. The cops were forced onto the stage itself, where they formed a wall of short-sleeved blue

shirts and dark blue pants between the Doors and their frenzied audience.

No one could see. Jim lay writhing on his side, his hands pushed between his thighs. The music was pounding.

Kids began climbing over the backs of other kids, gaining a grip on the stage, only to be grabbed by the cops and literally flung back into the darkness.

Hundreds of wooden folding chairs were hurled at the cops. Hundreds of teenagers were bleeding.

The concert was ended abruptly and that was Riot Number Two. In an era when rock "riots" were acquiring underground chic—and causing newspaper headlines—the group's reputation was enhanced. The momentum was still building in August. "Hello, I Love You" was number one in the nation for the fourth week. The Doors were featured again in *Vogue,* in an article about rock theater. Critics for *New York* magazine and the *Los Angeles Times* called the third album the band's best yet. And Europe was yet to come.

"Hello, I Love You" was the Doors' first major hit in Europe and it laid the groundwork for their explosive three-week tour. The hypnotic song was already high on the British charts when the band landed in London. They were met at the airport by hundreds of fans and a Granada TV film crew, who filmed not only their passage through customs but also the first of their four Roundhouse concerts as well.

Europe was ready for the Doors and the Doors knew it. The Roundhouse was an intimate theater, seating only twenty-five hundred. It was smaller than the venues the Doors had become accustomed to. Four shows in two nights was the booking, ten thousand tickets in all, quickly sold out. Thousands of people milled about outside the gates, hoping at least to hear the excitement being generated inside. Disc Jockey John Peel said in his *Melody Maker* column, "The English embraced the Doors as warmly as America did our Beatles."

The Roundhouse shows were an unqualified success. The audiences were highly appreciative and the band was at their best. In the intimacy of the small auditorium Jim's theatricality came across wilder than ever. At each show the audience demanded encores. The English press forgot all about the co-billed Jefferson Airplane, devoting nearly all their coverage to America's Kings of Acid Rock. The lucky ten thousand who saw the shows spread the word to those who hadn't. Granada would supply the missing piece to the absent. The Doors' reputation reached legendary proportions after they'd been in town only a week.

Morrison had met England, and it was clear the Yanks had won. On to Copenhagen, Frankfurt, and then Amsterdam.

The only real trouble during the tour came in Amsterdam. In Frankfort Jim was given a piece of hashish about half the size of his thumb, and as the Doors alighted from the plane

In England, at the Roundhouse,
1968

the next day in Amsterdam and approached customs, Bill Siddons asked, "Anybody holding anything?"

Jim said, "Yeah, I got this hash." Everyone else was clean.

Siddons said, "Well, get rid of it."

So Jim chewed it up and swallowed it.

Jim had had several drinks on the plane, and at a lunch with the show's promoters in Amsterdam he downed several more, then went off to explore the city's famous red-light district.

Siddons turned to one of the roadies. "Go with Jim, and be sure he gets to the show on time."

Jim continued drinking through the afternoon and early evening, and when a fan gave him another lump of hash, he promptly swallowed that. About nine o'clock the roadie got him into a taxi.

Once again the Doors were playing with the Airplane, who went on first. Jim arrived backstage about midway through their set and in the middle of a familiar Airplane song

he suddenly appeared onstage, trying to sing, trying to dance, whirling about, hopping drunkenly.

Precisely what happened next is uncertain—witnesses disagree. Some say Jim collapsed near the wings and was carried off. Others contend he was helped back to the Doors' dressing room, where he sat on a piano bench in a near-comatose state, head lolling, eyes glazed and lidded, as the others argued about what they should do.

A message was taken to the Airplane to stretch the set and

then the road crews for both bands were told to take their time breaking down the Airplane's equipment and setting up the Doors'. Backstage it was decided that Vince Treanor would announce that Jim was ill but that the three remaining Doors wanted to play anyway.

"And tell 'em, anybody who wants can have their money back immediately," Bill finished.

Suddenly Jim slid off his chair to the floor as if he'd been silently, instantly filleted. Bill ran over to him, pulled a small

Daniel Sugerman, Doors Library

Action sequence at the Roundhouse, London, England

mirror from his pocket, and held it over Jim's mouth and nose, looking for the mist of life.

"Back off!" he hollared at everyone else. "I can't see if he's breathing. Back off, goddamnit!"

Bill bent over Jim's form again, peering hopefully at the small piece of glass in his hand. Jim's face was the color of old ivory, his breathing was shallow. A doctor huffed out of the audience and after a quick examination pronounced, "The *monsieur* has passed out."

Hearing that broke the spell, and as Jim was taken away to a local hospital, honest concern was replaced by pent-up fury. So irate were the other Doors that they performed that night, with Ray singing, as if they'd always been a trio.

The next day at the hospital Jim's amazing recuperative powers brought color to his cheeks.

"You shoulda heard what the doctor told me this morning," he told the others. "He asked me how it happened and I said I musta been tired and, uh, he lectured me for twenty minutes about the dangers of being in entertainment. He said I had to watch out for greedy managers who push the talent too hard."

Bill and the others glared at him and Jim smiled shyly back.

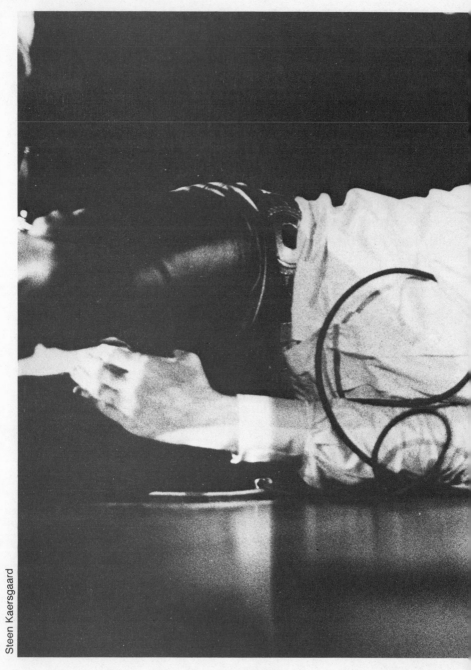

Steen Kaersgaard

Copenhagen, Denmark, 1968. Down for the count with the Airplane

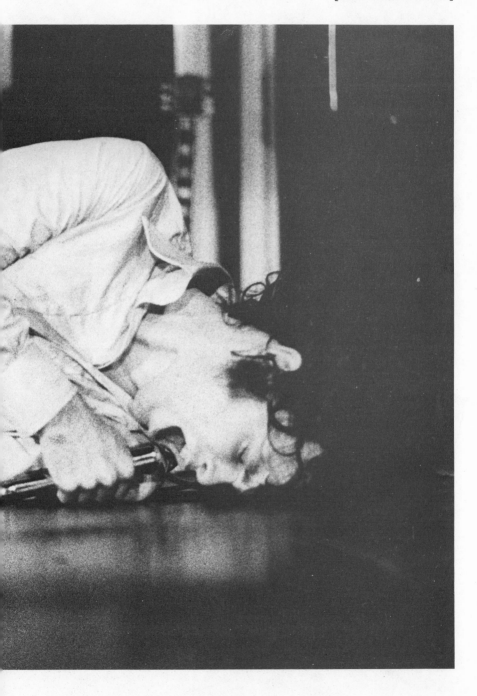

Frankfurt, September 1968

CHAPTER

7

Pamela stayed in London during the European tour, in a sumptuous flat she had found in expensive and fashionable Belgravia. In the first days she and Jim explored London together, walked through Soho and along Carnaby and Oxford streets, where Pamela bought some clothing. On October 6, they watched the Granada television show *The Doors Are Open,* which presented Jim in a revolutionary context, intercutting the concert at the Roundhouse with newsreel footage from the Democratic convention in Chicago and a recent demonstration at the American Embassy in London. It was obvious, but Jim thought the Doors came off quite well anyway.

They were joined a week later by the poet Michael McClure who had come to London to meet an American movie producer in exile, Elliot Kastner, who wanted Jim to play Billy the Kid in a film adaptation of Michael's play, *The Beard.* Jim and Michael quickly got over their awkwardness and in several boozy, talk-filled days in London cemented their friendship. For Jim and Michael and Pamela, getting drunk was an imperative in the rich poetic tradition, so on the first night they all got stiff and tried vainly to hire a taxi to drive eight hours north to England's Lake Country, home of Lamb, Scott, Wordsworth, and Coleridge. Each time they were stopped by the same neighborhood bobby, who threatened at 4 A.M. to run them in if they ventured from the flat once more.

In the morning Michael awoke with a hangover "so bad it was like a mescaline high" and he idly began to read some of Jim's poetry that he found on a table. He had known about Jim's poems, but he hadn't seen any of them before and he was "terrifically impressed." He had already begun to think of Jim as the human embodiment of Shelley's Alastor, an androgynous half-spirit, half-man who lived in the woods and worshipped intellectual beauty, and the poems he read before breakfast—many of which later appeared in *The New Creatures*—did nothing to change his mind.

When Jim appeared for breakfast Michael told him he thought the poems should be published. Jim's annoyance with Pamela for having left the poems so openly on a table was dissipated by the poet's high praise. He asked Michael what he thought about publishing the poetry privately.

"I said I thought when it was done for a very good reason, it was not the same as vanity publishing," says McClure. "Jim didn't want to get recognition for his poetry because he was Jim Morrison the rock star. He wanted to keep the poetry separate from that. I said Shelley had published his own work privately. I said I thought Lorca's first work was privately published. I published a book of mine privately."

The talk about poetry continued over drinks for two or three days. Jim said he'd dedicated the poems to Pamela, because she was his editor. "She goes through it and takes out all the 'fucks' and 'shits,'" Jim said, grinning.

Michael looked at him and said, "Mark Twain's wife did that, too."

Michael leafed through some of the poems and commented. "Do you know William Carlos Williams' poem 'The Red

Wheelbarrow'? It's one of the great objectivist poems and it relates to the Ensenada poem of yours. It reminds me of 'The Red Wheelbarrow' in its concreteness and length, although it's impressionistic in technique. It moves through space like film does, like a movie."

His first week back in Los Angeles Jim visited the office of Michael's literary agent, Mike Hamilburg. With him he had forty-two pages of poetry, accompanied by twenty photographs he had taken on a trip to Mexico. This was *The New Creatures.* He also had with him a long poem called "Dry Water." The agent showed great enthusiasm for the material and agreed that Jim's image as rock star should be deemphasized. By the end of October *The New Creatures* was on an editor's desk at Random House in New York and Jim was making plans to publish the book privately in Los Angeles.

At the same time there was a crisis over the documentary. Nearly $30,000 had been spent on it and all but Jim wanted to abandon the project. As things then stood, editing was far from complete and none of the planned fictional sequences had been filmed. They reached a compromise. Plans for more filming were dropped, Paul Ferrara and Frank Lisciandro agreed to work without salary, and the Doors agreed to put up the $3,000 to $4,000 needed to complete the editing. They hoped to sell the finished film to television.

In the last days of October Jim disappeared into the editing room, a cubicle behind the rehearsal room in the Doors' offices. Everywhere he looked there were cans and cans of film, and on a bulletin board were pinned suggestions for a title, most of them Jim's lyrics. "Mute Nostril Agony" was a favorite of John Densmore's, but it was one of Ray's recommendations that was finally picked: "Feast of Friends" from "When the Music's Over." Jim sat at the Moviola and made several suggested cuts and offered a tentative sequence of scenes, but he left all the final decisions to Paul and Frank. "Jim was intensely aware that film wasn't made in any one particular state," says Frank, "that it was made in a kind of evolutionary way, that each stage added to and enhanced the final product. He was tremendously interested in film editing."

It was while he was viewing the footage that Jim made a startling discovery. Babe and Frank and Paul had been alert at the Singer Bowl concert in New York to record the violence of the performance, of Jim writhing on the stage in mock agony, of police heaving teenagers bodily back into the audience only a few feet away from him. "The first time I saw the film I was rather taken aback," Jim said later, "because being onstage and one of the central figures in the film, I only saw it from my point of view. Then, to see a series of events that I thought I had some control over . . . to see it as it actually was . . . I suddenly realized in a way that I was just a puppet of a lot of forces I only vaguely understood."

However "taken aback" Jim may have been about the chaos and violence he inspired, on November 1 the Doors began the most riotous tour of their career, hiring four of the biggest bodyguards available at the Parker Detective Agency, an organization of good-natured black men each of whom weighed at least 250 pounds and was licensed to carry a gun.

The concerts in Milwaukee and Columbus on the 1st and 2nd were ordinary. The only noteworthy difference was that Jim was singing more blues material and fewer original songs, just as he had on some of the European dates. But in the eight days that followed there were injuries, riots, and arrests in Chicago, Cleveland, St. Louis, and Phoenix.

The *Phoenix Gazette*'s front-page headline read, "Near-Riot Erupts at Coliseum," and underneath the article stated, "Last night the State Fair being held at the Coliseum erupted into a war between kids and cops. Blame it on the Doors, possibly the most controversial group in the world. Lead singer Jim Morrison appeared in shabby clothes and behaved belligerently. The crowd ate up Morrison's antics which included hurling objects from the stage to the audience, cussing, and making rude gestures." There had been over twenty arrests.

When he was asked how he felt in situations of violence in a concert hall, Jim's answers were ambiguous. It was "just a lot of fun . . . pretty playful," he told one writer. "We have fun, the kids have fun, the cops have fun. It's kind of a weird triangle. [But] you have to look at it logically. If there were no cops there, would anybody try to get onstage? Because what are they going to do when they get there? When they get onstage, they're just very peaceful. They're not going to do anything. The only incentive to charge the stage is because there's a barrier. I firmly believe that. It's interesting, though, because the kids get a chance to test the cops. You see cops today, walking around with their guns and uniforms and everyone's curious about exactly what would happen if you challenged them. I think it's a good thing, because it gives the kids a chance to test authority."

He told another interviewer, "I tried to stimulate a few little riots, you know, and after a few times, I realized it's such a joke. Soon it got to the point where people didn't think it was a successful concert unless everybody jumped up and ran around a bit. It's a joke because it leads nowhere. I think it would be better to do a concert and just keep all that feeling submerged so that when everyone left they'd take that energy out on the streets and back home with them."

By now the public had become aware of what to expect from a Doors concert: riot and transcendence. Failing that, they'd at least get to see the Lizard King behave in a way that no one else could, or would. So stoned he'd stumble off the stage—so drunk he'd scream his way through forgotten verses—so high he'd hump amplifiers, then fall to the stage, unable to rise. The Doors gave you a show—a show unlike any other you had ever seen, a freak show.

The Doors worked hard to deserve these expectations. They were by far the most dramatic group on the circuit, and they appealed to the hip underground as well the teenyboppers. Morrison was capable of moving both past mere spectatorship into the arena of direct experience and awe.

But the more Jim realized the words and music were being overlooked, the more his frustration exploded onstage and off. He was also growing weary of the weight of the crowd's expectations. In the early days it had been effortless to transport audiences because they had come with an open mind. Now the crowd would be satisfied with nothing less than what they'd heard about, felt they'd been promised. And how do you deal with that?

The Doors had become larger than life. Their relationship with the audience was becoming more unrealistic with each passing show. Not only did Jim feel unworthy of the adoration, but he grew increasingly distraught over what to do about the situation. Contempt had merely added a sideshow to the main attraction. Perhaps, he reasoned, the way out was to stop conforming to his publicized image. It was not an immediate solution, but perhaps he could accomplish it little by little and in the long run lower the audience's demands and eventually maybe even radically amend their relationship with him.

The first week of December, after the band taped their first television show in more than a year, *The Smothers Brothers Show,* Jim went to the Troubadour bar, where after getting nearly too drunk to walk he convinced one of the waitresses to leave with him. On the way to his car, nicknamed the Blue Lady, he was approached by two homosexuals.

"Listen, that's not my trip," he said curtly. They continued to follow him and pushed their way into his car. Jim took off rapidly, pressed the accelerator to the floor, and wheeled onto Doheny Drive. He was on the wrong side of the road and speeding. There was a tree. There were screams, tires screeching, horns honking, and for some reason the car stopped when it hit the curb. The doors flew open, the passengers were thrown to the ground unharmed, and Jim roared off into the night again.

The waitress returned to the Troubadour to call a cab. Jim reappeared, screaming that she had to get into the car with him. She refused, he was too crazy, she said, and Jim sped off, ending his spree less than a mile away where he drove the Blue Lady into a tree on Sunset Boulevard. He was transported unconscious, but otherwise unscathed, to his motel room.

Half an hour later the waitress called and he begged her to come to him immediately. She rushed to the motel and Jim began sobbing. "I don't want to hurt anybody," he said, "I don't want to hurt anybody." She asked him what he meant. He only cried, "I don't want to hurt anybody, I don't want to . . ."

No one was hurt and a few days later the car was towed to the repair shop in Beverly Hills.

The following week, on Friday, December 13, the Doors made their first hometown appearance since the Hollywood Bowl, headlining at the eighteen-thousand–seat Forum. The band had been recording the first songs for its fourth album that afternoon and Jim left the Elektra studio a couple of hours before the limousines were to arrive. With his brother Andy, who was now nineteen and visiting from San Diego, he walked a block to a liquor store and bought six bottles of beer and a pint of vodka, all of which he drank on returning to the Elektra parking lot, smashing each bottle against the wall as he finished it.

The concert promoter had done an excellent job promoting the show. TV spots showing Morrison in leather with a sparkler advertised the event for weeks in advance, posters announcing the date covered Los Angeles from the beach communities inward to West Hollywood, every rock radio station in town was buzzing with the news: The Doors are back! The arena was packed and hopes were high.

The audience ignored the opening act, talked through the Chinese folk musician Ray had placed on the bill (Ray's walk-on introduction garnered more applause than the musician's entire set), hooted Jerry Lee Lewis every time he played a country song, and when the Doors came on, called for "Light

Jim, 1969. From a photo session to promote the Forum show

Elektra Records

My Fire" every opportunity they got. Someone threw a fistful
of lit sparklers on the stage, barely missing Jim. Jim came forward to the edge of the stage.

"Hey, man," he called to the crowd, his voice booming
through the thirty-two gigantic new amplifiers Vince had built,
"cut that fuckin' shit out." The audience was ready, murmur-
ing out loud. "Shut yer holes." There was a mixture of eager-
ness and laughter and scattered "all rights."

"What are you doing here?" Jim asked. "Why did you
come tonight?" There was no response. This wasn't what they
expected and Jim knew it.

"Well, man, we can play music all night, but that's not
what you really want, is it? You want something else, something more, something greater than you've ever seen before,
right?"

The audience roared.

"Well, fuck you. We came to play music."

The group rattled into "Celebration of the Lizard." The
sparse, sinister opening invited hecklers to speak up, but no
one did. As the musicians dove into the body of the song, the
audience was attentive. The performance was flawless—the
words emphasized and delivered with a new kind of passion.
Jim didn't dance. He didn't even jump. And he didn't scream
once. When he finished with the maracas, he set them back on
the drum riser. The song lasted nearly forty minutes, and
when it ended, the audience sat motionless. There was no riot
. . . no ovation. There was barely any applause. The band
didn't bow or wave their goodbyes—they silently walked off
the stage, then toward their dressing room. And the crowd sat
stunned. Then slowly they began to file out of the vast auditorium into the Los Angeles night.

Jim and Pamela were refused entrance to the press party
afterward because they weren't recognized by the security
guard and their names weren't on the guest list. Jim wasn't
belligerent, as Pamela expected. Instead he turned the situation into a comedy routine.

"But I have friends in high places," he told the guard.

"The answer's still no, you can't come in."

Jim was soon identified and ushered in. The crowd enveloped him and Pamela.

After the party he and his brother and Pamela played soccer with a beer can on the immense, silent, empty Forum parking lot.

For months Bill Graham had been trying to get the Doors to return to the Fillmore East in New York, but Bill Siddons consistently said no. The next time the Doors came East, he said, they'd play Madison Square Garden, the hall whose name and twenty thousand capacity made it the most prestigious and lucrative concert hall in the city. Graham said, "This is a little before your time, Bill, but I was the one who put the Doors into the Fillmore in San Francisco before they had a hit, I gave them their first break."

"Yeah, right, Bill," retorted Siddons. "I think you paid them three hundred and fifty dollars."

"Listen, you little shit . . ."

Obviously, the conversation ended badly and Siddons made arrangements to have the Garden shows produced by someone other than Graham. The Doors would be the first band to "graduate" from the Fillmores to the Garden, and Siddons had thought that Graham would have liked to have been there.

"You can't share anything with the public in anything that big," Graham said in parting. "You can't tell me about vibes in a cement factory. I'm happy for the guys that they're doing so well, but tell them I think it's bad for the business, playing houses that big."

In mid-January 1969 the Doors were doing well indeed. They were, in fact, the "American Beatles," the Biggest American Group. They refused to appear in halls that held fewer than ten thousand of their loyal fans and commanded as much as $35,000 a night, or 60 percent of the take, whichever was larger. Their latest record release, "Touch Me," a surprisingly traditional love song written by Robby, was soon to be another million-selling single, and to re-create its sound the band took a bass player and a jazz saxophonist to New York with them, and hired several violinists from the New York Philharmonic. In a readers' poll appearing that month in *Eye* magazine, the Doors were named top group and Jim was called the "sexiest man in rock and roll."

The day following the triumphant Garden concert Jim was entertaining in his Plaza suite. His mustachioed aide de camp from Elektra in Los Angeles, David Anderle, introduced him to someone he thought Jim would enjoy meeting, a cute little blond from his New York office, Diane Gardiner, who was his new publicist. Diane was an attractive and companionable twenty-one-year-old college dropout from California who'd helped publicize dozens of successful acts, Cream, the Bee Gees, and the Jefferson Airplane among them, but the Doors and most particularly Jim Morrison made her itch. He was getting drunk and telling jokes she thought embarrassing.

"What's the difference," Jim asked, "between a clever midget and a venereal disease?"

Everyone present looked at the floor.

"Well," Jim said, "the first is a cunning runt . . ."

Diane asked Jim to come into the bedroom. She said there was a telephone call he had to make.

Once in the room: "Now look, Jim, you're a great guy for meeting the press and all, but now you're . . . doggone it, you're falling down, and . . . and I've got this job to do, Jim, I could lose my job, so . . . I'll just go out there and tell them we called this man and you had an appointment to meet him and had to leave. Then you leave and I'll stay here and make your apologies." Diane looked up at Jim, who said nothing. "Goddamnit, I'm trying to help you, answer me . . . please, Jim."

Jim was wearing the same clothes he had worn at the Garden the night before: an unbleached linen shirt from Mexico, black leather jeans, and black boots. He stood near the bedroom door, one arm braced casually against the jamb, his opposite hip cocked sensually, a bourbon in his right hand. He gave her a lopsided boyish grin and collapsed onto his back on the bed. Jim looked up into Diane's worried face. "I want to fuck you," he said, one hand behind his head, the other resting over his crotch with the drink.

"Sure, Jim, sure." Diane nervously left the room.

The afternoon slunk into New York dusk. Vast quantities of alcohol were consumed, along with hashish chocolate chip cookies brought by Ellen Sander, the timid yet ballsy brunette who had called Jim a "Mickey Mouse de Sade" in her column in the *Saturday Review*. There was this weird feeling that everyone present had been born there, and no one was ever going to leave. Suddenly Jim crashed to the floor and walked on his knees to the couch where Ellen was sitting. He began to weave back and forth, moving his face closer and closer to Ellen's.

"Sing us a song, Ellen."

Ellen pulled her feet up under her rump. "I don't sing, Jim. I'm a professional audience."

"C'mon, Ellen," Jim begged, "please sing us a song."

"Really, Jim, I'm a writer, not a singer."

Jim reared back and roared, "I said *singgggg*!"

Ellen protested again. "I don't sing, you sing, you're the singer, you sing something for us, Jim." Her voice was weak, pleading. "I'm just a critic."

Jim continued his intimidating bobbing back and forth, glaring at Ellen menacingly. Finally Ellen began to sing, in a tiny, frightened voice, the beginning lines of the Beatles' "Hey Jude." Four lines only. Then everybody applauded and everything was okay again. Jim went into the bedroom and turned up the sound of the flickering TV.

"Mickey Mouse de Sade!" he snorted to himself.

Jim was in a bad mood all weekend. The Garden appearances went well, and the trip was an overall success, but something was bothering him and he didn't speak to the other

Doors that weekend in New York. It turned out that when Jim
had been in London with Michael McClure and Pamela, Jac
Holzman, who still controlled the Doors' music publishing,
was asked by an advertising agency if he'd allow Buick to use
"Light My Fire" in a commercial for $50,000. Jac said he
would ask the boys. When Robby, John, Ray, and Bill Siddons
were unable to find Jim, they voted without him. Jim heard
about "Come on, Buick, light my fire" when he returned to
the United States, and he went straight to Jac Holzman, cor-
nering him on the patio outside David Anderle's office, telling
him he held that song sacred even though he was tired of performing it publicly.

"I want it clear, Jac, I'm telling you now, I want it clear:
don't you ever do that again. That song is precious to me and I
don't want anybody using it."

The song was never sold. But still, Jim gave them all the
silent treatment without ever telling anybody but Jac what he
was so upset about.

That wasn't all that was upsetting Jim.

Jim made a new friend while in New York, the eloquent,
plump, gregarious Fred Myrow, who at twenty-eight was the
assistant to Leonard Bernstein and composer-in-residence at
the New York Philharmonic. Fred was brought to the Plaza by
David Anderle specifically to meet Jim.

Jim transferred a drink from his right hand to his left and
they exchanged a formal handshake. Jim immediately pulled
Fred aside, almost conspiratorially. He'd been told much
about Fred Myrow—that he was one of the up-and-coming
composers in the avant-garde classical world. But, Jim had
heard, Fred wanted out. He'd listened to the Beatles and decided that what he was doing was irrelevant, he wanted to get
into more popular forms. Jim was coming from the other direction, but their desires were nearly identical: They both
wanted meaningful change.

"If I don't find a new way to develop creatively within a year," Jim told Fred as soon as they'd met, "I'll be good for nothing but nostalgia."

Fred was much impressed by this statement, knowing it was rare for an artist to entertain such long thoughts the day following a huge success. But obsolescence was a fate Jim regarded with dread. He would never say so aloud to anyone but his closest friends, but he thought of himself as a revolutionary figure, one who had had to provide a social balance by opposing his father. Or so it seemed. Jim didn't like to admit it, but he was a lot like his father. Their goals may have been opposing, but they had the same kind of ambition and drive.

Jim did not necessarily want to lead the revolution, but if there was going to be one, he was all for it. Though he claimed that some of his songs came to him in a vision, he was never unaware of the mutinous and apocalyptic nature of that vision. When his fans and the rock public came to regard him as a figurehead in the political/social movement taking place, Jim was publicly unmoved, but secretly flattered.

For a long while he believed records could serve the same purpose that books and printed manifestos had in earlier revolutions. He wasn't yet certain he was wrong. But he felt he needed a new direction, and after making plans to meet again with Fred Myrow, he returned to Los Angeles and delivered himself into the hands of the disciples of the radical dramatic theorist, Antonin Artaud—the thirty-two members of the Living Theatre, who were on a tour of America.

Jim had been a believer in the Theater of Cruelty back at FSU when he'd first read Artaud. In the summer of 1968 he had questioned John Carpenter, a writer on the *Los Angeles Free Press,* about a friend of his who was in "Le Living." Then he pumped Michael McClure for more information when he learned that Michael knew the founders, Judith Malina and Julian Beck. In November Jim read and reread an article about the radical theater group in *Ramparts* magazine, until he could recite passages: "They are not really performers [wrote author

Stephen Schneck] but a roving band of Paradise-seekers defining Paradise as total liberation, practicing hypnology and advocating Paradise *now*; their presence and their function are in direct opposition to that repressive totalitarian state called Law and Order."

When Jim heard the company was coming to the University of Southern California campus in February 1969, he had the Doors' secretary reserve sixteen tickets for each of the scheduled five nights, then invited the group's advance man, Mark Amatin, home for dinner.

Home was now a comfortable, secluded house that Jim rented for Pamela in Hollywood's Beachwood Hills. Jim was coarse with Pamela and never introduced Mark to the other couple present. Then, after eating, he crudely dismissed everyone except Mark.

Jim was drinking and swallowing small white pills. He offered some to Mark, failing to identify them as benzedrine. They talked nonstop until morning.

Mark poured out his guts, told Jim how much he'd changed. "The night I saw 'Le Living,' I went home with thirteen people I'd never met before, stoned out of my head, after having taken my clothes off on the stage. None of those things I'd have dreamt of doing when I went. Well! By the end of the next day I knew that that was the way life was supposed to be. So I returned to my regular job as a travel agent, and when I was told to take my beads off, I told the guy to go fuck himself, and I walked out."

"I was doing what I thought was political and spiritual missionary work," Mark says now, "and that's what Jim wanted to find out about. His work had been a religious experience, but it had become entertainment, and he was extremely dissatisfied. The Living Theatre was made up of people who had come to see them and couldn't leave, and Jim wanted to know about that enthusiasm. He said he wanted to find ways to incorporate a political message into what he was doing, but he didn't know how to go about it, or where to begin. He felt everyone was waiting for him to speak, ready to obey his every word, and this was a tremendous responsibility, but Jim didn't know what to say."

"What is it about the Living that causes such enthusiasm?" Jim asked Mark. "How can we get that same sort of commitment and devotion? What do I have to do?"

The sequence of events that led directly to the Doors' fall from grace began on Friday night, February 28, 1969, when The Living Theatre staged its revolutionary *tour de force, Paradise Now.* For Jim, it had a cataclysmic punch.

He was seated with friends in the front row, as he had been all week long. The play opened with "The Rite of Guerrilla Theater," in which the actors mingled with the spectators, speaking the first of five key, cathartic phrases.

"I am not allowed to travel without a passport."

The Living Theatre was touring the United States after four years of self-imposed exile in Europe. During that time the troupe had become international in composition and knew the hassles of border-crossing firsthand. They engaged the spectators in dialogue, baiting them if necessary to get a response, shouting the words in anguish and frustration.

"I cannot travel freely, I cannot move about at will!"

"I am separated from my fellow man, my boundaries are set arbitrarily by others!"

"The Gates of Paradise are closed to me!"

In a few minutes' time the actors were close to hysteria, and the USC theater was transformed. Jim was on his feet with many others, shouting slogans, bellowing for Paradise Now.

The actors retired quietly, returning to the stage, paused for a moment, then began again, now with the second phrase: "I don't know how to stop the wars!"

And so it went: a catalogue of complaints, presented with explosive energy.

"You can't live if you don't have money!"

"I'm not allowed to smoke marijuana!"

And finally: "I'm not allowed to take my clothes off!"

"The body itself of which we are made is taboo!"

"We are ashamed of what is most beautiful, we are afraid of what is most beautiful!!"

"We may not act naturally toward one another!"

"The culture represses love!"

"I am not allowed to take my clothes off!"

The actors began to strip, removing much of their clothing, then standing in the aisles and on the stage, the forbidden areas of their bodies covered. It was an active demonstration of the prohibition. When the stripping reached the legal limit, the actors shouted once more, *"I'm not allowed to take my clothes off! I am outside the Gates of Paradise!"*

That was when the cops moved in and stopped the play from continuing.

A Doors concert was set for the following day. After it, Jim and Pam were going to spend a week together in a house that was already being readied for them in Jamaica. But before leaving for the airport, they had a fight. Then at the airport they had another fight and Jim sent Pamela home. Then Jim missed his plane. Cursing, and wishing he had a bottle with him, Jim reserved a seat on another plane, then went to the airport bar where he waited and drank. Once aboard the flight, he downed as many drinks as he could charm out of the stewardess in first class. There was a stopover in New Orleans, where Jim again went to the airport bar and again missed his scheduled departure. By the time he had made arrangements to catch still another flight, and had called the concert hall to tell the boys he'd be a little late, he was drunk.

Jim continued drinking. All the way to Miami.

The
Arrow
Falls

CHAPTER

8

A hot, steamy Southern night.

Jim's knees buckled. He caught himself with one hand on the huge black amplifier on the stage to his right and with the other hand raised a large brown beer bottle and guzzled. On his chin was a new beard, giving him a Mephistophelean toughness. A dark collarless shirt was worn outside his black leather pants to hide the whiskey paunch. Jim squinted into the smokiness at his audience.

It was a few minutes of eleven o'clock as he swallowed the last of the beer. The Doors were more than an hour late in starting and the audience was fever pitched. It was the band's first appearance in Florida—the result of their winning a popularity poll on the University of Miami campus—but even the most avid fans can grow tense when far too many of them are packed into an old seaplane hangar without seats and ventilation.

Ray and Robby and John moved toward their instruments in the darkness. Ray glanced nervously at John, who was so bitter about Jim's tardiness that his grip on his drumsticks was knuckle-white. Ray's eyes moved to Robby, who was cradling his guitar absently, as if unaware of the tension.

Backstage the Miami promoters were arguing angrily with Bill Siddons and one of the Doors' agents who'd flown down from New York to "straighten things out." Siddons had believed the promoters when they said their maximum box-office take for the show would be $42,000, and had agreed to accept a flat fee of $25,000 for the show rather than have the contract specify the usual 60 percent of the gross. After he had signed and returned the contract, the promoters removed the seats and sold another seven thousand tickets. Bill was insulted and furious.

Jim leaned over the mixing board behind the drums to ask Vince Treanor for another beer. Vince's official job was to supervise the setup, breakdown, and maintenance of the Doors' impressive sound system; his unofficial job was to dispense Jim's drinks. But this time he shook his head no. He didn't have any more beer, how about a Coke?

"Don't blow it," Vince said quietly. "This is the first time we've been in Miami."

Jim turned away, walked to the edge of the stage, and belched. Peering into the restless darkness, he asked if anybody had anything to drink. Someone came forward with a bottle of cheap wine.

First Ray called to John to begin "Break On Through," the song that began most Doors sets. They played the intro for nearly ten minutes. It didn't work. Jim wasn't listening. He was talking with some kids in the audience, sharing a paper cup. The Doors fell into silence again, as Jim clambered to his feet and grabbed the slim, gold microphone.

"I'm not talking about a revolution!"

The voice was a strident bark, a shot that sounded like the start of a recitation.

"I'm talking about having a *ggooooooood* time. I'm talking about having a good time this summer. You all come out to L.A., you all get out there. We're gonna lie down there in the

In Miami, 1969

sand and rub our toes in the ocean and we're gonna have a *good* time. Are you ready? Are you *readddddyyyy! ARRR yew rreeeadYY!!* Are you ready? Are . . . are . . . a-r-e yewwwwww . . . *Wowowowowooo* . . . Aahhhhwwwoooooo *suck . . . Aahhhh suck . . .*"

The band was crashing into the opening of a familiar song from the first album, "Back Door Man."

"Louder! Come on, band! Get it louder! Come on! Yeahhh. Yay-ehhh. Ahhhmmm uh *back door mannn . . .*"

Four lines into the song Jim stopped singing and began talking again. He sounded apologetic. Was he speaking to Pamela as well as to the crowd?

"Hey listen," he shouted, "I'm lonely. I need some love, you all. Come on. I need some good times. I want some love-a, love-ah. Ain't nobody gonna love my ass? Come on."

The crowd gasped.

"I need ya. There's so many of ya out there and nobody's gonna love me, sweetheart, come on. I need it, I need it, I need it, need ya, need ya, need ya, need ya. *Come on!* Yeah! I love ya. Come on. Nobody gonna come up here and love me, huh? All right for you, baby. That's too bad. I'll get somebody else."

The musicians were barely hanging in through most of the plea. When Jim paused, they began "Five to One" and he picked it up, singing the first verse fairly coherently. Then he made another speech, inspired by the greed of the promoters in jamming so many people together, but also by *Paradise Now.*

"You're all a bunch of fuckin' idiots!"

Again the crowd gasped.

"Lettin' people tell you what you're gonna do! Lettin' people push you around. How long do you think it's gonna last? How long are you gonna let 'em push you around? How long? Maybe you love it, maybe you love gettin' your face stuck in the shit . . ."

Jim was taunting them, just as the actors in the Living

Theatre taunted their spectators, trying to shatter their leth-argy.

"You're all a bunch of slaves!" Jim shouted. "What are you gonna do about it, what are you gonna do, what are you gonna do?" His voice was a hoarse shout. Then he resumed singing: "Your ballroom days over over, bayyy-beeee/Night is drawing near."

Somehow the song was concluded and Jim began to talk again. "I'm not talkin' about no revolution, I'm not talkin' about no demonstration. I'm not talkin' about getting out in the streets. I'm talkin' about havin' some fun. I'm talkin' about dancin'. I'm talkin' about love yer neighbor. I'm talkin' about grab yer friend. I'm talkin' above love. I'm talkin' about some love. Love love love love love love love. Grab yer . . . fuckin' friend and love him. Come *ooooooaaannnn. Yeahhhhhh!*

Then, as if to set an example, Jim pulled his shirt over his head and threw it into the audience, where it disappeared like meat thrown to a pack of ravenous dogs. As he watched, he hooked his thumbs into the top of his pants and started play-ing with the buckle. This was the moment that Jim had been planning since seeing *Paradise Now.* He had prepared for it carefully. But he hadn't said anything to anyone in the band.

Ray called for "Touch Me," hoping to draw Jim's atten-tion back to the music. Jim sang two lines and stopped.

"*Heyyyyyy,* wait a minute, wait a minute. Hey wait a min-ute, this is all fucked up—no, wait a minute, wait a minute, wait a minute! You blew it, you blew it, you blew it, now *come oannnn. Wait a minute! I'm not gonna take this shit! Fuck you!"* he hollered.

He was red-faced, his voice a bellowing growl, the micro-phone rammed into his mouth.

"*Bullshit!"*

The crowd roared.

Jim began to unbuckle the belt. Ray called to Vince, "Vince, Vince, stop him! Don't let him do it!"

Vince leaped over the sound board in front of him and in two strides was behind Jim, one hand stuck down Jim's pants at the small of his back, the other pushing against Jim's back higher up, making it impossible for Jim to undo the buckle.

"Don't do it, Jim, don't do it," Vince urged.

Although Jim rarely wore underwear, on this night he wore boxer shorts so large he had them pulled up and over the top of his leather pants. He had planned to shed his trousers, yet still not expose himself, to go the "legal limit" proposed in *Paradise Now*. Jim knew what he was doing. He had planned this carefully. Now Ray's decision and Vince's physical restraint aborted his plan. The arrival of paradise would be delayed.

Amazingly, the band was still playing "Touch Me," albeit haphazardly. Finally Jim relaxed and the concert resumed.

Jim remained obviously drunk, although the beer had been cut off and he stopped going to the audience for drinks. He slurred his words hoarsely. He forgot the lyrics to songs and got lost in the middle of verses, going back and repeating himself. He delivered an insulting rap about being born and going to school in Florida, "but then I got smart and I went out to a beautiful state called California." An acquaintance from Los Angeles, an eccentric named Louis Marvin, for whom the Doors had played one of their first parties in 1966, came forward carrying a lamb and gave it to Jim to hold. "I'd fuck her, you know," Jim said, "but she's too young." Then he removed a cop's hat and sailed it into the sweating mass before him . . . and the cop took a hat that had been given to Jim and tossed it in the same direction, to much laughter.

There were phrases he returned to again and again, between and in the middle of songs. "I wanna see some dancing, I wanna see some fun" was one. "There are no rules, there are no limits" was another. There could be no doubt about his inspiration and motivation. "Hey, listen," he called, "I used to think the whole thing was a big joke. I thought it was somethin' to laugh about, and then the last couple of nights I met

In Miami with young friend

some people who were doin' somethin'. They're tryin' to change the world, and I wanna get on the trip. I wanna change the world."

For nearly an hour Jim invited and badgered the audience to join him onstage and at the one-hour mark in the show they began to come forward. One of the promoters spoke into the microphone: "Someone's gonna get hurt," and threatened to stop the show. The kids kept coming. Now there were more than a hundred, milling around, dancing to the music the Doors somehow continued to play.

"We're not leaving until we get our rocks off," Jim shouted. He began dancing with two or three girls. The stage was vibrating so much, John and Robby thought it was going to collapse. Even more kids started scrambling for handholds on the rim of the stage to haul themselves up. Finally, one of the promoter's security men, who held a black belt in karate, reached into the onstage swarm and with a proficient flip tossed Jim off the stage. He landed in an empty space, got up, formed a human snake, and began trailing hundreds of kids behind him. He reappeared in the balcony a few minutes later, waved to the crowd, then disappeared into the dressing room. The show was over.

There were about two dozen present and all seemed to be talking at once, a few expressing concern over how much equipment was lost and the inevitable personal injuries to members of the audience. Bill Siddons would say later that Jim uttered something like, "Uh-oh, I think I exposed myself out there." While others contend he said, "Now let's see Buick use 'Light My Fire.'" Still others said he was laughing, still having a good time, saying nothing relevant or memorable. Generally, the mood was light. Part of this was from the relief everyone felt at the end of any concert. But it was also because of the jokes made when Siddons handed some money to one of the cops, to pay for the hat that Jim had taken and thrown into the crowd. Even the half dozen cops present were laughing, saying what a good time they had had.

Half an hour later only Vince and the Doors' road crew

and a few security people remained in the old airplane hangar-cum-concert hall, packing up and viewing the extensive debris. The stage was broken and leaning dangerously, but more impressive were perhaps a thousand empty wine and beer bottles and panties and brassieres in sufficient quantity to open a well-stocked lingerie store. The way Vince remembers it, "Every three or four feet there was another garment."

Jim may have been prevented from undressing and approaching paradise, but clearly his Miami audience had not.

In the three days that followed—with Jim vacationing, in Jamaica as planned, but without Pamela—his and the Doors' future was being plotted by Miami's politicians, police, and press. On Sunday one of the Miami newspapers wrote that Jim had thrown three policemen off the stage before being carried off by three more himself. On Monday a police sergeant was quoted as saying, "You've got to give the kids credit for this one. You can't do anything but commend them. That guy did his damnedest to start a riot and the kids didn't move." The acting police chief said that as soon as he could find a cop who'd witnessed any crimes, he'd issue warrants for Jim's arrest.

The same day the politically ambitious assistant city manager was aroused to ask, "How did this happen in a *city* auditorium?"

By Tuesday there was a scramble for the bandwagon as the president of the Crime Commission of Greater Miami, a former city prosecutor, called for a grand jury investigation . . . a state legislator, who was president of the Miami Exchange Club, wrote the mayor of Jacksonville, urging him to cancel the Doors' show scheduled there for the next weekend . . . the captain of the Miami police department's internal security division said he definitely would issue warrants for Jim's arrest . . . and a nineteen-year-old ex-football player named Mike Levisque began plans in the offices of a regional Catholic newspaper for an antiobscenity rally.

The ax fell on Wednesday, March 5, as Bob Jennings, a

```
                                              I.    LEWD AND LASCIVIOUS
                                                    BEHAVIOR (FEL)
                                              II.   INDECENT EXPOSURE (MISD)
                                              III.  OPEN PROFANITY    (MISD)
TO:     THE DADE COUNTY SHERIFF'S OFFICE    CHARGE IV.  DRUNKENNESS (MISD)


_____ Defendant __TO BE ARRESTED_____

JAMES MORRISON                                              69— 2355
        Name of Defendant

_____   Race __W__ Sex __M__ Age _____
Address                      Phone

                                            Height _____ Weight _____
_____
Business Address             Phone
        Member of musical group
        (The Doors)                         Hair _____ Eyes _____
              Occupation or Business

     3/1/69          Dinner Key Auditorium  Complexion _____
Date of Offense      Location of Offense    Marks or
                                            Features
REMARKS: Booking Agent for "The Doors" is   Comments

        Ashley Famous Agency, 1301 Ave. of the

        Americas, New York City, New York
Complainant (s) (Note: If filed by an officer, both the name of the victim and of the department are shown below)

        Bob Jennings, 495 NW 93rd St.
Name    Theodore Seaman, MPD        Address                        Phone

ASSISTANT STATE ATTORNEY: _____ALFONSO C. SEPE_____ alc

201.01—5
```

(Stamp: FILED MAR 5 1969 J. F. McCRACKEN CLERK)

twenty-two-year-old clerk in the state attorney's office, agreed to serve as a complainant in the case and Jim was charged with one felony—lewd and lascivious behavior—and three misdemeanors—indecent exposure, open profanity, and drunkenness. It was the felony charge that was most intriguing, and publicly controversial, for in the bill of particulars it was claimed that Jim "did lewdly and lasciviously expose his penis, place his hands upon his penis and shake it, and further the said defendant did simulate the acts of masturbation upon himself and oral copulation upon another." At a press conference held by the acting police chief it was announced that upon conviction of these charges Jim could be sent to Raiford Prison—one of Florida's meanest—for seven years and 150 days. The following day Jim's name and that of the Doors were smeared on front pages all over the country.

In the meantime Jim was having a miserable time in the Caribbean. His was the only white face in the old manor house that had been rented in his name. Ray and Dorothy were on the French island of Guadeloupe, and John and Robby and their girls, Julia and Lynn, were in another house some distance from Jim's on Jamaica. It was "spooky," Jim told friends later, and when he was offered some marijuana by one of the black servants, he said he was afraid to refuse so he smoked a joint the size of a Cuban cigar and experienced a subsequent "freakout that included the fantasy of my death." It was months before Jim would smoke pot again.

In a panic Jim left the house and joined John and Robby near the beach. But he had no interest in their water sports, so he soon returned, bored and visibly upset, to California.

It seemed incomprehensible that what Bill Siddons at first called "just another dirty Doors show" was attracting so much attention and having so vast an effect on the group. In the first week or so the group joked about it. When Jim entered the office and Leon Barnard asked, "How'd it go in Miami?" Jim grinned and said right back, "You would have *loved* it, Leon." When newspapers across the country began running stories about Mike Levisque and the decency rally he was organizing for the Orange Bowl, the Doors began planning their own decency rally—to be held in the Rose Bowl, with Jim presenting a large check to Levisque, who would be flown in from Miami for the occasion.

But the jokes stopped. In less than three weeks it became clear that what had happened in Miami was endangering the future of the group. The confidential newsletter distributed among members of the Concert Hall Managers Association warned of the Doors' unpredictability and the numerous charges against Jim. Result: the group was banned nearly everywhere.

The first city to cancel was Jacksonville. Then came Dallas and Pittsburgh, and after that Providence and Syracuse, Philadelphia and Cincinnati, Cleveland and Detroit. Even Kent State University canceled. Most ominous, the radio stations in several cities began removing the Doors from their play lists.

The press never let up. Every development, small and large, was amply covered and *Rolling Stone* even printed a full-page western-style wanted poster. For the first time in the Doors' career the media turned against them.

When the Orange Bowl rally attracted personal appearances by Anita Bryant and Jackie Gleason—and a crowd of thirty thousand!—reaction to Jim's performance became a national movement, prompting similar rallies in several other cities and drawing an endorsement from President Nixon.

At the end of March the FBI agreed to charge Jim with unlawful flight. It was a ridiculous charge because Jim had left Miami three days before any warrants were issued, but the FBI sent an agent to the Doors' office with a warrant for Jim's arrest. That was the day the Doors knew the situation was serious.

Bill Siddons issued (under the circumstances) a calm statement, but one that betrayed how anxious the Doors were for this bizarre nightmare to go away:

> There's nothing we can say that will make it any better. We're just letting everybody say what they want. We're letting everybody get rid of their wrath . . . and then when it's all over, we'll go on our way. We have nothing to say about it—good, bad, or indifferent.

For Jim, not a day passed without some reminder of Miami. On April 4, accompanied by his attorney, he surrendered to the FBI, and was released on $5,000 bail.

Meanwhile *Feast of Friends* was readied for its first screenings and Jim started on his new film. After forming his own production company, HiWay Productions, Jim put his friends

Frank Lisciandro, Babe Hill, and Paul Ferrara on the payroll, bought most of the equipment used in filming *Feast,* and moved it into two small upstairs rooms in the improbably named Clear Thoughts Building directly across the street from Elektra Records.

The filming was begun Easter week. Again, death in the desert dominated the plot, as a bearded Jim Morrison wandered out of the California mountains near Palm Springs, encountered a dying coyote while hitchhiking to Los Angeles, and then apparently murdered the first driver who offered him a ride.

While filming the ending in Los Angeles Jim made a mysterious telephone call to Michael McClure in San Francisco. He did not identify himself when Michael answered.

"I wasted him," Jim said.

Michael recognized Jim's voice. "Jim . . ." He thought Jim might've been drunk. But he wasn't certain.

Jim hung up abruptly, leaving the phone booth with a smile curling the corners of his mouth.

"Now we go to the 9000 Building," he said.

Jim had been drinking steadily for hours, but he was not drunk. Ginni Ganahl, then the Doors' secretary, and Kathy Lisciandro were along, with Frank and Babe and Paul and Leon. It was dark when they took the elevator to the top of the seventeen-story 9000 Building on Sunset Boulevard. The idea was for Jim to tie a rope around his waist—which wouldn't be seen in the shot—and then do a little dance along the eighteen-inch ledge, with nothing between him and the sidewalk seventeen flights below. The rope was to be held by friends, who'd keep him from death if he fell.

When Jim explained the scene, everyone was alarmed. They knew they couldn't prevent him from carrying on exactly as he wanted, but they wouldn't be his friends if they didn't at least protest.

"You don't want to do this really, do you?" Leon said.

Jim glared at him. He seemed to take the question as a

dare. Dramatically he removed the rope from his waist, jumped onto the parapet, ordered Paul to begin filming, and did his little dance, capping off the performance by urinating over the ledge onto Sunset below. The whole scene was senseless, unless you knew Jim. Then it was only drunkenly crazy.

If his films reflected the daredevil rock and roll star, his books shed light on Jim's other identity, the poet.

He was quite pleased with the poetry he'd had printed. *The Lords* was packaged the most extravagantly: eighty-two Rimbaudian observations about vision and cinematography printed on rich cream parchment paper measuring eight and a half by eleven inches, bound in a royal blue box with a red tie-string and the title in gold leaf. *The New Creatures* was presented more modestly: forty-two standard-size book pages of more recent poetry printed on pale yellow paper of the sort used for slick magazine covers, bound between brown cardboard similar to school workbook covers, and again, with the title in gold leaf. Jim had a hundred copies of each book delivered to the Doors' office, where they were stacked against a wall near Bill Siddons' desk. On the cover of each was the name he used for his poetry: James Douglas Morrison.

Throughout *The New Creatures* the words and phrases of sexual conflict interlocked with images of pain and death: There were assassinations, lynchings, earthquakes, ghost children, trenchmouth, gonorrhea, evil snakeroot, people dancing on broken bones, lootings, riots, and artists in hell. There was a grotesque otherworldliness, the hovering presence of Lovecraft and Bosch. Animal references were frequent: insects, lizards, snakes, eagles, cave fish, eels, salamanders, worms, rats, wild dogs.

The final poem in the slender volume was as despairing as the rest. In this, an untitled description of the aftermath of the apocalypse, there was a tour of the wasteland.

The poems provided a deep, long look into the raw wounds of Jim's profound despair, a despair that may never be adequately explained or understood, but which was in his poetry painfully clear and brilliantly expressed.

The four New York journalists assembled for the television panel seemed startled when Jim ambled into the Channel 13 studio. The last time they had seen him, at Madison Square Garden five months earlier, he had been clean-shaven and wearing his black leathers. Now he wore a full beard, tinted aviator glasses, and striped cotton railroad pants, and was smoking a long thin cigar, looking much like a handsome, beefy Che Guevara. As charismatic as ever, he was now sober and charming, telling everyone how delighted he was to be in an educational television studio where there was no censorship and talk and music were regarded seriously.

Jim's reference to no censorship was more than a casual remark, for the Doors planned to perform an unexpurgated version of a song called "Build Me a Woman." When this song was included in a live album a year later the lines "Sunday trucker/Christian motherfucker" would be excised. On the Public Broadcasting System, however, the lines remained, although Jim softened the blow by slurring the critical word when he came to it.

The Doors also performed the extended musical poem that would give their fourth album its name, "The Soft Parade," and during the band's ten-minute interview with Richard Goldstein Jim produced a copy of *The New Creatures* and read some of the poetry. When he was asked if he no longer wanted to be regarded as an "erotic politician," Jim admitted for the first time publicly that he had said that merely to give a writer the catch phrase all journalists seemed to be looking for.

This was the "new" Jim Morrison—honest, serious, politely declining to talk about Miami "at my lawyer's insistence," boyishly charming, spouting poetry. But to anyone watching closely, it was clear that Jim was manipulating the media again, that by changing his wardrobe, growing a beard,

Jerry Hopkins

emphasizing his poetry, and being candid about his Machiavellian past, he was building himself another image. This one was more honest. Not that the previous leather-clad incarnation hadn't been legitimate, but it had been limiting and he had obviously outgrown it. His new image was both easier to live with and easier to live up to. Jim was learning.

The PBS interview was Jim's first since Miami. The second began less than a week later and was with the Los Angeles

correspondent for the publication that had—Jim believed—hurt his image the most, *Rolling Stone.* Jim met Jerry Hopkins four times over a period of two or three weeks and gave what was his most extensive and probably deepest interview. He seemed eager to please, eager to make himself understood. Thus he picked his words slowly, carefully, almost as a gem cutter examines uncut stones.

As expected, he refused to talk about Miami—for legal

reasons, he said. But, unexpectedly, he did comment on his family, not in depth, but with honesty and perspective, something he had not previously allowed himself to do. Jerry asked Jim why he made up the early story. Jim thought for a moment before answering, then replied, "I just didn't want to involve them. It's easy enough to find out personal details if you really want them. When we're born we're all footprinted and so on. I guess I said my parents were dead as some kind of joke. I have a brother, but I haven't seen him in about a year. I don't see any of them. This is the most I've ever said about this."

The answer doesn't reveal much, but the fact that Jim was able to acknowledge his family's existence at all says much about the way Jim was beginning to come to grips with his life in other areas. Or, as Bill Siddons told an interviewer once, "Jim used to have lots of little demons running around inside him. I don't think he has so many anymore. He seems to be working them out of his system."

Some of his answers were finely polished: "I'm interested in film because to me it's the closest approximation in art form that we have to the actual flow of consciousness, in both dreamlife and in the everyday perception of the world." And this definition he offered of ritual: "It's kind of like human sculpture. In a way it's like art, because it gives form to energy, and in a way it's a custom or a repetition, a habitually recurring plan or pageant that has meaning. It pervades everything. It's like a game." And this thought: "the logical extension of ego is god" and "the logical extension of living in America is to be president."

At the end of the third interview session Jim stretched amiably and stared at Jerry, who seemed to have run out of questions.

"Don't you want to talk about my drinking?" Jim asked. He shifted in the chair, smiling.

"Well, yeah, sure," Jerry said. "You've got a reputation for . . ."

". . . getting drunk," Jim finished. "Well, it's true, all true.

Jerry Hopkins

Jim during the Rolling Stone *interview, early 1970*

Getting drunk is, uh . . . getting drunk, you're in complete control . . . up to a point. It's your choice, every time you take a sip. You have a lot of small choices."

There was a long pause. Jerry waited for more.

"It's like . . . I guess it's the difference between suicide and slow capitulation."

Did Jim really believe he was slowly drinking himself to death and not care because it fulfilled the poetic tradition of which he was so enamored? Or did he simply, for dramatic effect, choose to suggest that was his fate?

Jerry decided to try to find out. "What do you mean by that?" he asked.

Jim laughed easily. "I don't know, man. Let's go next door and get a drink. "

At the final meeting Jim told Jerry he wanted to read a long poem rather than answer more questions. Then untitled, it was later published as "An American Prayer." Like much of his earlier poetry and some of his best known songs, this poem took as its subject the onrushing American apocalypse and the form of still another catalogue of mid-century complaints, ofttimes personal and voiced with anger.

When he held the published interviews in his hands a few weeks later (a leather pants and shirtless Jim photographed by Paul Ferrara graced the cover) and saw the poem included, laid out as he'd requested, with the copyright credited to James Douglas Morrison, he was immensely pleased.

"At last," he told friends, "that rag is beginning to recognize real talent when it sees it."

By June the Doors' fourth album was finally complete. A full year in preparation, this album had been the most frustrating yet, with Jim contributing only half the material. His energy, obviously, was being directed more toward poetry than lyrics. For this reason, and because Jim didn't want anyone to think he wrote the song that would be their next single, "Tell All the People," individual writer's credits replaced the traditional, "Songs by the Doors."

But, as in previous albums, there were in *The Soft Parade* several "Jim Morrison lines," lines thought to be too weird and colorful to have been written by anyone else. In "Shaman's Blues" there was the image of "Cold grinding grizzly-bear jaws/Hot on your heels," and in "The Soft Parade" the singsong "Catacombs, nursery bones/Winter women growing stones/Carrying babies to the river," the latter line prompting the question: to bathe or drown?

"Easy Ride," a song Jim hoped would also be a single, had sharp and accessible lyrics throughout, but in the last stanza he couldn't resist the poetic twist: "Coda queen now be my bride/rage in darkness by my side/seize the summer in your pride/take the winter in your stride/let's ride."

But overall the lyric impact was less than it had been on previous albums, and the use of what Vince Treanor called "The La Cienega Symphony"—strings from the Los Angeles Philharmonic, horns by some of the top local studio jazz musicians—further blurred the once-lucid Doors sound.

It was imperative that the Doors find work. The new album had cost $86,000, but even more dismaying was the continuing economic blight that Jim was now referring to as the "Miami incident." Ray remembers losing twenty-five concert dates, which John described at the time as "a million dollars in gigs."

Promoters in a dozen cities were suing for money they lost when local do-gooders officially banned the Doors from appearing. Although their last hit single, "Touch Me," which had been released about the same time as the Miami incident, sold nearly as well as "Light My Fire," the money was quickly spent on lawyers, and subsequent record sales plummeted when the band was blacklisted by radio stations in twenty important markets. This dip was short-lived, however, and when the news hit the nation in the face, record sales leveled.

Though "Touch Me" was recorded before the Miami incident, its release date made it appear as if the two were related.

Indecent exposure in the news and the plea "Touch Me" storming up the charts—the teenyboppers innocently ate it up, and the Doors' fans were proud of their band, despite the horns and strings, for what they took to be bravado.

Finally, Bill Siddons had some good news. "We've got some firm dates," he said. "Chicago and Minneapolis, June fourteenth and fifteenth. Eugene, Oregon, on the sixteenth. The Seattle Pop Festival on the seventeenth."

"Hey," Jim said quietly, turning away from the office refrigerator, a can of Coors in his hand, "I thought we agreed: no more outdoor shows."

The other Doors stared at Jim blankly.

"These dates are *firm*, Jim," Bill said. "We really need the work. It's been three months since Miami. That's a long time between gigs."

"So how come we got four in a row? What'd the agency promise? They promise I wouldn't drop my pants?"

"We have to post a bond, Jim. Five thousand dollars a show. We lose the bond only if it's an obscene show. It's written into the contracts."

"A 'fuck clause,'" Jim grumbled. He dropped into the couch and pulled on his beer. "I bet it's a rock and roll first."

Jim was careful in both cities not to wear leather and not to use any obscenities. There was reason for caution. In Minneapolis, just before they went on, the hall manager and police were standing in the wings in case of "indecent exposure." The post-Miami paranoia had begun.

On the 16th the Doors flew to Eugene, and then on the 17th to the festival outside Seattle. Again they were cautious (to the audience's disappointment), but they were also beginning to get the feel of performing again. The festival wasn't that satisfying. Since performing at the Hollywood Bowl, they'd believed their music wasn't right for an outdoor arena. But it was clear, nonetheless, that the four Doors could still perform as one. Each concert was better musically, and freer, more spontaneous, than the show before it. Jim's on-the-road behavior had become more civil as well—gone were the days of ordering seven meals just to taste each. He spent his time reading, going to the movies, and sight-seeing—avoiding the hotel bar as well as the night spots.

He was content, even pleased with the way things were going. Audience expectations seemed lower. Perhaps he had succeeded in Miami when, as he told a writer, he had "tried to reduce the myth to absurdity, thereby wiping it out." However, there was still that element who came not for the music but to see the naked Door sing "Touch Me."

More dates were added as summer came—in Toronto, Mexico City, San Francisco, Philadelphia, Pittsburgh, Las Vegas, and Los Angeles. But by now America was hip deep in what *Rolling Stone* called "The Age of Paranoia." The year before, Martin Luther King and Robert Kennedy had been assassinated and the police had rioted at the Democratic convention in Chicago. The Manson murders were being used to smear the youth culture that only a short time before had been embraced so warmly. It was abundantly clear that the Doors formed part of the target.

In Toronto they were told as they mounted the stage that city police were ready to pounce if Jim so much as twitched. Two days before their show in Philadelphia the mayor unearthed a law from 1879 giving him the power to revoke a permit for any performance that "may be immoral in nature or unpleasant and harmful to the community," and after the promoter fought the ruling and won, the Doors were warned that their limousine drivers were narcs. In Pittsburgh the show was halted when hundreds of teenagers rushed the stage. In Las Vegas the sheriff came to the show with blank warrants made out for each of the Doors, the charges to be filled in—or not—according to how the band performed.

The shows tightened and shined despite the pressure. Jim enjoyed the opportunity to simply sing and entertain and even developed a sense of humor about the situation. But he was irritated at the small-mindedness of the authorities and began to think he might just do something about it, once and for all.

It was with mixed feelings that they anticipated the shows

Mural on the Forum wall in Mexico—Ray supporting

in Mexico City scheduled for the end of the month in the Plaza Monumental, the city's largest bullring. Again it meant playing to a large outdoor audience (forty-eight thousand), but the Doors felt the prestige of the show was more important than aesthetic reward, and because tickets were to be priced from 40 cents to $1, they believed they would not be excluding the poor. It was also planned that the band would perform a United Nations or Red Cross benefit at the Camino Real Hotel as well as in an expensive supper club.

But the promoter in Mexico City, a young bearded interior decorator named Mario Olmos, was unable to get all the necessary permissions, so he went to Javier Castro, a twenty-six-year-old singer who owned the Forum, a one-thousand–seat supper club that was roughly equivalent in decor and clientele to the Copacabana in New York. He told Javier he could deliver the Doors for four nights at $5,000 a night. Together they found a friend who provided a $20,000 cashier's check to take to the Doors as a guarantee, and the next morning Mexico City newspapers carried a full-page ad heralding the appearance of the Doors at the Forum that weekend.

The Doors had not been consulted on these plans and they were furious when Mario and Javier entered their offices with the newspaper ad and check in their hands, wild promises on their lips. The office that night was dimly lit, the desk of Bill Siddons was littered with empty beer bottles and posters and Forum newspaper ads. Members of the band were sitting around with long faces, talking about how they should have called in a psychic. That idea came when Alan Ronay and Leon Barnard both had reported premonitions of Jim's death. This wasn't the first time, but it seemed to be the harbinger of doom.

Bill Siddons never came to accept such reports comfortably. On a dozen Monday mornings in the past year Jim had been rumored dead, the victim of a weekend of self-abuse, and each time Bill had panicked, calling around frantically to find Jim, until Jim himself squelched the wild tales by arriving at the office to read his mail.

"You're supposed to be dead," Bill would say, smiling, obviously relieved.

"Oh?" Jim would reply, opening the refrigerator in Bill's office and pulling out a can of Coors. "Again? How did I go this time?"

Jim was not told about the premonitions Leon and his close friend Alan felt. The packing for Mexico resumed.

"Jeem! Jeem! Where is Jeem?" Thousands of Doors fans had come to greet the band and welcome them to Mexico.

The Doors walked through customs and into the lobby of Mexico City's airport. In his full beard Jim went unrecognized: he didn't look like the Jim Morrison who had been painted on the front wall of the Forum, and there were dissatisfied rumblings within his party. Siddons was asked to talk to Jim, which he did. But the beard stayed.

The performances were among the best they ever gave. The Doors were far more popular in Mexico than they'd thought and the response from the rich teenagers who packed the club each night fired them to unusual musical highs—although they remarked how *strange* some of the popularity seemed. It was the reaction to "The End" that puzzled them most.

The first night Jim and the others ignored the repeated calls for that song, but the second night they acquiesced. As they approached the Oedipal section, so many in the audience began to shush each other that it sounded like a roomful of snakes.

"Father?" "Yes, son?"

Jim recoiled at the response that line elicited, as instantly every young man in the room called out, "*I want to keeeeel you!*"

Jim looked into the darkness, visibly stunned. "Mother?" he offered tentatively. "I want to . . ." and again the audience erupted.

Jim was impressed.

In Mexico, 1970

Ray Manzarek

Paul Ferrara

Jim and friends in Mexico, 1970

So popular was this song in Mexico, it had been released on an extended-play 45, and was played so often on jukeboxes that the lyrics were barely intelligible. "Mexico is an Oedipal country," someone later told Jim. "It's all wrapped up in national *machismo* and 'Mother Church.' "

The Doors were treated as royalty, and in a week's time grew to appreciate the comfort that accompanies an extended engagement. There was time for sight-seeing and for this there were matching black and white Cadillacs, chauffeurs, and a woman named Malu, who normally served as the Forum's publicist but was now the Doors' interpreter and den mother. All were available on a twenty-four–hour basis. The motel was situated in the best residential neighborhood. They were introduced to the Mexican president's son, who was dressed in the latest Carnaby Street styles and in whose wake traveled a covey of American girls, known locally as "presiden-

Lynn and Robby Krieger in Mexico

tial groupies" (the one Jim picked for himself while visiting the anthropology museum looked a lot like Pamela). Backstage someone appeared carrying what looked like a pound of cocaine in a large plastic bag, offering the boys as much as they wanted.

Throughout the week Bill Siddons held meetings. First he tried to arrange a free concert in a park but was rebuffed because the government was wary of allowing so many young people to gather in one location. (A year earlier there had been student riots and massive strikes.) After that, Siddons tried to set up a television show, and finally a contract was signed for a two-hour special on the Doors, their music, and their ideas. However, nothing came of it.

The Doors returned to their motel after the last of the five shows. The chauffeur of Jim's Cadillac sped along the broad tree-lined boulevard at eighty miles an hour, slowing to fifty for the ninety-degree turns. The speed made everyone laugh nervously.

Jim formed a gun with his finger and thumb and made the throaty sounds of pistol shots. *"Andele! Andele!"* he shouted. ("Go! Go!"). The Doors thundered into the Mexican night.

The band was still finding it difficult to work. Before leaving for Mexico, two more concerts had been canceled, in St. Louis and Honolulu, leaving them with only one firm booking for all of July, and that was in a Los Angeles theater that had been leased for a series of Monday night concerts by the Doors' own record company. Tickets sold out the same hour they went on sale.

There were two shows, and before each Jim distributed to members of the audience copies of an impressionistic poem he had written about the recent death of Rolling Stones guitarist Brian Jones, "Ode to L.A. While Thinking of Brian Jones, Deceased." As in "An American Prayer," there was Joycean word-play and a pervasive contemplation of death.

The stormy journalistic tide that had followed the Miami incident was finally receding. In June, July, and August, at a time when the Doors remained virtually unemployable, several publications important to Jim began to publish flattering articles.

One of the Los Angeles newspapers called the Aquarius show "one of the most exciting rock concerts in years," and the other headlined, "Audience Hears a New Jim Morrison." *Rolling Stone,* the publication that had made Jim seem such a fool in the immediate aftermath of Miami, had printed a pleasant review of *Feast of Friends,* then followed that with the cover picture and Jerry's interview, which ran more than eight thousand words, and then printed a four-thousand–word report from Mexico. In the July issue of Pat Kennely's *Jazz & Pop* there was a flattering report of the Doors' appearance on New York's Channel 13. Finally, the first week of August a long appreciation of the Doors written by the young playwright Harvey Perr appeared in the *Los Angeles Free Press.* In time, Harvey would become a friend of Jim's and this article would be included in *The Doors Complete,* a compilation of all the Doors' sheet music.

I'm not altogether sure that my own admiration of the Doors has anything to do with their songs [*he wrote*]. Some of them are, admittedly, weak, but I find the degree to which they give themselves to simplicity is more strikingly impressive than the degree to which lesser artists consciously avoid simplicity. It seems to me that if a group has truly reached the poetic heights, they should enjoy the luxury of making gross mistakes; too few do either one or the other. It's like Morrison's poetry; most of it is the work of a genuine poet, a Whitman of the revolutionary 60's, but some of it is embarrassingly sophomoric. There is no crime in going from one artistic extreme to another; these are, after all, human flaws, and there is no art if there is no humanity. But, again, it's not their music at all, and maybe not even the poetry or the musicianship or the charisma, neither the albums nor the Aquarius concert, all of it as strange and beautiful and exciting as it is, that really makes me admire the Doors. Instead it's the vibes I get from them because of the thing I feel they're trying to get into and get us into, a world that transcends the limited one of rock, and moves into areas of film and theatre and revolution. Seeing Morrison not on stage but living his life, in those quieter moments: seeing him at a production of Norman Mailer's *The Deer Park,* at every performance of The Living Theatre, at the opening of The Company Theatre's *James Joyce Memorial Liquid Theatre;* always at the right place at the right time, involved furiously in the kind of art that is pertinent rather than tangential to living. That kind of person doesn't have to have poetry in him, but if he does, when he does, you tend to look at it more closely, take it more seriously. In the case of Jim Morrison

and the Doors, it is worth the trouble. They have approached Art, no matter how much they have offended, amused, or even thrilled the rock critics. The standards by which their art must be measured are older and deeper.

A few days after the Aquarius show, Thursday, in the late afternoon, Jim walked into the office and then into the bathroom. Denny was at Jim's desk, mail spread out before him, and on the phone. "Oh shit!" Denny shouted.

"Poetic today, aren't we?" someone remarked.

"Waz up?" Jim asked, pulling up his fly, walking back into the office.

"Nothing," Denny mumbled, pretending to read the mail.

"What do you mean nothing? Don't tell me nothing," Jim teased. "I take time off from my busy schedule to inquire and possibly aid in what appears to be a mild case of misfortune, a gesture you, uncaringly, reject." Jim was obviously in a good mood.

Denny had been trying desperately to get tickets to a local Rolling Stones concert now only a few days away. It had been sold out for weeks, and with the last phone call, he had not only exhausted all his sources, but had received final notice that there were no tickets to be had.

"Can you get me Stones tickets?" Denny asked hesitantly.

"What do you need Mick Jagger for when you got me?" Jim asked with a mixture of bravado and hurt.

Denny couldn't answer. He hadn't meant to hurt Jim, but he very much wanted the tickets and he was sure Jim could get them in one easy call. Jim played Denny along.

"I mean, what night is that concert? This Friday, isn't it? I thought we were gonna do something together that night," Jim said, then improvised a bit more before being called into the back office for a meeting.

The next afternoon, Friday, the day of the show, Jim came into the office. Denny was again at Jim's desk poring over the day's mail. They both behaved as though the conversation of the day before had never taken place. Jim pulled a pair of concert tickets from his jacket pocket.

"Look what somebody gave me last night. For no reason at all. He just said, 'Here, Jim, I have this pair of Rolling Stones tickets, I want you to have them.' And he just handed them to me. Can you imagine that?" Jim looked at the tickets. "Goddamn, look what it says here: third row! Well, shit, I don't want to hassle that. I can't use these. Anybody else want 'em?"

There were three people in the room, besides Jim, who had been present the day before. "Sure, Jim, I'll take them if you aren't going to use them," a secretary said.

Bill said he already had his. So did Ray. Denny was silent, confused.

Jim sat down on the desk in front of Denny and put his right hand over the letter Denny was reading. "Today is your lucky day, my man. I'm prepared to make you a deal."

Denny looked up. "I don't want to make a deal with you!" he said.

"Doncha at least want to hear what it is?" Jim said, soothingly.

Denny nodded.

"Okay," Jim continued, "the deal is, you give me back my fucking desk and I'll give you these tickets." Jim put the tickets on the desk.

Denny leaped up, dashed around the desk, gave Jim a bear hug, grabbed the two tickets, and ran to the door.

"Hey?" Jim barked.

"What?" Denny stopped.

"You could at least say thank you."

Back at their West Hollywood apartment on Norton Avenue, within walking distance from the office, Pamela was on downers and cranky, and Jim was on the telephone, trying to talk with Babe Hill. Pamela kept interrupting, providing a constant, nagging drone in the background.

"Yeah, hey, Babe . . ."

"Jim, listen to me," said Pamela. "just put that phone down and listen, this is more important than where you and Babe are going to meet . . ."

". . . I'm sorry, Babe, what was that?"

". . . to do what you usually do, get drunk. I'm talking to you, Jim. *Jim!*"

Jim ignored her, hunching over the telephone, turning his back. "Babe, I'm sorry about the background noise. You know how it is with Pamela . . ."

"Jim! Are you trying to provoke a fight?" Pamela's voice rose half an octave and twenty decibels. "Jim, goddamn it, every time you start a fight, you go out and get drunk and then you do something outrageous. Goddamn it, Jim."

Pam did not care for many of Jim's friends. More to the point, she was bitterly jealous of anyone Jim chose to spend time with other than her. In time she grew to object vehemently to Jim's role as perpetual host and hated even more his stubborn reticence. In return, Jim's friends tolerated Pamela with the understanding that Jim truly did love her and that she, despite her fun-killing possessiveness, was good to and for him.

Jim didn't like many of her friends, some of whom were homosexuals. Pam tried to point out to Jim that he didn't like in others what he didn't like or couldn't accept in himself. At any rate, these were the companions who satisfied Pam's social urges, who responded to her needs and offered sympathy in a way Jim could not, demanding nothing physical in return. Jim, however, privately felt they were using her to get near him. He was partly right, but he didn't have the heart to tell her. So he voiced other objections instead.

Jim also hated her choice of drugs. He thought downers were dangerous. At the same time, he felt somewhat guilty about being the one who had introduced her to drugs. So he swallowed that objection as well. He did not know of Pam's heroin experience. And she, in turn, felt guilty about conceal-ing it.

The mutual deceit would create separation, and since nei-ther party was the sort to confess to the truth, the separation would usually surface as a fight. It was almost always triggered by something trivial, like which movie they would see that night. Once they quarreled ferociously over the average life expectancy of a golden retriever. (They had one named Sage.)

Pots and books and dishes flew. Once, when Pamela com-plained about how messy his books were, he dumped several hundred of them out a second-story window. The house would resound with bellows and screams. Then Jim would dis-appear, or Pamela would stalk next door to her homosexual neighbors in the Beachwood hills and announce, "Today's at-titude is . . . shitty."

Sometimes Pamela sought revenge by hiring the sleek limousine that Jim used for his occasional trips to Mexico with the boys. With Jim's usual chauffeur taking her shopping, she knew her spree would be reported back to him. It was not un-usual for her to spend $2,000 or more on these splurges.

Once, after an especially dramatic episode involving Jim's drinking, Pam furiously rummaged through her makeup draw-er, found what she was looking for, and as Jim walked out of the house, scrawled in red lipstick across the bathroom mirror, "Some sex symbol—can't even get it up!"

After other fights Pamela would get whacked out of her skull on downers or, occasionally, smack, and be seen in pub-lic, tongue-wrestling with a bartender from the Beverly Hills Polo Lounge, under a table at the Troubadour bar, moving from party to party in the rich-rock-star circuit, asprawl in the back seat of limousines playing rock 'n' roll finger pie. She had dozens of affairs. One of them, with a young French count who had land in North Africa and who shared her affection for heroin, was considered serious. Another, this one with the son of a dead movie mogul, was also more than just a fling.

Jim resumed his old affairs, calling his sometime girl-friends Ann Moore, Pamela Zarubica, or Gayle Enochs. Jim's days as a sexual philanthropist were largely past. Although he saw Anne, Pamela, and Gayle only two or three times a month, at most, the relationships were well established.

Gayle was the gentle brunette he took to New York when the Doors appeared on educational television and it was to her house, not far from Pamela's in the Beachwood hills, that he occasionally went, usually for an all-night talk. Other times they walked along Hollywood Boulevard and dined in the small ethnic restaurants that Jim preferred, or took a bottle of wine to one of the movie theaters on Western Avenue that specialized in foreign films.

His relationship with Anne was even more cerebral. She was a student of archeology and anthropology at USC and wrote for some of the teenybopper magazines. They would lose themselves in rambling conversations about the Egyptian and Talmudic flood epics, or Ginsberg, Corso, and Kerouac. Jim suggested she read those authors and take some of the film courses at USC.

Pamela Zarubica he saw less frequently, usually coming to her small Hollywood home late at night, dead drunk, to argue about poetry. "Poet?" she'd lovingly taunt. "Give me a break. Poet? Lord Byron? How you ranking yourself, baby? Not bad for a boy from L.A."

Jim loved it. Like the others, Pam loved Jim dearly, and Jim told them all that he loved them. Sometimes he meant it. But most of the time he was simply trying to be loved and ac-cepted as a person rather than a star.

It was, however, to Pamela Courson that Jim made his firmest commitment, calling her, still, his "cosmic mate." In August Jim's accountant told him his cosmic mate was spend-ing money in cosmic proportions, and he said Jim's latest "gift" to her could cripple him financially. Jim advised Bob Greene not to worry, claiming he'd rather spend the money on

Pamela than on lawyers. Pamela wanted a boutique of her own and Jim was footing the bill.

The space they found was a convenient one for Pamela. It was on the ground floor of the Clear Thoughts Building, practically underneath the HiWay offices, where she could keep an eye on Jim during the day. An artist friend from Topanga was hired to design the shop and carpenters were put to work. Initially they were going to call it Fuckin' Great—they even had some business cards printed with this name—but in the end they settled on Themis, for the Greek goddess of justice, law, and order.

Downstairs, carpenters were setting tiny bits of mirror into the ceiling. Upstairs in Room G, the HiWay cutting room, Jim sat smoking a tiny cigar, his feet up on a table, talking about the Sharon Tate murders of the week before. One of those killed, Jay Sebring, had given Jim his "Alexander the Great" haircut in 1967.

Only two years had passed since then, but Jim was much changed. No longer was his hair curly and carefully tousled, no longer were his cheeks gaunt, no longer was his torso lean and muscular, as if made from knotted rope. Gone were the leathers and beads. Now Jim looked almost ordinary: like a handsome, beer-drinking college student with longish hair and an angular jawline. And he was beginning to smile more.

CHAPTER

9

Although Jim's relationship with Pamela turned noncombatant as the summer ended, he spent more and more time with those Pamela liked least: Frank Lisciandro, Babe Hill, and Paul Ferrara, with whom he was finishing the film begun in Palm Springs in March. By now it had been titled *HWY*.

Some of his greatest disappointments came out of his interest in film. Over the months he, Frank, Babe, and Paul planned many projects. They talked with Timothy Leary about documenting his California gubernatorial campaign, and then Leary was arrested. They met with Carlos Castaneda about securing the film rights to *The Teachings of Don Juan* and were told they were too late. Jim was approached by an American screenwriter to score an Italian film, but backed out when he learned he was expected to star in it as well, playing a rock singer who committed a public disgrace in London's Albert Hall.

Then he was introduced to Steve McQueen by his old friend from the Whiskey a Go Go, Elmer Valentine.

McQueen's production company was casting *Adam at 6 A.M.*, and after meeting Jim once, McQueen turned him down cold. Apparently he talked too much, told them how the film should be made and the script rewritten. Although he had shaved for the interview, he looked unwell—overweight, wearing a night-club pallor. "They were afraid of his drinking," Elmer recalls, "that was the worst of it."

Then Jim met Jim Aubrey, the legendary ex-president of CBS Television who was known as the Smiling Cobra and had been the inspiration for Jacqueline Susann's *The Love Machine.* At the time Aubrey was between show business empires (he would soon take control of MGM).

First he screened Jim's two films, then arranged a long lunch at the Luau in Beverly Hills. Bill Belasco, Aubrey's voluble personal assistant, was one of those present. Once they said good-bye to Jim, Aubrey turned to Belasco and said, "Jim Morrison's going to be the biggest motion picture star of the next ten years. This guy will be the James Dean of the seventies." He told Belasco to sign him up, at any cost.

Jim came away from the lunch suspicious. "Those guys say they want to produce the screenplay I wrote with Michael," he told his friend Frank Lisciandro. "I think the truth is they just want to hang my meat up on the screen."

Jim's legal problems were increasing. Florida was trying to extradite him on the ridiculous "fugitive from justice" charge and the FBI was conducting an intensive investigation of his background, calling on former friends and faculty at Florida State University.

On November 9, 1969, Jim appeared in Judge Murray Goodman's Miami courtroom and entered a formal not guilty plea. Bail was set at $5,000 and the judge said the trial would begin the following April.

On the 11th, back in Los Angeles, Jim and Pamela fought bitterly. Hours later, in late afternoon, Jim entered the Doors' office. He looked around.

"Hey, Leon . . . Frank. How'd you like to go to Phoenix and see the Rolling Stones?"

Bill Siddons and a Doors promotor, Rich Linnell, were promoting the show and Jim had four front-row tickets. He called Tom Baker and the four bought a six-pack and a bottle of Courvoisier, consuming it on the way to the airport.

"My name is Riva," said the stewardess, starting her pre-flight warmup.

"If your name is Riva," Baker called out, "then your old man must be called *Old Man Riva.*"

Jim and Leon and Frank joined Tom in a chorus of the song: "That *old man riva,* he just keep rolling . . ."

The stewardess was visibly upset, but began giving instructions about oxygen masks. As the mask fell down from her hand, Tom called out again, "My girlfriend has one of those, but she calls it a diaphragm!"

Tom then went to the toilet and on the way back dropped a bar of soap into Jim's drink. Jim pushed the button for the stewardess, and when she came, he whined, "He put soap in my drink."

"All right, Jim, all right, keep it cool, okay? I'll bring you another."

Instead she brought the plane's captain, who said, "If you young men don't change your attitude, we'll turn this ship around and return to Los Angeles, where you'll be arrested, all four of you."

They were quiet for a while, but as a stewardess named Sherry went by, Tom reached for her thigh.

Soon after, Jim threw Leon the sandwiches he'd been served and Tom threw an empty plastic drinking glass at Jim.

The stewardesses and ship's officers seemed to ignore the rowdiness, but as the plane rolled to a stop in Phoenix, it was surrounded by cars with revolving top-lights.

An announcement came over the plane's PA system: "Ladies and gentlemen, please accept Continental's apologies . . . disembarkation will be delayed for just a few short moments."

Suddenly the pilot appeared before Jim and Tom.

"As captain of this ship, I am placing you both under arrest. The other passengers will exit first and you will be escorted off by the FBI."

The FBI? They were stunned.

"For what? What'd we do?"

"Hey, man," Baker called after the departing captain, "read me my rights."

"What are the charges?" asked Leon.

The plane was empty except for the four and FBI agents from the Phoenix office, who cuffed Jim's and Tom's hands behind them before taking them out for the gathered photographers.

"What are the charges?" Leon asked again, assuming a take-charge role.

Tom held his head down as he exited the plane, his eyes and face turned away from the cameras. In distinct contrast Jim exited arrogantly, his chest thrown forward, head back, a proud grin upon his face.

After spending the night and most of the following day in jail, Jim and Tom were charged with being drunk and disorderly and interfering with the flight of an aircraft, the latter an offense against the new skyjacking law that could result in a $10,000 fine and a ten-year sentence. Jim was not yet twenty-six, and this possible sentence, added to the three years hanging over him in Miami, meant he could spend the next thirteen years of his life in prison.

Elektra Records was pressuring the Doors to produce another album as quickly as possible. It had been under six months since the release of *The Soft Parade,* but Elektra wanted a live album by Christmas. The Doors started rehearsing their new songs in September and by November were trying to get them on tape.

Ironic—considering the depressing aftermath of Miami— was the strength and vitality of the new songs. Lyrically, the new album would be Jim's best work in years, and Ray, Robby, and John rose to the challenge by providing their strongest support yet.

Part of the reason for their renewed vigor was that Jim had gone through an extremely productive period in the spring. In the midst of his involvement with films he had continued to write songs and bits of poetry. He seemed, finally, to admit to himself that he was destined to make a lasting impact on music, not cinema, and this admission was the impetus for the creation of such quality lyrics only a year after he feared he had "dried up" creatively.

Morrison Hotel was named for a real hotel in the skid-row district of downtown L.A. where rooms went for $2.50 a night, which was discovered by Ray and Dorothy during one of their weekend drives around the city. The album had many gripping songs significant to America in the year 1969. One included a powerful two-line reflection from Jim's childhood. The song was "Peace Frog," a tune whose smouldering melody appealed so much to Robby, John, and Ray that they recorded it even when there were no lyrics. But then Ray found a poem in one of Jim's notebooks called "Abortion Stories" and they used nearly all of it. It was startling how closely the lines Jim wrote fit the music created by the others.

> There's blood in the streets, it's up to my ankles,
> There's blood on the streets, it's up to my knee.
> Blood on the streets in the town of Chicago,
> blood on the rise, it's following me.

During one rehearsal Jim improvised the next two lines for the bridge of the song:

> Blood in the streets runs a river of sadness
> Blood in the streets it's up to my thigh.
> The river runs down the legs of the city
> The women are crying rivers of weeping.

When the bridge came up again he sang:

> She came into town and then she drove away,
> Sunlight in her hair.

Dipping back to the poem for the rest of the song, beginning with the two lines inspired from the witnessing of a car accident involving the truckload of Indian workmen, he grew sullen:

> Indians scattered on a dawn's highway bleeding,
> ghosts crowd the young child's fragile eggshell
>   mind.

Then sang:

> Blood in the streets of the town of New Haven,
> blood stains the roofs and the palm trees of Ven-
>   ice.
> Blood in my love in the terrible summer,
> bloody red sun of Phantastic L.A.
> Blood screams the pain as they chop off her fin-
>   gers
> blood will be born in the birth of a nation.
> Blood is the rose of mysterious union.

"Roadhouse Blues," which was originally intended as the album's title song, was written, like so many of Jim's songs, about Pamela. When he sang (wrote), "Keep your eyes on the road/Keep your hands upon the wheel/We're going to the Roadhouse/Gonna have a real good time," he was repeating lines he threw at her as she drove them to the cottage he'd bought her in the funky Topanga section of Los Angeles. Again, in "Blue Sunday" he sang of his love to her: "Now I have found/My girl . . ." Pamela was also the inspiration for "Queen of the Highway": "She was a Princess/Queen of the Highway/Sign on the road said/Take us to Madre/No one could save her/Save the Blind Tiger/He was a Monster/Black dressed in leather . . ." The ride-out line was a sardonic reference to their troubled love: "I hope it can continue/Just a little while longer."

Edmund Teske

Jim and Pamela Courson Morrison,
Bronson Caves, Hollywood hills, California

Although the songs came quickly, Jim was usually drunk during the sessions and it often took all night to record the vocals for one song. Once when Pamela came to the studio and found Jim's bottle, she drank it to keep him from drinking

"So here were the two of them, completely out of their minds and crying," says engineer Bruce Botnick, the only other person present at the time. "He started shaking her violently. I think he was putting me on. She was crying out of control, telling him he shouldn't drink any more and that's why she drank it. And I'm cleaning up and I said, 'Hey, man, it's pretty late.' He looked up, stopped shaking her, said, 'Yeah, right,' and hugged her and they walked out arm in arm. I felt he had done all that for me. I'd seen him do that sort of thing before, because he'd always give you a funny look afterward, to see your reaction."

The problems were piling up.

Jim had another accident in the Blue Lady, this time leveling five young trees on La Cienega Boulevard near the Clear Thoughts Building. He abandoned the car and ran to a phone booth to call Max Fink to say his car had been stolen.

Feast of Friends was described in *Variety*—whose word could greatly affect the film's booking potential—as a disappointing waste of time, "made either from the outtakes of some larger project or an unsold try at daytime TV slotted to meet the kids home from school." *Rolling Stone* in Random Notes called it "corny, pretentious, silly, sloppy, fantastically boring, and mainly just unending first-try amateur movie-making." If this weren't enough to bring Jim down, the catcalls the film got at the San Francisco and Santa Cruz film festivals were.

The Doors' latest single from *Soft Parade,* a tribute to Otis Redding and the third single in a row written by Robby, "Runnin' Blue," limped onto the charts and crawled to number sixty-four.

The Miami and Phoenix trials were waiting in the wings.

The first screenings of Jim's hitchhiking film, *HWY,* were held and the opinion was that it seemed somehow . . . unfinished.

One of Jim's girlfriends was pregnant.

Jim's accountant was harping on Pamela's extravagances. Her allowance he could accept; even the spending sprees and charge accounts were within the limits of sanity. But the boutique was madness. It had already cost Jim $80,000, and Pamela was in Europe buying more stuff. That was the worst part for Jim. They had fought and Pamela had gone off to see the French count she told her girlfriends she loved.

Jim drank.

They were *all* drunk. Tom and Frank and Babe, and Jim, of course, hanging onto the Barney's Beanery bar.

"You're a pussy, Morrison," said Tom, baiting his friend. "You're a goddamn no-count pussy."

Jim ignored the taunt. Frank and Babe stared into their drinks.

"Tell us now, Mr. Jim Morrison, rock star," Tom went on, in a voice that traveled the length of the bar, "tell us what happened in Miami."

It was a tiresome subject for Jim. He glared at Tom, took another swallow from his drink.

"Come on, Jim, tell us once and for all."

"Yes," said Jim quietly, "I did it."

"Did what, Jim?" Tom's voice was strident, triumphant.

"I showed my cock."

"Why, Jim? When I showed mine in my movie, you said it wasn't art."

"Well," Jim said in a low voice so everyone present had to strain to hear, "I wanted to see what it looked like in a spotlight."

There was a moment's pause before Babe and Frank simultaneously burst out laughing, spraying the bar with their drinks. Jim grinned mischievously.

The scene at Ahmet and Mica Ertegun's was less amusing.

Ahmet was the charming Turkish diplomat's son who had created Atlantic Records and made himself a very wealthy man. His wife was one of Manhattan's most fashionable hostesses. Ahmet knew the Doors' contract with Elektra was running out and he wanted Jim on his label, so he invited him to a party. All Ahmet remembers today is that one minute Jim was a Southern Gentleman, dispensing interesting stories and good manners, and the next he was a raging drunk, standing on a couch, tearing at the expensive paintings on the wall. Jekyll and Hyde.

Jim celebrated his twenty-sixth birthday on December 8, 1969, with Bill Siddons and his wife Cheri, Frank and Kathy Lisciandro, and Leon Barnard at the Siddonses' house in Manhattan Beach. After supper a bottle of brandy was placed in front of Jim, joints were rolled for the others. By now marijuana only made Jim nervous. Or paranoid.

Jim and Leon talked casually about doing a comic strip together, then the conversation turned to Mick Jagger. Jim was unexpectedly (perhaps sarcastically) generous, calling Jagger a "prince among men." He then thanked everyone genuinely for the party and, the bottle emptied, nodded off.

"Oh, Christ, look!" Leon soon cried. "Look at Jim!" Leon leaped from his seat. Slumped unconscious in his chair, Jim had managed to extract his penis from his pants and was pissing on the rug.

"Jesus!" Bill rushed across the room, grabbed a large crystal goblet and held it under the stream.

To his surprise, Jim filled it.

Bill took another goblet from the table and Jim filled that, too, then a third one.

Leon, Frank, Kathy, and Cheri were falling down with laughter.

Afterward, Frank and Kathy took Jim to the Doors' office and dropped him, still asleep, on the office couch.

The pressures were growing intolerable. Jim was being

pulled and twisted this way and that. Frank, Paul, and Babe wanted more money to finish the films and the Doors wanted the filming stopped, believing it was draining Jim of energy he should be devoting to the group. They also wanted Jim to shave his beard and shed a few pounds for the string of concerts starting in New York in just a few weeks. Pam was incessantly demanding that Jim give up his singing career with the Doors and begin a domestic life with her, in which she envisioned him peacefully at work on his poetry. At the same time no less than twenty paternity suits were pending. Jim knew that the audiences on the upcoming tour would be expecting the grotesque when all he wanted to do now was to stand still and sing. His lawyers forbade him to speak of Miami and he desperately needed to proclaim his innocence as well as his disgust at the hypocrisy of the whole affair. Vince had recently put the "new manager" bite on him again. And there was the clearly felt pressure of being unable to walk down the street anonymously (hence the beard), an inconvenience Jim was becoming aware of more and more.

Jim was sitting on the couch drinking a beer the day after his birthday party, trying to sort out this list of demands when Bill and the others came in. He nodded absently as each one entered, then turned his gaze to the *Los Angeles Times* that had been put on his desk. He stared blankly at the newspaper: "Vietnamization" was continuing in Southeast Asia; the Indians were in their third week of occupation of Alcatraz Island; the day before—his birthday!—there had been a four-hour shoot-out between LA police and the Black Panthers; a grand jury had indicted Charlie Manson and four others for the slaying of Sharon Tate and others.

Jim put the paper down. He shifted the bulk of his body and cleared his throat.

"I think," he said slowly, "I'm having a nervous breakdown."

Everyone rushed to console him, urgently wanting to say something to cheer him up, but at the same time frightened by the possibility that he was, finally, about to fall apart. Bill went to the door to call Vince Treanor from the rehearsal room downstairs.

Jim looked balefully at Bill. "When you put that bottle of Courvoisier in front of me last night, you were saying, 'This is for the man who drinks.' I had to drink it all."

He turned to Vince as he entered the room. "I knew what I was doing, Vince. In Miami I was wearing boxer shorts. Didn't you see them? I knew what I was doing and you stopped me."

He turned to Leon and recalled the scene on top of the 9000 Building, when Leon suggested he get down off the ledge. "Don't you see?" Jim asked. "I had to do it. I couldn't stop."

It was a strange and frightened plea. Never before had he let these people see him so bleakly vulnerable.

A week later they hired another babysitter for him, a six-foot, four-inch black football player from the University of Southern California who'd served as Mick Jagger's personal bodyguard during the recent Rolling Stones tour.

Jim liked Tony Funches immediately. "Let's go have a drink," he said.

"Sure, Jim. Anything you say." Tony winked. "Maybe you can turn me on to one of those topless dancers."

Jim was in Mexico, vacationing with Frank. The other Doors were in New York, anxiously waiting for Jim to show. After much work, and the posting of the usual "fuck clause" bond, the band was booked into the prestigious Felt Forum.

The telephone rang in Bill Siddons' hotel room.

"Uhh . . . I missed my plane."

"Jesus, Jim." Bill instantly remembered Jim's call about a missed plane en route to Miami. "Jim, are you sober?"

"Wellll . . ."

The January 17 and 18 concerts—two shows each night—were regarded seriously by Siddons, the other Doors, and

Elektra alike. The performances were to be recorded for the live album begun the previous summer. New York was where most of the editors and writers worked, and the Felt Forum appearances were supposed to prove that the Doors were still capable of performing as a band. A no-show—or, worse, another exhibition like the one in Florida—would be suicidal.

Siddons spoke in the exasperated tones of a parent. "Jim, did you make another reservation?"

Jim said yes and gave Bill the flight number.

"We'll have a limo waiting, Jim."

"Uh . . . Billy? Uh . . . there's a stopover in Miami."

"Jim? Will you *please* stay on the plane?"

After hanging up, Bill called for Tony Funches. "Get on a plane and get to Miami immediately. Intercept Jim. Meet the plane when it lands at Miami and make sure Jim stays on it. We'll book you back to New York with him."

The concerts were successful. Most of the songs they played were older ones: "Moonlight Drive," "Back Door Man," "Break On Through," "Light My Fire," "The End." There were memorable moments, as when John Sebastian and Dallas Taylor, the drummer for Crosby, Stills, Nash, and Young, joined the Doors for a few songs during one show; and when a young homosexual heaved himself at Jim, locked his arms and legs around Jim's knees, and, after he was finally peeled off and carried away, Jim said casually, "Well, that's New York for ya. The only ones who rush the stage are guys." That line would be used (unexplained) in the live album. One that wouldn't be used came when someone tossed Jim a joint that was about as big around as pencil lead. "That's what I like about New York joints," he said, "you can pick your teeth with them."

There were meetings while the Doors were in New York. Some were held to discuss the advertising and promotion of *Morrison Hotel*, and the Doors were always invited. Jim hated meetings and seldom attended them. He preferred to let others make decisions for him. However, he was present at the

Elektra offices when the subject of his image came up and a memo was circulated proposing a new public relations campaign. Jim sat slumped on a couch, his sheep-lined suede jacket riding up around his ears while the publicity department talked earnestly about "Jim Morrison as Renaissance man."

It was made abundantly clear in the four-page memorandum that Jim's feelings must be considered:

> Jim Morrison is a public figure seeking to broaden his artistic horizons. All public figures must have public images. The best public image is one that both the public and the artist can live with happily. The figure comes first because he has to live with it most intimately. Since being a Renaissance man implies limitless explorations of all and any creative processes and endeavors, I think Morrison can live with it pretty easily. Once established in that frame of reference, he can try, do, live anything he pleases without endangering—or even bothering with—a Good/Bad reputation.

Besides, the memo added, "There aren't any Leonardos on the scene, and they'll love it in Poughkeepsie."

Jim didn't like having his image played with by a corporation. Besides, Elektra had reversed three years of Doors publicity policy and started to promote Jim Morrison rather than the group. He got even the following day at an Elektra party.

It was part of the company's courting ritual. Most record companies throw elaborate parties for their most successful groups as contract renewal time approaches.

This party was exceptional, with Alaska king crab, fingertips of black caviar, Dom Pérignon, and a cast of hundreds, including Ingrid Bergman's daughter Pia Lindstrom and a gallery of Warhol stars in drag—all contained within a forty-fourth-floor penthouse with an impressive view of Manhattan. At the end of the evening there was a screening of Alfred Hitchcock's *39 Steps*.

It was after two in the morning. Jim and Pamela were leaving, and as they passed their host, Elektra's president Jac Holzman, Pamela dropped a devastating exit line. Jac was convinced Jim had put her up to it.

"Well, in case we're all on Atlantic next year," Pamela said sweetly, "thanks for the swell party."

Jim merely smiled.

The Renaissance Man campaign was dropped.

The first week in February the new album was released and there were surprisingly satisfying concerts in the Arena at Long Beach and at Winterland in San Francisco. All were sold out and well reviewed. Jim had shaved, donned black jeans and a black shirt, and sung his best. And, finally, an agreement was signed by Jim and Bill Belasco and Michael McClure concerning the production of *The Adept.* Jim's company, HiWay, and Belasco's company, St. Regis Films, had together taken a one-year option on the film rights to Michael's unpublished novel, paying him $500 against a total purchase price of $5,000.

In March there were stories in all the trade papers reporting the certification of the Doors' fifth Elektra LP, *Morrison Hotel,* as gold, and pointing out that the group was the first American hard rock band to achieve five gold albums in a row. Although a concert was canceled in Buffalo, other dates were set in Salt Lake City, Denver, Honolulu, Boston, Philadelphia, Pittsburgh, Columbus and Detroit.

While *Morrison Hotel* didn't produce a hit single, it did reestablish the Doors as favorites of the critics, garnering favorable reviews in nearly all the important publications. Not only were there no strings or horns, but the band had had time to work up several of the songs on the road before recording—the first time they'd had this luxury since recording their first album. It showed. *Morrison Hotel* possessed an intensity the last two albums had lacked. Jim's voice had matured, deepened, and the others had grown as musicians. It was an artistic comeback: the Doors had managed to pull off a collection of songs that ran together with frightening force.

Under the Venice Pier. Doors publicity photo, 1970

Dave Marsh, then editor of *Creem* magazine, wrote, "The Doors have presented us with the most horrifying rock and roll I have ever heard. When they're good, they're simply unbeatable. I know this is the best record I've listened to . . . so far."

Rock Magazine raved as well: "Morrison isn't sexy anymore, you say; he's getting old and fat. Well, you can't see a pot belly on record, but you can hear balls, and the fifth Doors album is, without any doubt, their ballsiest (and best) album to date."

The May 1970 issue of *Circus* magazine echoed similar sentiments: "*Morrison Hotel* is possibly the best album yet from the Doors, it will convert new adherents to Morrison's faith, and reassure those like me who thought the last two sets were bummers. Good hard, evil rock, and one of the best albums released this decade. More power to Morrison's leather pants."

Only *Rolling Stone* withheld praise, maintaining the Doors' first two albums were the ones that really counted and for the time being "*Morrison Hotel* could only be truly recommended to those with a personal interest."

Jim remained distracted throughout this period. His thoughts were on the impending Phoenix trial and the possible heavy sentences he faced: up to three months and $300 on the assault charge, up to *10 years* and $10,000 on the federal charge of interfering with airline personnel on a commercial flight. Jim, Frank, Tom, and Leon flew to Phoenix on Wednesday, March 25, for a brief pretrial meeting with Bill Siddons and Jim's lawyer, Max Fink. Drinks were ordered from room service. As usual, Jim and Tom began to compete.

Tom was getting belligerent. He wanted to go *out* drinking. "Fuck this drinking-in-the-room bullshit! C'mon, Jim." Jim said sure and lurched to his feet. Siddons suggested they stick around. He didn't want Jim out in public, not tonight. He figured sure as hell he would get arrested for drunkenness, at least, which would have made for a lovely press the day of the trial.

Suddenly Leon was standing on a coffee table screaming at Jim, "Asshole! Asshole! Asshole!"

"Why are you calling me that?" Jim asked. "Why are you talking to me like a child?"

"Because you're acting like one!"

Frank moved in and told Leon to mind his own fucking business, when they were interrupted by a knock. Someone went to the door and admitted a pneumatic blond. "I'm looking for Jim," she said.

Jim was quickly all over her, running his mouth down her blouse. Everyone else tiptoed out.

Next morning Jim and Tom both wore white shirts and ties and double-breasted blazers. Their long hair was brushed back behind their ears. Leon and Frank were called as witnesses, as were the stewardesses, Riva Mills and Sherry Ann Mason. It was Sherry's testimony that convinced the judge. She said she'd been pawed throughout the flight by one of the defendants, despite several warnings to him to keep his hands off her. She identified Jim as her assailant.

Jim was bewildered. Each time Sherry described something she said he had done, she was actually describing Tom's actions. She had the two of them confused. It was like a scene from *Alice in Wonderland.* Finally the prosecution asked his witnesses not to refer to Jim and Tom by name, but as "person in seat A" and "person in seat B." Jim was found innocent of the federal charge, but guilty of "assaulting, threatening, intimidating and interfering with the performance of" the two stewardesses. Tom was acquitted of all charges. Sentencing was set for two weeks later.

Jim, Leon, Tom, Frank, Bill Siddons, Max, and the local lawyer who'd worked on the case went back to their hotel and stopped in the cocktail lounge. Surprise! There were the two stewardesses and the pilot who had arrested Tom and Jim.

Bill and Leon went over to offer friendly congratulations. Jim ordered his first double.

Bill charmed them, chatted amicably for half an hour, then returned to his table with the two girls. Sherry sat next to

Jim, who'd had four doubles by now and who told her she was lovely.

"Y'know," he said, "under any other circumstances, we might've gotten something going."

A while—and more doubles—later Jim decided to sing. He lurched out of his chair and staggered toward the piano bar.

"Y'don' care if I sing along, do ya?" Jim asked the startled pianist.

The bar's manager was on Jim as quickly as a football player falls on a fumbled ball. "No, no, no. I'm sorry, Mr. Morrison, but no, no, no."

Jim was enraged by this incursion of authority. *"Fuck you, man, fuck you! Fuck you! Fuck you!"*

Max and the younger lawyer pulled Jim out of the room and the rest of the party followed. In the lobby Tom dared Jim to jump into an outside fountain.

Jim glared drunkenly at Tom and took off for the fountain at a run.

Now it was Bill's turn to stop Jim and, with help, he got him into the hotel elevator. As the doors closed, Jim was screaming again, "Fuck you!"

The next morning they all returned to Los Angeles, where Jim went to the Palms bar with Tom and some girls— one of them mysteriously brought back from Phoenix by Jim, the other a long-time Doors groupie. They drank heavily and played pool. Tom got drunk and tipped over the pool table. The bar owner called the sheriff's office and Jim and Babe wrestled Tom back to the Doors' office nearby.

On the way Tom bellowed, "Morrison, you're no fucking good! Whole world hates you! Hates you! You're no fucking good at all!"

In the office Jim and Babe and some of the others suggested that Tom leave. Finally, Jim explained what was eating him. He had paid all of Tom's Phoenix expenses: the plane tickets, the hotel rooms, meals, drinks, lawyers, the whole shot. He had also taken the rap for Tom, and all he got back was crap.

Jim threw himself at Tom and tried to wrestle him toward the door. Tom was laughing. "You gotta get outta here," Jim grunted, "this is a place of business."

A friend of Tom's appeared and threw himself at Jim; then Tony Funches arrived and grabbed Tom's friend. Tony was joined by Babe in punching the friend. Jim slipped away into Bill Siddons' office to call the sheriff. A car came quickly, direct from the previous call to the Palms.

"You mean to tell me you called the cops?" asked Tom. He was standing apart from the others now, looking at Jim, stunned.

"You mean it was *you* who called us?" asked the cops, equally stunned.

Babe began bad-mouthing the sheriff's deputies, who chose to ignore him and leave. Tom got into his friend's car and drove away, leaving Jim standing with Babe and Tony on the sidewalk. When Tom returned ten minutes later to throw a rock through the Doors' office window, Jim had already gone to Barney's Beanery to have another drink. It was the last time Jim saw Tom Baker for almost a year.

Throughout April Jim became more preoccupied with his legal difficulties. Before returning to Phoenix on the 6th he had reviewed the impressive sixty-three–page document that Max Fink had prepared for the Miami case. Jim had been pleased by Max's eloquence in the Phoenix courtroom—he called him a "reg'lar Perry Mason"—and he was very happy when he saw that the brief contained a challenge to the constitutionality of the laws under which he had been arrested.

The first ten pages explained "contemporary social attitudes and community standards" as Max (and Jim) saw them: "Youth (and a large segment of our mature population) have rebelled against the hyprocrisy, falsity, 'lily-white' surface and decaying sub-surface of our society. False, ephemeral, Victorian concepts have disappeared in the face of knowledge, scientific developments and education. . . ."

Max took as his legal precedents the court cases involving the films *I Am Curious Yellow* and *Midnight Cowboy,* and made reference to Henry Miller's *Tropic of Cancer* as well as the paintings of Gauguin, Picasso, and Michelangelo. Many pages were devoted to arguing that the First and Fourteenth amendments protected theatrical performances, and the brief reviewed the historical "fear of the political potential of the theater." U.S. Supreme Court rulings protecting free speech were cited. Finally, Max attacked the charges individually, asserting that they were all either in direct violation of the First, Eighth, or Fourteenth amendments, "unconstitutionally vague," or unsupported by facts. Of the four laws Jim was alleged to have broken, the brief pointed out, the most recent had been enacted in 1918.

On April 6, Jim returned to Phoenix with Max, ostensibly for sentencing on the skyjacking law violations. When Max told the court that the stewardess named Sherry had made a mistake and wanted to change her testimony, the judge deferred sentencing and rescheduled Jim for another appearance later in the month.

On the 7th the first copies of his book arrived from Simon and Schuster. Jim held the slender volume in his hands, admiring it. *The Lords and The New Creatures,* it said, and under that the word "Poems." Jim was not happy about the way his name appeared. He had asked for James Douglas Morrison, but they had used Jim Morrison. They'd also used that "Young Lion" picture on the front and back covers and made reference on the dust jacket to his rock career and called his audience "kids"—none of which he liked. Nor did the dust jacket copy relate in any but the most superficial way to Jim's poetry. It said, "He sees and speaks of contemporary America—the cities, the drug scene, the movies, the money hustle, the old hang-ups and new freedoms in love. . . ."

Still, Jim sent a telegram to his editor in New York that began, "Thanks to you and Simon & Schuster, the book is great beyond my expectations." And to Michael McClure he said, "This is the first time I haven't been fucked over." Michael swears Jim had tears in his eyes.

The next day Babe Hill fell from a moving car and broke two vertebrae in his neck after a drinking bout with Jim at the Phone Booth, and the day after that Jim was drunk on a Boston stage.

The concert was running late and at 2 A.M. the hall manager decided to pull the plug, cutting off the band's electricity. Mysteriously, Jim's microphone was still working.

Jim blinked. Then he took the slim gold mike from its stand and mumbled audibly, "Cocksuckers."

Ray leaped forward swiftly. This was what he and the others had feared. Abruptly, he clamped one hand over Jim's mouth and lifted him with one arm, carrying him offstage as if he were a statue.

The audience was stomping for more music.

A moment later Jim broke away from Ray and reappeared. He lurched to the front of the stage and shouted, "We should all get together and have some fun . . . because they're gonna win if you let 'em!"

By the time Jim woke up the next morning, that night's concert in Salt Lake City had been canceled. The Salt Lake hall manager had been in the Boston audience and he didn't like what he saw.

The Miami paranoia continued. At almost every date Vince was being asked by the hall managers to cut the sound whenever Jim said anything "controversial." Each day the Doors wondered if their next show might not be canceled, literally at the last minute.

The Miami incident was affecting the whole industry. Anti-obscenity clauses were being written into or added as riders to concert contracts for other bands in dozens of cities, with the group required to post a cash bond, which they would forfeit if there was any "illegal, indecent, obscene, lewd, or immoral exhibition" while they were onstage.

On April 17 and 18 the Doors played a huge convention center in Honolulu. Then, leaving the other Doors behind to begin a short vacation, Jim flew back to Phoenix with Siddons to meet Max Fink and the stewardess named Sherry. Sherry reversed her testimony on the 20th and the final charge against Jim was dropped.

Jim had begun calling and writing New York editor and critic Patricia Kennely the previous September, had renewed his communication in March, and in April, when she reviewed his book of poems in her magazine *Jazz & Pop*, he telegrammed his thanks.

Patricia was an initiated, practicing witch, high priestess of a coven—something that fascinated Jim—and the day after his telegram arrived, she was in Philadelphia visiting other witches. The Doors were in Philadelphia the same day and she attended their concert at the Spectrum and talked with Jim briefly backstage. The band was working in Pittsburgh the next day, he told her, but after that he'd come to New York. Once there, Jim spent half the week with Pamela at the Navarro Hotel, the other half with Patricia in her small apartment.

With Pamela and Bill Belasco, who was still tagging along on so many of Jim's out-of-town trips, Jim went shopping along Fifth Avenue and dined at Lüchow's and Mamma Leone's, established show business restaurants. With Patricia he went to the Fillmore East to see the Jefferson Airplane, sitting in the lighting booth with Allen Ginsberg.

By now Grace Slick had developed a new put-down for hecklers. Someone yelled, "Sing 'White Rabbit,' Gracie!"

"Oh, I see Jim Morrison is here tonight," Grace sneered back. Jim muttered, "Thanks, Grace," and left it at that. He had been reluctant to attend the concert to begin with, and afterward told Patricia that he thought the Airplane "was the most boring band I ever heard in my whole life. Everything's up front, everybody plays as loud as they can, and nobody gets to show off. There is no delicate interplay like my group has."

Another negative story about the band appeared the end of May in *Amusement Business,* the magazine most popular with concert promoters and hall managers. The publication had pursed its puritanical lips over the Doors' exploits since the days of the New Haven obscenity arrest, and now the front-page story read, "Jim Morrison and the Doors have developed a new wrinkle to irritate building managers." The magazine quoted the manager of Detroit's Cobo Hall, which the Doors had filled, as saying that the group "literally took over the building, and as a result they are banned from the facility." That night's show had been regarded by the band and fans alike as very special.

Jim seemed to have shaken off his impending "nervous breakdown." He impressed people as aloof, relaxed. The last week of May he went with Babe to San Francisco for the opening of a new play and sang with the backup bands in some of the North Beach topless clubs. Then he took off for a few days in Vancouver, where he roamed the city with Ihor Todoruk, a painter who edited a Canadian pop magazine and had staged a Jim Morrison Film Festival a month earlier. To Todoruk, Jim talked endlessly of Paris, saying he'd like to go there as soon as he could settle everything that had to be settled.

After a disastrous concert in Vancouver and a moderately successful show in Seattle, Jim's calendar was marked not by concerts but court appearances. The Miami trial was scheduled for August and his attorneys were making a last-ditch attempt to stave it off. On June 9 they filed a motion in federal court to halt the trial on the grounds that the three statutes under which Jim had been charged were vague and punished conduct that was not within police jurisdiction. The motion was denied and three days later the attorneys went into another Miami court to request a jury trial.

In between the court dates on Jim's calendar there was another screening of *HWY* for agents and friends. *HWY* had been screened several times, but only once publicly, at the film festival in Vancouver. Most showings had been held at Synanon and in private screening rooms. Finally a couple of young producers, Bobby Roberts and Hal Landers, approached Jim to do a film with Michele Phillips, formerly with the Mamas and the Papas. Instead of an answer Jim provided them with a screening of *HWY* and soon Landers and Roberts were talking about providing development money to expand the film to feature length. When Jim detected what he thought was another exploitation plot, he cut off the negotiations. Frank argued with him, but he was adamant.

Negotiations with MGM seemed more promising. Jim had been meeting regularly with both Belasco and Aubrey about *The Adept* and they had convinced him that the screenplay could be shortened satisfactorily. Wryly, he remarked that they intended to cut it "from a sequoia to a toothpick."

Belasco and Jim looked for a new director, finally settling on Ted Flicker, who was best known for his direction of an improvisational theater group called the Premise Players and an underrated satire made with James Coburn, *The President's Analyst.* Slowly, the deal came together. Aubrey wanted Jim as an actor, not only in *The Adept* but also in a film called *Corky.* Jim didn't like the script (the part Aubrey wanted him for would be played by Robert Blake) but agreed to lose some weight for his own film—after all, whoever heard of a fat coke dealer?—and to shave off the beard he had allowed to grow back following the Phoenix trial.

By mid-June MGM had offered Jim substantially what he wanted: $35,000 for final development of the script, and if the script was acceptable, another $50,000 for his services as coproducer (with Belasco) and star. The figures weren't large by Hollywood criteria, but Jim was pleased. He instructed his attorneys to carry through on the deal, authorized payment of the $600 fine levied by the Federal Aviation Agency in connection with the Phoenix flight (and independent of the trial), and began to pack a single suitcase for a trip to France and Spain.

CHAPTER

10

Patricia Kennely was panicking. When she and Jim woke up, Jim had over a 100° F. temperature and she stayed home from work to take care of him, going out only to buy invalid food—some soup and ginger ale. Two hours later Jim's temperature was 103° F. She gave him aspirin, tetracycline, water, and alcohol rubs, and she tried to find Leon Barnard. Her doctor, who lived only two blocks away, wouldn't make a house call. Jim's temperature rose to 105° F.

Jim had arrived in New York the day before, en route to Europe, with Leon and one of Leon's friends and the final tapes for the live album. Although he was fairly drunk when Patricia met him at his hotel, they had spent a pleasant and uneventful evening watching Mick Jagger's new film, *Ned Kelly*, and sitting through Ingmar Bergman's latest, *The Passion of Anna*, twice. The only notable occurrence was that Jim pulled out Patricia's diaphragm before they went to bed, flinging it across the room like a Frisbee. Now, in Patricia's apartment the following gloomy New York afternoon, Jim felt as if he were dying.

At two o'clock Patricia decided to take his temperature one more time before calling for an ambulance. Suddenly the fever broke, dropping from 105° to 101° F. in fifteen minutes. Within three hours Jim was up and walking around as if nothing had happened. He returned to his hotel, changed clothing, and, joined by Leon, he and Patricia had dinner, went to another movie, and bought some books at Brentano's.

The following night Jim and Patricia were married.

Twenty-four years old at the time, Patricia was the editor-in-chief of a rock magazine, and one of the several Doors loyalists in the East Coast rock critical establishment. She had adored Jim from the moment they met, eighteen months previously when she had interviewed him at the Plaza Hotel. He'd stood up at her entrance into the room, and upon being introduced he had shaken her hand formally. She remembers the scene: "All I could think was, 'Good God, his mother taught him manners and he actually *remembers* them!' When we touched hands, sparks went flying. Static friction from my boots on the carpet, no doubt, but genuine storybook sparks. Jim loved it. 'An omen,' he said. He was right."

Since then, Patricia had written about Jim and the Doors often in her magazine, in a mature and critical style that incorporated literary references and quotations. Always she took Jim seriously—criticizing his work, not his image. "If T. S. Eliot had been a rock group," she once wrote, "he would have been the Doors and done *The Soft Parade*." In a review of *The Lords and The New Creatures* she suggested that "a re-reading at the earliest opportunity of Aristotle's *Poetics,* or better, the *Preface to the Lyrical Ballads,* might assist in a reestablishment of poetic priorities sorely needed."

Patricia had well-thought-out opinions on nearly every subject; a facile, lashing Irish tongue, much like Jim's own; much better than average looks, with long auburn hair, brown eyes, and a voluptuous figure; an extensive knowledge of the occult; and a superb gift for storytelling.

In many ways their relationship was fairly typical for Jim. Except for Pamela, there was no one girl that he saw very often or for periods of more than a few days, and in the months since they'd met, Jim and Patricia had been in the same room probably no more than seven or eight times. Nor had there been many phone calls. A sheaf of oddly personal letters, gifts of jewelry and rare books and copies of his three privately printed works, but nothing that signaled a passionate courtship.

Nor was the manner in which Jim behaved toward Patricia much different from his style with others. With her, too, he drank and passed out and played his endless games. "We'd be sitting in a bar," Patricia recalls, "and he would come out with these complete non sequiturs––apropos of absolutely nothing—like 'I fell asleep in the light of the full moon one night and when I woke up it was the face of my mother looking down at me. Now what do you think about that? What do you think it means?' He was forever testing people, forever trying to see how much you were willing to put up with from him, how you were going to react to him. He didn't trust anyone. He never seemed to believe me when I said I loved him. I expect he heard that from every woman he ever slept with. I meant it, though. Even so, I felt that when I said I loved him I was handing him a weapon to use against me, something to hold over my head. The first time I told him how I felt about him, he said, 'Well, now that you love me I guess I'll never be able to get rid of you.' I asked, 'Do you want to get rid of me, then, Jim?' He just smiled and closed his eyes and said, 'No.' And then he told me he loved me. He probably even meant it, too."

Midsummer Night, 1970. Candles were lighted in Patricia's Victorian Gothic apartment. The wedding ceremony was explained. Witches, or Wiccans, are not Satanists; they worship the ancient forces of nature, the Triple Goddess, the Great Mother, and her male counterpart, the Lord, the

Horned God. It is a religious tradition that predates Christianity and Judaism, and is thought by many scholars to be a survival of the oldest universal religion.

A Wicca wedding, Patricia explained, is a blending of souls on a karmic and cosmic plane that has an effect on future incarnations of the two involved: death does not part, and the vow taken is "forever in the Goddess's sight." Patricia told Jim there was a legend that Henry VIII and Anne Boleyn had been married in the witch ritual—probably for some of the same reasons.

One of Patricia's friends, a high priestess of a coven, conducted the ceremony, assisted by a high priest. They led Jim and Patricia through a traditional handfasting, with prayers and an invocation of the Goddess, blessings, the making of two small cuts on each partner's wrist and forearm, and the mixing of a few drops of their blood into a consecrated cup of wine from which they later drank, a ritual stepping over a broomstick, the exchanging of certain vows, and the final calling down of the Goddess's presence.

To Patricia, this was a perfectly natural ceremony in her religion, but Jim was totally caught up in the ritual. He gave Patricia a silver claddagh, the traditional Irish wedding ring, and she gave him a matching gold one. The officiating priestess and Patricia, in her capacity as a priestess, made out two hand-printed documents, one in English, one in witch runes. Everybody present signed, with Jim and Patricia required to mark their signatures in blood. The pair were declared wedded, and Jim fainted.

On Saturday Jim and Leon left for Paris, where they checked into a $60-a-day room at the fashionable Georges V Hôtel and began to explore the city—drinking at dozens of sidewalk cafés, visiting the haunts of Left Bank existentialists, mingling with gypsies performing on the streets of Montmartre, making pilgrimages to Balzac's home, Napoleon's tomb, and the catacombs. Then Leon went to Copenhagen and Jim ran into his friend Alan Ronay, who had begun his annual vacation in Paris a week or so earlier.

Alan had often talked to Jim about Paris—he was, in fact, one of the reasons Jim was now in France. Jim had had the film for *Feast* and *HWY* processed at the company where Alan worked and they had seen each other often over the years since they first met at UCLA. Alan was one of Jim's "mystery" friends and not too much was known about their relationship. Alan loved Jim dearly, and although he was forced to share him with Frank and Babe and all the rest, he did not have to share him in the same room or at the same time. Except when Jim and Babe barged in at 3 A.M., drunk, to harass him, Alan usually saw Jim alone.

For a week Jim was the quintessential American tourist, a rumpled figure slogging through the summer rain. But the day before he left for home, he began to feel feverish again.

"Pneumonia? Jesus, *where* is he? *How* is he? Does Max know? We'd better delay the trial."

Bill Siddons was playing nervously with a pencil as he listened to Babe on the telephone. Jim had returned from Paris, Babe said. He was staying with Pamela in the apartment she had on Norton Avenue and he had pneumonia, but he was all right. Later in the day Bill talked to Jim, who said that after leaving Alan Ronay in Paris, he had gone to Spain and Morocco, traveling by train and in rented cars. He'd been sick in New York before he left, he said, and in Europe he'd encountered a lot of rain.

Jim had been gone nearly three weeks. Just after he returned to Los Angeles the federal court in Miami rejected the motion to halt the trial on constitutional grounds. The judge said that if Jim were found guilty, the appeal could cover that area. Nor would the trial be delayed because of Jim's health. Typically, Jim recovered rapidly, and by the time the live album was released at the end of July, he was back prowling the Sunset Strip and the bars along Santa Monica Boulevard.

On August 4 he was alone at a club called The Experience. At closing, he asked the owner, Marshall Brevitz, if he would drive him home. A year earlier Jim would have driven no matter how drunk he was. But now he was practically too drunk to walk.

"I hada club in Miami once," Marshall told Jim, loading him into his car. "You'll be interested to know my partners were the same two guys who tried to cheat you when you played there and got busted. They're the reason I *left* Miami."

Jim nodded and slurped, "Turn lef' here . . . I think."

Marshall turned left and kept on talking. "Did you know those guys ran a gift shop in one of the hotels? And they floated a suntan lotion business, had a billboard. . . . Shouldn't we be coming to your place soon?"

Jim mumbled something that sounded like, "Turn lef' here . . . I think."

After an hour of being driven up one street and down the next and circling ten or fifteen blocks, Jim finally found the small West Los Angeles house he was seeking. Or rather, he thought he did.

"This's it," he said.

Marshall accompanied Jim to the door.

"Shhh," Jim hissed. "There's a chick here, she's mad at me and . . . shhh!"

Jim knocked timidly at the door.

Silence.

Jim knocked more loudly.

Still no response.

Jim knocked even *more* loudly.

"Hey, Jim," Marshall said nervously, "I'll see you later, okay." And he retreated quickly, leaving Jim slumped against the front door of the house.

In the morning Jim was found curled up asleep at the door by the sixty-eight-year-old woman whose home it was. Believing the bearded, long-haired figure was another Charlie

Manson, she called the sheriff's substation nearby and Jim was arrested and charged with public drunkenness.

That was Thursday morning.

On Friday Jim flew to Miami to stand trial.

"Look!" Jim was pointing overhead to a small plane towing a banner that read, "We Love Spiro Agnew."

"Anybody believe in omens?" Jim asked.

The temperature and humidity were both close to the 100 mark, and without the rich winter tourists Miami rattled with emptiness and the big hotels on the beach looked like tombstones. Jim was standing in front of the Carillon Hotel, a medium-priced tombstone with a beige marble lobby, crystal chandeliers, and an activity board by the swimming pool. So far his stay in Florida had been uneventful. Sunday he had wanted to see a jai alai game, but was told the courts were closed for the summer, so he went to the dog races instead. The rest of the time he stayed close to the hotel, lying by the pool, drinking in the air-conditioned bar, baking in the sauna on the roof. At a meeting with Max they discussed whether all the Doors would testify—they decided yes—and held informal talks about doing a free concert. Not much was said about the trial, though everyone made little reassuring jokes.

Now, on Monday, August 10, while waiting for a taxi to take him to court, Jim was joking about the Agnew banner. He was wearing cowboy boots, black jeans, and a Mexican peasant shirt, and was carrying a pebbled school notebook. "Okay," he said finally, "let's go." He got into the cab with Babe, his attorney, Max Fink, and his publicist, Mike Gershman. The other three Doors and Tony Funches took a second cab.

Half an hour later Jim was deep inside the Metropolitan Dade County Justice Building, standing outside Division "D," shuffling through a stack of 150 photographs just given him by his Miami attorney Bob Josefsberg. He was enjoying the pictures. He stopped occasionally to explain one to Babe and the others present: "Look, this is the one where I'm supposed to be giving head to Robby's guitar, right? And this one, with the lamb . . . that lamb remained absolutely still and, I swear it, was purring amidst all that chaos. I look sort of satanic there, taking the lamb to slaughter. Yeah, yeah, and the band played on. You know, I'm beginning to believe I'm innocent."

He was still making jokes, but he was worried. As casual and cool as he tried to be—publicly he maintained he was fighting a battle to preserve artistic freedom—he could not shake his fear. Or his anger. In the five days they had been in Florida they had learned a lot about Miami politics and the backstage psychology of the case. The judge, Murray Goodman, had been appointed to fill a vacancy on the court and faced his first election in November. Given the times, a Morrison conviction would win the judge popular support. It was possible that Goodman was antagonistic toward Jim's Miami lawyer, Bob Josefsberg, because Josefsberg had been offered the judgeship before Goodman, and turned it down. The State of Florida vs. James Morrison, Case No. 69-2355 seemed like Them vs. Us, again.

Max Fink was arguing along just those lines to the press. A week earlier he had said that he was going to request that the jury be taken to a performance of *Hair* and to a theater to see *Woodstock,* so that they could put Jim's performance in proper context. Now he was saying, "You have to accept the fact that what the generation-gap people like Morrison's group, the Doors, are protesting are the problems created by their forebears."

Max said he expected the trial to last six to ten weeks, in part because he planned to call up to one hundred witnesses for the defense. For months he'd had a young lawyer named Dave Tardiff interviewing potential witnesses, all of whom were ready to testify that Jim did not expose himself. They had also lined up several expert witnesses, including two psychology professors from the University of Miami to discuss the

Jeff Simon

Miami: Jim simulating fellatio, 1969

concept of contemporary community standards; an assistant professor of English to contribute his understanding of etymology, the branch of philology concerned with the origin and derivation of words; the minister of the university to say Jim's language wasn't profane but controversial; and the entertainment editors of Miami and Miami Beach newspapers to place Jim's act in a local context by testifying about all the foul-mouthed hotel comics whose acts went unharassed.

Then Judge Goodman announced that his docket was too crowded to allow the trial to start until Wednesday. So on Tuesday Ray and Robby and John rented a car and drove to Key West, while Jim stayed in his room and read.

"If," Max asked each prospective juror two days later, "the evidence shows that Mr. Morrison did things that are described in best-selling books and shown in plays, will you consider whether he has as equal protection of the law as everyone else?" And: "If Mr. Morrison used slang expressions which you as an individual considered crude—some four-letter words—and those same expressions verbally and physically are part of the dissenting scene in this country, as evidenced by plays, books, and the young people of this country, would you be shocked?" It is debatable how effective these questions were. The four-man, two-woman jury that was sworn in on Friday consisted of a former army cook, now a machine worker; a tile setter for a flooring company; a mechanic with twenty-three years in the Coast Guard; an elementary school art teacher; a Miami Beach housewife with a twenty-three-year-old son and a thirty-year-old daughter; and a housewife who once had been an insurance underwriter. Immediately, Bob Josefsberg challenged the entire panel, saying that if Jim were to be tried by his true peers, all the jurors would have to be under thirty years of age. The judge smiled wryly and took it under advisement, then court was adjourned for the weekend.

As Jim was leaving the courtroom he was approached by the young prosecutor, Terrence McWilliams, who was dressed in an olive green suit and an orange shirt. He seemed embarrassed, hesitant. Finally he asked Jim if he happened to have a copy of his new album with him; the prosecutor said he'd already bought all the others and the local shops had run out of *Absolutely Live.* The tone of his voice told all: he was sorry; he didn't want the case, he had been assigned to it; he was only doing his job.

This didn't mean that McWilliams would diminish the severity of his professional attack. How he really felt about the case may have been more clearly revealed in a note he later passed to Jim, an original piece of doggerel:

> There once was a group called The Doors
> Who sang in dissent of the mores
> To youth they protested
> As witnesses attested
> While the leader was dropping his drawers

That night, Jim, Babe, and Tony went to hear Creedence Clearwater Revival at the Miami Beach Convention Center, then on to the Hump Room in the Marco Polo Hotel, where Jim joined Canned Heat for four songs. "After that," Babe wrote in his diary, "Jim 'n I 'n Ina [Gottlieb, a stewardess they'd met on the plane to Miami] went up to the Fontainebleau where Creedence Clearwater Revival were staying and shot pool and drank until I passed out on a couch next to the pool table. When I woke up, Jim was out under it. . . ."

Monday it was back to Division "D," where now the prosecutor was wearing a bright red shirt and standing by Jim as he finished his opening statement with a dramatic reading of the charges:

"The defendant did lewdly and lasciviously expose his penis in a vulgar or indecent manner with intent to be observed, did place his hand on his penis and shake it, and further the said defendant did simulate the acts of masturbation upon himself and oral copulation upon another. . . ." When he finished, McWilliams slowly raised his eyes from the charge sheet and gave Jim not the customary glare of condemnation, but the vacant gape of awe. Jim looked back impassively.

McWilliams quoted from the record what was purported to be the language of the performance: "... You are all a bunch of fucking idiots. Your faces are being pressed into the shit of the world. Take your fucking friend and love him. Do you want to see my cock?" The jury sat motionless, expressionless.

At noon Max Fink began his opening statement, establishing his personality as that of a slightly reproachful but ultimately understanding grandfather. It was an image that he thought the jury might be persuaded to identify with.

"Your imagination may run rampant, but there's a small difference between the prosecutor's evidence and their witnesses. There is no question about the use of the words. I'm sixty-two and I haven't been to one of these concerts, but it is what they say these days. Young people use these words with no prurient intention whatsoever. That is what they say and do. A rock concert is an expression of dissent. Let's have oneness. There were twenty-six officers present in uniform that night and many officers not in uniform. No one arrested him for his performance onstage. Now a rock singer works very hard. He leaves the stage swimming in perspiration to join his friends for a few laughs backstage before heading to the hotel and then to Jamaica. There was no arrest, there was no crime. The words we admit, that's free speech. The evil is in the mind."

The state's first witness seemed perfectly turned out. She was wearing white shoes and a pink minidress, and her blond hair was pulled back into a ponytail. She had been only sixteen when she'd attended the Doors concert, she said, and she had seen Jim drop his pants to his knees, exposing himself for ten seconds, then (she paused) she saw him touch himself. When asked what unusual words Jim had used onstage, she said, "The one that starts with *f.*" Asked how the experience affected her, she replied, "I was shocked, it was disgusting."

During Max's intensive cross examination he read from a sworn statement the girl had made in April in which she'd said she had seen Jim rubbing against a girl onstage but didn't know if Jim's pants were up or down. "Has your memory been affected in the last few months?" Max asked her. She burst into tears and Judge Goodman called a brief recess to give the witness time to recover.

After the break the girl contradicted herself two more times and said that she and her boyfriend had not paid to see the concert, but had been admitted free by her brother-in-law, a city policeman.

The girl was followed on the stand by her boyfriend, who confirmed her testimony. Again Max attacked inconsistencies between the testimony the witness was offering in court and a sworn statement he had given earlier. In the latter he had said that he had only a "vague memory" of what Jim had or had not done. Now his memory was precise. In answer to a question from the prosecutor the boyfriend said he hadn't been embarrassed for himself, being twenty at the time, but for his young date. In answer to another question put by Max, however, the witness admitted taking the girl to see *Woodstock,* though he said he knew it featured nudity.

He was followed on the stand by the girl's mother, who hadn't been at the concert but testified that her daughter was visibly upset when she returned home that night.

Monday night a second drama began with the arrival of Patricia Kennely. Jim had talked to Patricia by telephone on Friday, the 14th, learned that she was pregnant, and asked her to join him in Miami. He sent his publicist and one of his lawyers and the lawyer's wife to meet her at the airport.

Jim was most cordial as they drank at the hotel bar, but whenever Patricia tried to direct the conversation toward her pregnancy, he skated away. At his request she had brought thirty copies of the latest issue of her magazine, with a picture of Jim on the cover and inside a new poem called "The Anatomy of Rock." Jim glanced at the brooding pictures and read through the poem's text.

Finally, Jim looked up at Patricia. He told her he thought it might impress the judge to know that he wasn't just a rock star, but was contributing to society by writing poetry. Then he told her to return to her room and he would join her later. He never went.

By now, Judge Goodman had determined that the trial would be held on alternate days, so Jim had Tuesday free. Again he dodged Patricia, telling her twice by telephone that he'd see her, then twice failing to show up, spending the day with Babe instead.

Wednesday Jim was back in court. Patricia was there, too, in a rage but managing to control herself. A television camera crew filmed them arguing in the hall. Just as Jim was promising that they'd get together that night, the judge arrived.

The prosecution called three witnesses this day. The first was a policewoman who in June had said she'd heard no profanity, but now testified otherwise, embarrassing the prosecutor when she blurted out that in the interim she had heard a tape of the show. The second witness was the university student who had taken photographs and said he had seen no genital exposure. This witness was a disappointment to the prosecution, but with the next one, the train was back on the track. This was a twenty-two-year-old redhead named Bob Jennings, who had signed the original complaint against Jim and now quoted extensively from Jim's concert monologue and swore that Jim had exposed himself for between five and eight seconds. He was a convincing witness, and the only damage Max was able to inflict on cross examination were the revelations that for the past three years the witness had been a clerk in the state attorney's office, while his mother worked in the same building and his sister was a secretary to a local judge. Jim and his friends were now convinced he was being railroaded by people who worked for or were related to the Man.

"Go to your room," Jim told Patricia after a couple of drinks back at the hotel. "I'll go change and be up in half an hour."

Half an hour later the long-promised talk began. "I know it's not exactly the best time and place to ask you to deal with this, with the trial and all," said Patricia, "but the fact remains, it happened and now—"

Jim smiled awkwardly and said, "We'll manage."

"Listen, I'm not exactly thrilled by the idea either, you know. But you happen to be the only man I ever considered good enough to father a child of mine, and now it's come to pass and I don't know what to do. I do think you owe me a bit more than your checkbook."

Jim glanced at her, then away. "If you have that baby, it'll ruin our friendship. A baby isn't going to change my life at all, but it would alter yours tremendously, forever."

"I could take it to court."

He looked surprised by the idea. "Another trial? Well, of course, you could do that, and it'd be just like this one we're doing now. It'd take a long time, though. First you'd have to have the baby; that's, what, another six months. Then you'd have to set up a preliminary hearing, with blood tests and all that, just to find out if you had a real case. And I'd deny the charges, and you'd have to find witnesses, and maybe there wouldn't be any witnesses because I'd buy everybody off first. And even if you finally got it to court, you might not win, and there would be incredible publicity, which you would hate. And even if you won in the end, what would you have gotten out of it? Some money and some satisfaction and a lot of bad feelings. I don't think you think it's worth it."

"I can't believe you said that." By now, tears were streaming down her face.

"Well, what did you want me to say?"

"I don't *know*, goddamn you! I suppose it makes no difference that it's *our* baby, yours and mine, not yours and Pamela's?"

"I—no, *no* difference. I won't support a kid. *Any* kid. I can't afford it and I don't want the responsibility."

"The only way you can't afford it is emotionally," she shot back at him.

"Well now, wouldn't it be better to have a kid with somebody who wanted to be its father?"

"Obviously. So what do you suggest?"

"It's really up to you. If you have the kid, it'll be your kid. If you want the abortion, I'll pay for it and I'll come to New York to be with you when you have it, I promise I'll come. I'll be right there with you and everything will be just fine, you'll see. You can go in to have it on a weekend, I'll be off from the trial, maybe we could go away together afterward."

Patricia studied her fingernails, her rings, the ends of the waist-length red hair, then looked up straight into his eyes. "Done," she said in a cold little voice.

There was a long, long silence, then Jim gave her one of his famous boyish smiles and said in an odd voice, "It'd be an absolutely amazing child, you know, with a genius for a mother and a poet for a father."

"Very likely," Patricia answered dryly. "But that hardly seems a fit reason to have it. This isn't some kind of experiment, you know, to see if two terrific people can turn out a terrific product between them. I don't much like kids anyway, and the only reason I'd have it was because it was yours. And that's probably the worst reason of all to have *any*body's kid."

Jim did not react to this, but said, "You know, this subject has never come up with me before."

Patricia exploded. "Don't give me that bullshit! I know it has. I've been told about at least four, and I know for a *fact* about Suzy Creamcheese and—"

"No, no, it's not true, none of it—it's never happened before. Don't you think this is just as hard for me as it is for you? As you point out, it's my baby too. You'll just have to be brave."

Patricia chose not to reply. Finally Jim suggested they return to the hotel bar, and she agreed. "I just want to be sure I have this straight now: I'm going to have an abortion, you're going to pay for it, and you'll come to New York to be with me for it, is that right?"

"That's right."

"And what do you expect us to do about it after?"

"Weep about it together, I guess."

"Well then," she said, "let's go get those drinks."

Because the Doors were to perform two concerts in California Friday and Saturday nights, the judge agreed to continue hearing testimony the following day, Thursday, and then recess until Tuesday. It was a day of mixed but ultimately disastrous results. Patricia had allowed Jim to stay the night with her and their relationship was good again, or as good as it could be. Then in the courtroom the 150 photographs were introduced as evidence and none showed him doing anything illegal, while the only witness called testified that he hadn't seen anything, either. But then Judge Goodman ruled that no evidence pertaining to "community standards" would be allowed in his courtroom, thereby wiping out the entire thrust of Jim's defense.

As Jim's eyes flew down the two-page ruling, his face turned the color of wet cement. Quietly, he placed the order on the table in front of him and glanced at Max, who was rising in anger to protest. "Your Honor," the attorney said in an urgent tone, "may the jury be removed?"

The jury was instructed to leave the box and Max began his argument. "To exclude evidence concerning community standards in regard to words we freely admit were used," Max cried, "to exclude expert testimony concerning the effect of these words on the audience in this day and age, would be a denial of a fair trial." Max argued strenuously for nearly half an hour, tracing the development of freedom of speech, showing how it tracked the development of drama and the right of the artist or dramatist to state his views. It was, Jim said a few months later, "a brilliant summary of that historical process, but it didn't have any effect." Goodman listened with his chin on his hands, his horn-rimmed glasses on the end of his nose, and then denied Max's argument and motion without comment.

Friday morning Jim and his entourage flew to Los Angeles, where they rejoined the other Doors—who had returned earlier in the week—and then went by bus north to Bakersfield for the first concert, south to San Diego the following night for the second. The shows were strong, but they tired Jim.

Apparently getting a second wind the next evening, Jim set out with Babe to get ripped. "We were fucked up!" Babe remembers. "Just laughin' and laughin', rollin' in the street." The stewardesses with Jim and Babe were not so mirthful. They stalked off. Jim and Babe continued to laugh. And laugh and laugh.

Then they returned to Florida, where Jim stayed up all night, snorting coke and rapping nonstop from midnight until eight in the morning with his playwright friend Harvey Perr, who now was doing some of Elektra's publicity.

At 8 A.M. Jim stopped talking, ordered a watermelon from room service, ate most of it, and met his lawyers back at Division "D." Today the prosecution had four more witnesses scheduled, all of them policemen and undercover agents who had either heard profanity or claimed they had seen Jim's genitals. One of them even described his penis as being "in the process of becoming erect."

Wednesday Jim, Ray, and Babe drove to the Everglades, where they took a ride on an airboat and watched an alligator-wrestling exhibition and ate frog's legs and hush puppies.

Thursday it was back to Division "D" for another wave of witnesses for the prosecution: three more policemen and a "civilian" who worked on the police switchboard and had been admitted to the concert by a cop she knew. They all said something incriminating, and in answer to Max's question, "If Jim was so obscene, why didn't someone arrest him backstage after the show?" one of the witnesses said they feared the crowd would riot.

"What crowd?" Max asked. "There wasn't anyone in the dressing room except for the Doors and their friends and police."

The question went unanswered and was quickly forgotten as the prosecution put into evidence a tape that had been made on a small cassette by someone in the audience. The recorder was placed on the railing of the jury box and the "play" button was depressed. For the next hour and five minutes the courtroom was filled with the smoky sounds of the Doors and the growl of Jim Morrison's voice.

"... ain't nobody gonna love my ass? ... you're all a bunch of fuckin' idiots! you're all a bunch of slaves! ... I'm not talkin' about no revolution, I'm talkin' about havin' some fun ... I'm talkin' about love ... I wanna change the world ... *Aw ri, aw ri, I wanna see some action up here, I wanna see some action up here, I wanna see some people come up here and have some fun. No limits, no laws, come on!*"

"You see," says Harvey Perr, "Jim and Max agreed to having the tapes played because they wanted to show that everything was in context, that everything came out of a rhythm. It was kind of like a poem, a feeling, and they were saying that the obscenity was integral to it. When he said 'fuck,' he was using it in the love way. 'Fuck' meant love. I mean, for all the obscenity, he was really telling the audience to revolt, to revolt against the overpriced tickets, to revolt against the system, and to love each other. He said, 'Fuck your neighbor.' And it all had this rhythm, almost like one of his poems. It was like this big, brawling, drunken poem, telling them to revolt. It was like Dylan Thomas."

Friday night Jim flew to London where he took a small plane to the Isle of Wight to join the other Doors in the only concert salvaged from their aborted European tour. It was Saturday night and Jim had been awake for thirty-six hours. The

Doors went on at 2 A.M. and were followed by the Who, the band the audience was staying awake for. The Doors were performing in the wrong venue—outdoors—and under the worst of conditions, with cold wind, inadequate lighting, and questionable sound equipment. It was, as described by one of the British pop papers, "something like listening to a Doors album through a bad record player that runs slow." Jim really wasn't up to it and throughout the performance he hung onto the microphone limply. Afterward he wandered around the festival site for several hours, giving a short, superficial interview to a British magazine writer, but mostly watching the audience. By the time he returned to London he had made his decision: the Isle of Wight Festival had been his last public performance.

The state rested its case on Wednesday after presenting two more shocked witnesses to Jim's profanity, and then it was Jim's turn at bat.

Bob Josefsberg asked for an acquittal on the grounds that the state itself had raised reasonable doubt. Judge Goodman perfunctorily denied the plea and then set limits on the defense. Only seventeen witnesses would be permitted, he said—the same number the prosecution had called—and there were to be no "so-called experts" among them.

For the remainder of that day and all of the next Max and his courtroom partner questioned the first five witnesses for the defense. All testified that they had been in positions of prime observation and had not seen Jim expose himself. The witnesses were convincing, but so were the prosecution's witnesses who said they *had* seen something. A pall of ennui settled over the courtroom, as invisible but noticeable as the air conditioning. It was almost a relief when at the end of the day an eleven-day recess was announced. Jim and Babe took off for Nassau, where they met Frank and Kathy Lisciandro for a week of booze and sun.

Back in court on September 14 the defense called no fewer than ten witnesses in two and a half hours, and on the following day questioned another five. (The defense had now passed the judge's limit of seventeen, but no one was counting inasmuch as Max was hurrying.) They were housewives and students, doctors and cops, and all echoed previous defense testimony: they hadn't seen Jim expose himself. It was as if a broad cross section of Miami were auditioning for the same small part in a play, the statements sounded that much alike. Each time judge asked Terrence McWilliams if he wanted to cross examine, he declined.

After limping along for more than a month, the trial was now dashing to an end. Not even the testimony of Jim and the other Doors on the 16th and 17th was particularly memorable. "I didn't have to testify," Jim said later, "but we decided it might be a good thing for the jury to see what I was like, because all they could do was look at me. I don't think it meant anything one way or the other."

Jim's testimony was calm and rational. He answered questions from Max and Terrence McWilliams with equal courtesy and grace, selecting his words slowly and carefully, pausing contemplatively, running his fingertips along his mustache, appearing articulate, soft-spoken, convincing.

Finally Max said, "The defense rests."

Judge Goodman agreed to keep his court open on Saturday to hear the closing statements and give the case to the jury. Before court that morning, Jim read in a Miami newspaper that Jimi Hendrix had died in London. Again he wondered aloud, "Does anyone believe in omens?"

The "contemporary standards" defense having been denied them, Max and Bob Josefsberg had to resort to attacking the prosecution's case in their summation. For more than three hours Max dissected the evidence and reviewed the conflicting and contradictory testimony. Then for over an hour more, Bob Josefsberg took the text of "The Emperor's New Clothes" and created a contemporary parable, turning to the prosecutor at the conclusion and saying with a courtly bow, "Mr. McWilliams will now carry the train."

McWilliams made a half-hour speech that seemed almost apologetic and sat down without looking at Jim.

At 9 P.M. Saturday the jurors began their deliberation and

by 11:30 had reached a decision on three of the four charges. Jim was, they concluded, innocent of charges one and four— lewd behavior (the simulated masturbation/simulated oral copulation charge, a felony), and public drunkenness (a misdemeanor)—but guilty on charge three—profanity (another misdemeanor). (When on the stand, Jim was asked if he had exposed himself. In his answer, he accidentally confessed to one of the charges: "I don't remember. I was too drunk." Yet he was, ironically, acquitted of the drinking charge.) The jury told Judge Goodman it was "hung" on charge two: public exposure (another misdemeanor), so he sequestered them in a Miami hotel and recessed court until 10 A.M. Sunday, when the jury was to resume its deliberation.

Sunday morning Jim was reading Irving Stone's biography of Jack London, *Sailor on Horseback,* when the jury came in and the foreman read the verdict. He had been found guilty of exposure.

Sentencing was set for late October. Because Jim could not be extradited from California for misdemeanors, the bail was raised from $5,000 to $50,000 to give him a reason to come back.

Solemn as he left the courtroom in black jeans, boots, an embroidered sweatshirt a fan had given him, Jim stopped to talk to reporters. "This trial and its outcome won't change my style, because I maintain that I did not do anything wrong."

The months after the trial were in some ways worse than the trial itself. In Miami Jim had seemed to be marking time. Now he was moving toward disaster with abandon.

He went into a desperate funk almost as soon as he returned from Florida, when he heard that Janis Joplin was dead of an overdose. First Jimi. Then Janis. Jim's line to friends while out on the town was, "You're drinking with Number Three." And then he fought so bitterly with Pamela that she left him—threw up her hands, packed, and flew off to Paris to be reunited with her rich French count.

Wide World

(MH1)MIAMI, FL, October 30—MORRISON SENTENCED—Singer Jim Morrison leaves the courtroom in custody of a police officer today after he was sentenced to six months in jail and fined $500 for using profanity in public and indecent exposure. Morrison remained free on $50,000 bond pending disposition of an appeal. The charges stemmed from a 1969 performance by Morrison in an appearance at Miami, Florida, with the Doors.

The days that followed were spent in bars and the nights were passed in the Strip hotel, where Jim and Babe had adjacent rooms.

"Hey, Babe, look at this!"

Jim was hanging from the balcony railing outside his room in the Hyatt House Hotel, ten stories above the Sunset Strip. He had been drinking and snorting coke.

"I wish you wouldn't do that," Babe said, "you make me nervous."

He walked onto the balcony and looked over the edge and then at Jim, still hanging by his hands. "You're pulling a purty good crowd," he said. Babe looked over the edge again and saw the hotel manager on the sidewalk, waving his arms. Minutes later there was a thundering knock at the door. Babe helped Jim inside and sat him down, then opened the door to the angry manager and a small knot of sheriff's deputies.

"What's going on up here? What the goddamn hell do you guys think—"

"Everything is okay," Babe said, pointing to Jim. The cops came marching in. Later they'd claim that Babe's opening the door wide was an invitation to enter, that his pointing to Jim was a "gesture of welcome." While they were searching the room, Babe was able to hide their cocaine stash inside a triangular folded card on the dresser that said "Visit the Saber Room." But the police did find some marijuana, and as it was Babe's room, Jim was not arrested. But he was moved to the back of the hotel, overlooking the parking lot.

Asked about the Miami concert by Salli Stevenson, an interviewer for *Circus* magazine, Jim finally relented and spoke of it. "I think I was just fed up with the image that had been created around me, which I sometimes consciously, most of the time unconsciously, cooperated with. It was just too much for me to really stomach and so I just put an end to it in one glorious evening. I guess what it boiled down to was that I told the audience that they were a bunch of fucking idiots to be members of an audience. What were they doing there anyway? The basic message was realize that you're not really here to listen to a bunch of songs by some good musicians. You're here for something else. Why not admit it and do something about it?"

He said he regarded the interview as "an increasingly important art form with antecedents in the confession box, debating and cross examination." He worried about Los Angeles cops who "are idealists and . . . are almost fanatical in believing in the rightness of their cause. They have a whole philosophy behind their tyranny."

The interview was reflective and articulate. For perhaps the first time Jim intimated in public that he might not live much longer. "I'm not denying that I've had a good time these past three or four years. I've met a lot of interesting people and seen things in a short space of time that I probably wouldn't have run into in twenty years of living. I can't say that I regret it." But, he added, "If I had to do it over . . . I think I would have gone for the quiet, demonstrative artist-plodding-away-in-his-own-garden trip." What would happen if he had to go to jail? He hoped the other three would "go on and create an instrumental sound of their own that didn't depend on lyrics, which aren't really that necessary in music anyway."

On October 30 Jim flew to Miami to face Judge Murray Goodman. Before delivering sentence, the judge had a few words. "The suggestion that your conduct was acceptable by community standards is just not true. To admit that this nation accepts as a community standard the indecent exposure and the offensive language spoken by you would be to admit that a small minority who spew obscenities, who disregard law and order, and who display utter contempt for our institutions and heritage have determined the community standards for us all."

Jim thought it was a pretty fair campaign speech, bound to win the judge some votes the following month. The sentence was what he had expected: the maximum. For profanity he was given sixty days of hard labor in the Dade County jail, and for exposure he was sentenced to six months of the same, after which he was to serve two years and four months of probationary time. He was also fined $500.

The first week of November Patricia Kennely entered a

hospital in New York and Jim's child was aborted in the twentieth week of fetal development. Jim was not present and he did not call.

Within a fortnight of the sentencing Max Fink filed an appeal of the convictions with the U.S. District Court and Elektra released its first album of repackaged Doors songs, a record called *13*, the number of songs lifted from the first five Doors albums.

The Doors' relationship with Elektra was tenuous. In no way did Jac Holzman want his company associated with the Miami convictions; he instructed the Elektra staff to avoid the subject whenever possible. Communications remained cordial, but when Elektra asked the Doors' office to approve release of the anthology album, it was understood that the request was a formality. *Morrison Hotel* had sold well, considering the circumstances under which it had been released and considering that it had done without the aid of a hit single. *Absolutely Live,* which had followed it by several months, had cost a bundle and had sold poorly, only 225,000 copies, (half of what *Morrison Hotel* had sold). Elektra wanted product for the Christmas customers, so *13* received the Doors' reluctant blessing. Jim even consented to shave for the photo session needed to produce the album's rear cover.

Jim hated the cover for *Absolutely Live.* Originally the cover was going to be an effective grainy, bluish rear-view photo of the band on stage at the Aquarius Theatre where the included "Celebration of the Lizard" had been recorded. Elektra Records art department decided that photo alone wasn't eye-catching enough. A color photo of Jim, taken during the Hollywood Bowl concert well over a year before, was superimposed squarely over the existing front-cover photo, and before the Doors office knew anything about it, the album was shipped. Jim was furious.

He would also dislike the front cover of *13*, which also pictured a younger Jim Morrison, considerably larger than the

Edmund Teske

Photo session for Doors' Album 13, *1970*

band. Elektra obviously wanted the "pretty" Jim Morrison. Surprisingly, Jim only expressed his anger to a few close friends. Although Ray, Robby, and John had become accustomed to the attention directed toward their singer, it upset Jim.

The week following *13*'s release, Jim's old friend from UCLA, Felix Venable, died of cancer of the stomach.

With rehearsals for the new album under way, Jim's schedule was turning productive again, despite the psychological trauma. Because much of the material that went on the album had been written long before, the album came together more quickly than expected. The sinister "Cars Hiss by My Window" ("Window starts to tremble with a sonic boom/A cold girl will kill you in a darkened room") was from one of the few surviving Venice notebooks. The poetry of "The WASP (Texas Radio & The Big Beat)" was included in the Doors' original souvenir book, distributed in 1968, the same year that Jim wrote the lyrics to another song, called "The Changeling." "L'America" was left over from Antonioni's *Zabriskie Point.*

The new material included two songs that ran seven and eight minutes in length, respectively, both of them starkly and poetically autobiographical, and both strong lyrically and musically. The first of these, "L.A. Woman," was Jim's despairing salute to Los Angeles, a city he now saw as diseased and alienated. "Are you a lucky little lady in The City of Light?/Or just another lost angel—City of Night." Los Angeles *was* a "city of night" for Jim (he took the phrase from a novel by John Rechy) and in another verse he described it: "Drivin' down your freeways/Midnight alleys roam/Cops in cars, the topless bars/Never saw a woman—/So alone, so alone. . . ." To this he added a grimmer thought: "Motel money murder madness/ Let's change the mood from glad to sadness." In the next verse he addressed himself in an anagram for "Jim Morrison": "Mr. Mojo Risin'/Keep on risin'/Got to keep on risin'/Risin', risin' . . ."

"Riders on the Storm" had no word tricks and was slower,

J.M. / Doors

L.A. Woman

Well, I just got into town about
an hour ago
Took a look around, see which
way the wind blow
Where the little girls in their
Hollywood bungalows
Are you a lucky little lady in
The City of Light?
Or just another lost angel—
City of Night (4)

L.A. Woman (●) (2)
L.A. Woman Sunday afternoon (3)
Drive thru your suburbs
Into your blues (●) (2)
Into your blue-blue Blues
Into your blues

Lyrics to "L.A. Woman," in Jim Morrison's hand

Break
I see your hair is burning
Hills are fill'd w/ fire
If They say I never lov'd you
You know They are a liar
Drivin' down your freeways
Midnite alleys roam
Cops in cars, The topless bars
Never saw a woman —
So alone (2)
So alone-lone Lone
So alone

_____

Motel money murder Madness
Let's Change The mood From glad
                    To Sadness

Break

Mr. Mojo Risin' (4)

Keep on risin'

Got to keep on risin'

Risin' risin' (8)

Repeat 1st Verse
          down to ... 'City of Night'

L.A. Woman (2)

She's my woman

Little L.A. Woman

L.A. Woman C'mon

jazzier, more melodic than "L.A. Woman." It was also generally thought to be more autobiographical. "Riders on the storm/Into this house we're born/into this world we're thrown/like a dog without a bone/an actor out on loan/Riders on the storm." And in another verse a familiar theme reappeared—a cry to love and Pamela: "the world on you depends /our life will never end/girl you gotta love your man." The "There's a killer on the road" image surfaced in song, inspired by *HWY.*

The Doors took these songs to Paul Rothchild. Their relationship with Paul had been deteriorating from the time they had finished recording *Morrison Hotel* in January. Paul's habitual insistence on perfection, which necessitated so many dozens of starts and stops in the studio on previous albums and caused so many concerts to be recorded live, was, as John put it, "starting to wear on us." Worse, Paul didn't like the new material. "It was awful," he says, *even* now. "The material was bad, the attitude was bad, the performance was bad. After three days of listening I said, 'That's it!' on the talk-back and canceled the session. We went out to dinner, and I talked to them for three straight hours. I said, 'Look, I think it sucks. I don't think the world wants to hear it, it's the first time I've ever been bored in a recording studio in my life, I want to go to sleep. The tensions between you guys are phenomenal.' I said to Jim, 'This is *your* record. This is the record you've wanted, so you've got to get it together. Why don't you guys produce it yourself? I'm gonna drop out.' "

The criticism hurt, especially when Paul called "Riders on the Storm" "cocktail music." The Doors admitted that they hadn't played the songs well, that perhaps they were not ready to record, but they did not lose faith in the material. After dinner they returned to the studio with their engineer, Bruce Botnick, and agreed to co-produce the album with him.

Pamela remained in Europe and Jim went on the prowl in search of a girl who'd go—as Bill Siddons described it—"all the way."

"Jim took things all the way," Bill says. "Jim—especially Jim drunk—would follow a line of action to its conclusion, whether that led him into the morass of hell or into heaven. That's one of the reasons people went with him, because they sensed that. My wife Cheri told him that one day he would want to be with a woman who could go as far as he could, a woman who could take him as far as he could take someone else."

Jim might have thought he found that woman in Ingrid Thompson, a large, buxom Julie Newmar look-alike from Scandinavia. On November 19, when her husband went to Portugal on business, Jim moved into the Chateau Marmont, another Sunset Boulevard hotel, and they started seeing each other.

Ingrid opened her front door a crack and Jim put his foot in it. He was drunk, and with his beard full grown again and wearing a ratty army fatigue jacket, he looked like a befuddled mountain man. Ingrid opened the door wider. "You know I've always loved you," Jim told her.

In the next weeks Jim returned to Ingrid's home probably two to four nights a week, often arriving with another girl, someone he'd sweet-talked into taking him "home," and with whom he'd neck on the doorstep before going in. Ingrid hated that and told him so, but Jim merely shrugged, saying he was giving Ingrid as much as he could. At the end of the month he told her he wanted her to have his baby and dramatically threw her birth control pills into the fire in the fireplace.

"We really got it on," says Ingrid. "Neither of us was expecting it. He really loved life and so did I. The only bad thing was there was too much cocaine, which blew our minds. He thought I was crazier than he was and he wanted to see how far I'd go."

Jim had been snorting cocaine for over a year, first getting into it heavily when he and Michael McClure got MGM to provide them with $1,000 in "research money" while writing their script, again when Paul Rothchild was into it during the recording of *Morrison Hotel*. Once Jim and one of the MGM executives bought an ounce of it and Jim said, "You keep it in your safe and only give me a little bit at a time, no matter what I might say, okay?" To Patricia Kennely he once said, "If I had a mountain of coke in my backyard, I'd do it—because it was there."

One night, returning to Ingrid, he brought champagne and a larger than usual amount of cocaine in a 35-millimeter film can. Holding both arms aloft with glee, he entered the house and sat down in front of the coffee table. After he toasted Ingrid's intelligence, good looks, and European charm, he emptied his glass in a single swallow. Then he unscrewed the film can and dumped a pile of coke onto the glass coffee table. Slowly, silently, he pushed it into thin two-inch rows with his BankAmericard. Then he produced a crisp one-hundred-dollar bill and rolled it tightly. One after another they snorted the powder, consuming about fifty dollars' worth apiece.

The hit was almost immediate. Their heartbeats accelerated, body temperatures rose slightly, pupils dilated, faces flushed. Minutes later they were garrulous, restless, excited. They felt confident and larger-than-life. They snorted another fifty dollars' worth.

A cocaine rush is short and sweet. If the user can afford it, he does more. Jim recently had gone through huge quantities of the drug with Steve Stills and some others, and now he did the same thing with Ingrid. After three hours the film can was nearly empty. They had taken their clothes off and were dancing in the moonlight. They tossed themselves into bed. Ingrid began talking about her native land, her strange friends there. She said that sometimes she drank blood.

"Bullshit!" said Jim.

"No. It's true," Ingrid swore, nodding her head earnestly. "I do. Sometimes . . ."

"Okay," replied Jim, smiling, "let's you and me drink some right now." He seemed to be serious.

Ingrid tried to turn it into a joke. Snapping her fingers she said, "I forgot—the bloodman didn't come today."

"Let's drink some blood now," Jim repeated.

Jim remembered the blood Patricia had drawn from his wrist and forearm for their marriage ceremony, an act that probably contributed to his passing out. Jim was inordinately afraid of sharp objects.

"Ya got any razor blades?" he asked.

Ingrid knew by the way he asked that she would contribute the blood. She went into the bathroom to search. Moments later she held a blade with one corner barely touching the fleshy pad of skin where her thumb joined her left hand. She nervously struck herself, eyes closed. When she opened her eyes, there was no blood. She closed them and jabbed again.

On the fifth stab blood spurted everywhere and Jim whooped, grabbing a champagne glass to catch it in. They made love and danced some more, smearing their bodies red.

The next morning when he awoke on blood-caked sheets, with dry brown streaks from Ingrid's blood over much of his body, Jim was scared. The paranoia increased.

From the end of November through the first week in December Jim was visited almost daily at his cottage at the Chateau Marmont by Larry Marcus and another screenwriter, a friend of Larry's named Syrus Mottel. First they gave the "secret knock," at which Jim would peer from a window on the second floor to see who was outside. Finally they would be admitted to Jim's sanctuary, which was decorated with wall-to-wall books, many of them collections of poetry. Although the refrigerator was full of beer, there was no food.

The film ideas they discussed had to do with identity. They decided (Jim's idea) to tell the story of a young film editor in Los Angeles who one day walked away from his job, wife, and children to disappear into the jungles of Mexico in what Jim called a "frantic search for absolute zero." Jim and

Larry shook hands and an agreement was drawn up with Max's help. For Jim's services as co-writer, co-producer, and star, Larry personally guaranteed him $25,000.

In the evenings they sometimes went to the Cock 'n Bull, a restaurant on the Strip. Once, with Frank Lisciandro, Jim began a verbal parody of the script idea and virtually destroyed it, squashing all Larry's hopes and cruelly destroying his own. Another time, with only Syeus and Larry present, Jim went through three bottles of scotch in the course of a meal and afterward dashed onto Sunset to direct traffic with his coat as if the bulls of Pamplona were thundering past.

Still another time Jim collected Larry Marcus at the Columbia studios in the latest of a series of ugly rented cars he had. Without saying a word, he drove around Los Angeles for half a day. He didn't even turn on the radio. Larry sat there silently. Trapped.

CHAPTER
11

On December 6 Jim called a phone number Jac Holzman had given him and spoke to the engineer who had built the Elektra studio. "It's my birthday the day after tomorrow," Jim told him, "and I'd really like to record some poetry." On the 8th they were in the Village Recorders, two blocks from the bar where Jim drank when he was at UCLA, the Lucky U. He had a drink with Frank and Kathy, Alan Ronay, and a Swedish girl before going to the studio. When they got there, the engineer gave Jim a fifth of Irish whiskey. Jim began to read, and to drink.

Like his "An American Prayer," much of what Jim read that night took the form of an invocation. For four hours Jim read his way through a thick sheaf of neatly typed sheets, becoming drunker and drunker.

Elated by his readings, Jim agreed to try performing again in Dallas on Friday, December 11, and in New Orleans on the following night.

Dallas was a triumph. For that one night, the Doors and

Jim proved to themselves, and to their detractors, that they were still a mighty force to be reckoned with. They sold out two shows in the six-thousand–seat auditorium and trotted out to do two encores after each set. Jim was in good spirits, the band tight and strong. They previewed "Riders on the Storm" to a delighted audience. Backstage after the second show the four Doors toasted one another for the successful rally.

New Orleans, though, was a tragedy. If Dallas was the good, Miami the ugly, then New Orleans was the end. That night Ray saw Jim's spirit go. "Everyone who was there saw it, man. He lost all his energy about midway through the set. He hung on the microphone and it just slipped away. You could actually see it leave him. He was drained." As if to defy his own weakness, Jim picked up the microphone stand and repeatedly bashed it into the stage, over and over and over until finally there was the sound of wood splintering. He threw the stand into the stunned audience, turned, and plopped down on the drum riser, sitting motionless.

The Doors never again appeared in public as a quartet.

Back in Los Angeles Jim's life brightened when Pamela returned from France. She took delight in learning that Jim had gone bananas in her absence, but she also admitted to friends that on her end things hadn't gone so well either. She was, she said, glad to be back on Norton Avenue, even if Jim was still staying at the Chateau. He needed the space, he said, for his business meetings. Pamela knew Jim would be back at her bed and board soon enough.

When Jim shambled into the Doors' office a few days before Christmas, Kathy Lisciandro, Frank's wife and the Doors' secretary, told him there was a message on his desk.

Indeed there was. "I'm in town," it said. "Call me. Patricia." The note was pinned to the desk with a dagger.

Jim hadn't seen Patricia Kennely since Miami, had failed to hold her hand through the abortion. She left the telephone number of Diane Gardiner, his former publicist. Jim recognized it because Pamela lived upstairs over Diane and, not having a phone of her own, used Diane's. Patricia was staying at Diane's.

Jim called half an hour later. The Doors had decided to record their album in the rehearsal room under the office and Jim invited Patricia to come over while he finished a song. She declined, saying recording sessions bored her ... why didn't he come over there. He said he would, but didn't.

Four days later, Christmas Day, Patricia answered Diane's telephone and it was someone calling for Pamela. Patricia decided to trek upstairs to get Pamela. She'd avoided the confrontation long enough. Patricia had met Pamela briefly at the Hilton Hotel party in New York, and after Pamela took the call they began to talk. Pamela was already *very* stoned on downers, so Patricia companionably smoked enough grass to get half a dozen people high. They drank wine and talked for nearly three hours. There was no ill feeling, no antagonism. Pamela told Patricia that she and Jim weren't really married— something she seldom admitted, except to close friends, calling herself Mrs. Morrison even when phoning the Doors' office. Patricia told Pamela about the abortion, but not about the Wicca wedding.

"Oh, wow," said Pamela, "that's beautiful." She paused. "But it would've been even more beautiful if you could've loved Jim enough to have the baby."

Patricia snapped, "I like to think I loved Jim and loved myself and loved that kid enough *not* to have it."

"Yeah, but if you'd had the kid, you could have gone away and lived in the country. Of course, Jim woulda never sent you any money, because that's the way he—"

There was a bark from Pamela's dog Sage. Jim was coming up the walk. Patricia tensed and Pamela went dead white, dashing outside to meet him with a rush of words. "Jim, Jim, don't go in there. Don't go in there. It's only Diane ..."

Jim was laughing as he climbed the stairs to Pamela's apartment. Pamela returned to Diane's and frantically faced

Patricia: "What am I gonna do? Jim's gonna kill me. He knew I was in here talking to you, he knows it was *you*." She then climbed the stairs, following Jim.

Jim came down alone and treated Patricia with charm and grace, keeping her wine glass filled, speaking with feeling, nodding apologetically when she said he had made her feel like a groupie in Miami. He told her it was just bad timing, with the trial and all. "But you of all people should understand," he said. "You were there."

By the time Pamela returned, the room was full of people. Diane had come home with more houseguests. Jim and Patricia were sitting on the floor, bow-legged drunk, noisily playing the card game War. Jim dealt Pamela in and beat them both, twenty games in a row.

After a while Pamela tried to get Jim to go upstairs with her. He said no, he was staying where he was. The clash of wills embarrassed everyone in the room. Finally, Diane good-naturedly gave Pamela some amyl nitrate and took her upstairs, as if she were half-friend, half-juvenile ward.

Later, when everyone else had gone to bed, Jim asked Patricia to go to the Chateau with him. Then he changed his mind, said he was too drunk to drive, told her he loved her again, and suggested they sleep on the floor. Patricia shrugged. They found a spare quilt, wrapped themselves up in it, and fell asleep in the middle of the room.

At ten in the morning Pamela came downstairs and knocked on Diane's door. Diane came out of her bedroom, opened the door a crack, and told Pamela, "I'm not going to deny he's here."

Pamela strode in and stood over Jim and Patricia, who were still huddled nude under Diane's quilt. It was like a French farce—so ludicrous, so horrible, and so funny all at once that no one knew whether to laugh, cry, or commit mayhem.

"I have only one thing to say to you," Pamela intoned, "and I'm gonna say it in front of all these people: Jim, goddamn it, you've ruined my Christmas. You spoil it for me every year. This is the fourth year you've done it. I just can't stand it anymore!"

Jim was grinning; Patricia, who had recognized the moment instantly as one of the high points of her life, was biting her lip to keep from laughing, and tried to be tactful. "Pamela, it isn't what it looks like, I promise you—"

Now Diane interrupted. "Pamela, what you need is some vitamin pills and orange juice. Come out to the kitchen with me." Pamela dutifully followed, and Jim began to pull on his pants.

"Christ," he muttered, "I'm never going to hear the end of this—"

"Oh, *spare* me, Jim," said Patricia, but she was laughing with him. "You *wanted* this to happen. Whose idea was it to stay here?"

"Yeah, yeah. You're right—as usual."

When Pamela and Diane returned with some wine, they all sat cross-legged and got cross-eyed again. "Don't worry about it," Jim finally said to Pamela, putting his arm around her waist. "It's all in the family."

In the end, Pamela's loyalty and patience won him over and most nights during January and February 1971, Jim returned to the Courson bed. He finally seemed to be enjoying a period of domestic calm.

That winter he was simultaneously at work on four major projects in the four artistic disciplines that interested him: poetry, film, music, and theater. For all these projects Jim was not just the writer, but also the performer. Max Fink was negotiating a modest advance from Elektra to produce a poetry album. Meetings were resumed with Larry Marcus, the screenwriter who now wanted Jim for a film in Italy. He was also meeting again with his friend, "Philharmonic Fred" Myrow, to discuss a stage show in which Jim was to play a Vietnam prisoner-of-war.

The most satisfying project was the Doors' new album, now being recorded in their office and rehearsal room and referred to as "The Doors' Workshop." They were producing it themselves, with the help of their longtime engineer, Bruce Botnick.

"At last," Jim told everyone, "I'm doing a blues album."

It was true. The gritty, randy Doors were back, with the Brechtian bite and the nightmare carnival bounce of the band's early "Whiskey" days.

The antidrug group, the Do It Now Foundation, had been directing all their energies toward subduing, if not eliminating, the alarming rise of methedrine (speed) abuse in America. To accomplish this task, they had been approaching various youth leaders soliciting public service "Speed Kills" radio messages. Frank Zappa had consented and so had several other "name" rockers. Jim had ignored the foundation's requests for months until one day he answered the phone in the Doors' office and found himself agreeing to a visit that afternoon to tape his own antidrug rap. Those present were surprised when Jim consented. "Well, why the fuck not? Speed puts worms in your ears. I know this chick who thinks she can talk to you without using her voice—I don't want my fans listening to my music with their brains bleached and poisoned."

It had been understood, however, that Jim would never allow himself to be used to influence his following, in any way, at any time, for any reason. Why the sudden turnabout?

"I thought you said you wanted your fans to think for themselves, Jim?" Denny Sullivan asked. Denny was still handling Jim's fan mail and had become a virtual fixture in the office. Jim had lectured Denny before on the dangers of hard drugs.

"I do, damn it, but they *can't* think with that shit. That's the whole damn point. Besides, who appointed you custodian of my affairs?" Jim was joking, but he was also serious. Speed was bad news, and he knew it.

Jerry Hopkins

During rehearsals at Doors workshop in West Hollywood, 1969

When the Do It Now representative finally arrived with his tape recorder to produce the sixty-second spot, Jim found himself a seat and graciously offered the rep the one on the other side of his corner desk. He appeared eager to please.

"Okay, now, what we want you to say," the rep nervously started, "is 'This is Jim Morrison from the Doors,' and then just, umm, in your own words, tell them speed kills."

Jim thought for a moment and then conceded.

"Okay, is this thing on? Testing, testing . . . you better play it back, make sure it's working. We don't want to go through all this trouble and then discover, only too late, you missed your only chance."

The tape was rewound, played, checked out, and rewound again back to the start. "Ready, Jim?" "Ready." "Okay, now, go."

Jim thought for a moment and then began. "Hi, you little assholes out there listening to the radio instead of doing your homework, this is Jim Morrison of the Doors—"

The Do It Now representative stopped the recorder.

Jim shot a wink at Denny. "What are you doing?" he asked the rep. "I hadn't finished!"

"Please, Jim, we can get this whole thing done in just a minute if you'll be straightforward. Remember, this is a public service spot."

Jim listened attentively and nodded. "I think I understand. Can I try it again?"

The recorder was switched back on to record: "Hey, how you guys out there doin'? This is your old buddy Jim Morrison, I sing with a group called the Doors, you mighta heard of 'em. We done a few songs, but I never, never did a song on speed. Drunk, hell yeahhhh . . ."

The exasperated representative told Jim, "Please, you must understand what we need. Frank Zappa had fun. You can have fun, too, but you must be serious."

Jim seemed to understand. "Okay, got it. Turn the sucker on. We'll get it this time. I promise."

"Hello, this is Jim Morrison of the Doors, I just want to tell you that shooting speed ain't cool, so snort it." The recorder was turned off and the representative sat motionless. The room was silent.

"Something the matter? Was that all right?"

The rep only shook his head. Jim stood up and put a hand on his shoulder. "Hey, man, I'm sorry, come on, turn that back on. I'm real sorry, I'll give it to you straight this time. Honest."

The rep looked at Jim. "You promise?" Jim was solemn. "I promise."

The tape was set and rolling.

"Hello, this is Jim Morrison. Don't shoot speed. Christ, you guys, smoke pot."

The rep looked up. "I think we're getting closer, Jim, if you could just change those last few words."

"I know exactly what you mean," Jim assured him. "One more time, roll it."

This time Jim gave his formal introduction, warned that shooting speed "isn't that smart, shooting speed kills geese, if you shoot a goose fulla speed, that goose is gonna swim in circles forever."

The Do It Now man had lost all patience and was nearly in tears. Jim was begging him, "Come on, man, I'm sorry, I was just having fun you know, we'll get it right this time, I promise."

"I don't know, Jim"—the rep was shaking his head—"I can't spend all day here."

"One last time," Jim insisted.

"Okay, but if you don't get it right this time, that's it."

"I'm sorry. This will be a take—you know what a take is?"

Jim held the hand microphone carefully before his mouth. He paused and then began. "Hello, this is Jim Morrison from the Doors and I just got one thing to say." Jim smiled at the rep, who smiled back hopefully. "Don't shoot speed. Speed kills. Please don't shoot speed, try downers, yeah, downers, barbs, tranks, reds, they're much less expensive and—"

The tape machine was still running but the rep had hit the end of his rope. He got up, pulled on his jacket, and grabbing the recorder, stalked out of the office. The room erupted in laughter. Jim had given his speech in a way so that it was impossible to edit.

"Wassa matter with him?" Jim asked "I heard Alice Cooper say if he caught anybody shooting speed, he'd come over to their house and hang their puppies. I didn't say anything like that."

The Do It Now Foundation never got their Jim Morrison antidrug spot.

Jim hadn't met with the local press for quite a while. It had been even longer since he had granted them an exclusive.

Jim liked the *L.A. Free Press* for its antiestablishment stands, and because he felt it was "part of everybody's life," he gave the paper's music writer, Bob Chorush, time enough to get a good interview and once again displayed his thoughtful side. When asked about rioting at early Doors concerts, Jim said rock concerts were a form of "human swarming to communicate an uneasiness about overpopulation," much like the swarming of insects and certain animal species. "I haven't got it all worked out yet," he said earnestly, "but I think there's something to it." Some of his answers were aphoristic: "I think in art, and especially in film, that people are trying to confirm their own existence," and on Charles Manson: the trials were "society's way of assimilating the horrible event."

The subject of drinking came up casually when Jim said he had missed a lot of good music in the two years since he and Babe had been barred from the Troubadour. The interviewer asked a question. Jim paused, cocked his head to outline his full moustache with his fingertips. "I, uh, went through a period when I drank a lot," he finally said. "I had a lot of pressure hanging over me that I couldn't cope with."

Jim paused again. "I also think drinking is a way to cope with living in a crowded environment and also a product of boredom. I know people drink because they're bored. But I enjoy drinking. It loosens people up and stimulates conversation sometimes. And, uh, it's, I don't know, it's like gambling somehow. You know? You go out for a night of drinking and you don't know where you're going to end up the next day. It could work out good and it could be disastrous. It's like a throw of the dice. Everybody smokes grass. I guess you don't consider that a drug anymore. But three years ago there was just that wave of hallucinogenics. I don't think anyone really has the strength to sustain those trips forever. Then you go into narcotics, of which alcohol is one. Instead of trying to think more you try to kill thought—with alcohol and, uh, heroin and downers. These are painkillers. I think that's what people have gone into."

Jim was speaking as an observer of American society in the early 1970s, but he also must have been speaking for himself and Pamela. Thus far she had kept her occasional use of heroin a secret from him, but he did know she qualified as a "downer freak," just as he satisfied nearly all the criteria for alcoholism. Though he told the *Free Press* that his hard drinking days were over, the people around him were astonished by the quantities of alcohol he consumed.

Jim ended his rap about drinking even more offhandedly than he'd begun it. "I like alcohol," he said, "because it's traditional, and also I hate scoring. You know? I hate the kind of sleazy sexual connotations of scoring from people, so I never do that. That's why I like alcohol. You can go down to any corner store and it's right across the table."

Indeed, with all his projects going so well, Jim was no longer drinking to escape boredom. As in his youth, he was drinking for the hell of it. He drank to get drunk.

Once he entered Pamela's boutique singing "Back Door Man" at full volume, accompanied by two drinking partners of recent acquisition; he looked at Denny, who was helping Judy, Pamela's sister, in the store.

"Sell these gen'elmen some clothes," he slurred. He turned to them. "What would you like? We have some excellent material and some fine garments designed by our own factory of pygmies in Switzerland. Their nimble hands and precise eyes, you can be sure, provide the finest production."

Suddenly he collapsed into a chair, his head drooping on his chest. His voice fell into a snore.

When Jim awoke, his friends were gone and Denny's older sister was there. Denny introduced her. "Tha's yer sis'er?" Jim asked. "You nev'r tol' me you had a sis'er who looks like this. Whooooooopppppeeeee! Looka those tits!"

At that moment a well-proportioned matron of fifty entered the boutique. Assuming Jim's remarks were directed at her, she tore into him with her handbag, chasing him around the jewelry counter and leaving only after she had scored two or three clouts.

"Christ," Jim groaned after the incident.

"I haven't had a workout like that since my father chased me around the kitchen with a baseball bat."

Another time Jim wheeled into the boutique, crashed into a shirt rack, knocked it over, and fell on the shirts. Pamela was there this time and she exploded. "Oh, Christ, oh Jesus fucking Christ! He's drunk. Goddamn you, Jim Morrison, you son of a bitch!"

"Drunk?" said Jim, getting up slowly, smiling innocently. "Not me, ma'am. I tripped. It was an accident." Babe then came in and took him off to the Palms to drink.

That night at the Chateau Marmont Jim did a Tarzan act. He got up on the roof and tried to swing into his bedroom window off the rain gutter. "The only reason he didn't get killed," says Babe, "is he bounced off the roof of the shed attached to the back of his cottage. It was outta sight, man."

Jim had no regard for what he drank: gin stingers one day, whiskey with beer chasers the next, Black Russians on the third, tequila neat the fourth, Singapore Slings or some other "tropical" drink with fruit when he was hungry. Only the end was invariable: total inebriation.

His health was not good. From bumming occasional cigarettes at his concerts, Jim had worked his way up to three packs of Marlboros a day. He had a rasping cough. Once, he told Robby, he had coughed up blood.

His voice still had much of its rough-edged, throaty sexiness, but it was irreparably damaged. When Jac Holzman heard the first work tapes for "L.A. Woman," he thought: "I'm listening to Jim's final album as a vocalist."

And he was soft, weighing 175 pounds—40 more than he had when the first publicity photographs had emphasized his wiry torso. He was eating poorly, consuming most of his calories in alcohol. He had the bloated body of a drunk.

Michael McClure went on the wagon in December and wrote to Jim, suggesting he try it, too. Jim never replied. When he met Michael and their agent, Sylva Romano, for lunch, Sylva introduced a game.

"I think," she said, "we'll all agree that regardless of how old any of us might be chronologically, inside, deep down, we feel a certain age, and we believe that's the way people should see us."

Michael said he never got past eleven.

Sylva said she'd always secretly thought of herself as nineteen.

Jim, who was only a few weeks past his twenty-seventh birthday, gloomily said he felt *forty*-seven.

The first week of January 1971 Jim sat at his desk reading *Rolling Stone.* He was startled to see that one of the magazine's first-line critics liked the Doors' last album, *13*.

Downstairs the other Doors were recording. Elvis Presley's bassist, Jerry Scheff, was there, and so was Marc Benno, on rhythm guitar. Jim was killing time, waiting for word that all was ready for him to sing. For this one, he was going to use the tiny downstairs bathroom as a vocal booth. Jim was singing "live" with the others on most of the songs. It was going so easily. In ten recording days they'd have everything on tape, and on only two of the nine songs (the tenth was "L'America," recorded for *Zabriskie Point* months earlier) would Jim's vocals be overdubbed.

The material was good, and varied, giving all members of the band equal opportunity to show off. Jim got to sing one of John Lee Hooker's blues, a song from the Doors' early repertoire, "Crawling King Snake." In another, original blues, "Cars Hiss by My Window," Robby threw in a distinctive Jimmy Reed–styled guitar line, as Jim adopted a black blues voice and at the end of the song provided a better-than-passable vocal impression of a blues guitar. Ray's wry sense of humor showed up in the middle of "Hyacinth House." After Jim sang an absurd line, "I see the bathroom is clear," Ray slid into the melody line from Chopin known as "Til the End of Time." "Riders on the Storm" was clean and jazzy, eerie and hopeful. "Love Her Madly," the song of Robby's that would be released as their first single in exactly a year, was bouncy and carnivalesque, reminiscent of an earlier, funkier, more spontaneous, but also extremely commercial, Doors.

Jim's lyrics once again reached soaring peaks, notably in the longer songs, "L.A. Woman," "Riders on the Storm," and the long-germinating "The Wasp":

> The Negroes in the forest
> brightly feathered;
> & they are saying:
>   "Forget the Night.
>   Live w/us in forests
>   of azure. Out here
>   on the perimeter there
>   are no stars; out
>   here we is stoned—
>   immaculate."

Later, in the same song: "I'll tell you this, no eternal reward will forgive us now for wasting the dawn."

Each of these three songs gave clues of Jim's growing wish

to escape. Jim claimed that the "Mr. Mojo Risin'" in "L.A. Woman" was not just an anagram for his name, but the name he'd use when contacting the office after he'd "split to Africa." No one took him seriously.

"Been Down So Long" took its title and refrain, "been down so Goddamn long/That it looks like up to me" from the book of the same approximate title by Richard Fariña and included some blatant male chauvinism:

> I said, Baby, baby, baby
> Won't you get down on your knees
> C'mon little darlin'
> C'mon, & give your love to me

This same male supremacy appeared in the John Lee Hooker song:

> C'mon, crawl
> C'mon, crawl
> Get on out there on your hands & knees, baby
> Crawl all over me

In a period when women's liberation was beginning to command attention, such a message would not go unnoticed.

At Denny's insistence Jim wrote a description of the album in his large, childlike scrawl to Dave Marsh, at *Creem*, then slid into an autobiographical appraisal. He described the album as his vision of L.A. as a microcosm of America. He told Dave that he had originally gone to L.A. to make films and happened into music. He went on to describe many of his upcoming projects, including a long essay on the Miami trials. He closed his letter with:

> I am not mad.
> I am interested in freedom.
>
>   Good luck,
>   J. Morrison

The solitary, overweight figure in the rumpled fatigue jacket and jeans, with massive head and face of hair, moved slowly along the Hollywood streets. Day after day Jim walked, looking at the stucco wonderland as if for the final time, returning at last to the apartment on Norton Avenue. Most nights and many days in January and the first half of February were spent "at home" with Pamela—Jim reading, Pamela designing clothes for Themis. Sometimes Jim would get down on the floor with their dog and hum.

"Mmmmmmmmmmmmmmmm-ah, hummmmmmmmmmmm."

Sage answered in perfect harmony: "Mmmmmmmmmmmm-mm."

Jim would do it again and this time Sage would go up one note.

Pamela would join in and Jim would complain that she was ruining it. Sometimes they'd go downstairs and talk with Diane Gardiner about going to France. They'd decided. They actually were going to do it—live in Paris as exiles for six months or more. Pamela was enthralled. Even Jim seemed relieved.

Jim's leaving Los Angeles was inevitable, and so, perhaps, was his going to Paris. The Doors' last album was nearly complete and he no longer owed them, or Elektra, anything. He was not bitter, but he desperately craved a change of direction, and had come to believe that so long as he stayed in California, the people and places he had long comforted himself with would remain a dominant force in his life. Jim had no real enemies—he had to escape from his friends.

Paris was a natural choice. Alan Ronay talked of the city constantly, visited it annually. Fred Myrow had lived there and he, too, filled Jim with romantic tales. Jim's continuing fondness for Rimbaud and Céline and Baudelaire was a factor as well. Paris was also a traditional choice for American writers and lovers. "He had a thing about Paris that was really incredible," says writer Salli Stevenson, who saw him before he left. "He thought it was a place where he could be himself and not have people hounding him and making a circus out of his life, making him into something he wasn't."

None of his current projects kept him. *Hwy* was either going to find a distributor or it wasn't, and his presence in Los Angeles was irrelevant; Frank could handle that. Deciding on a cover for the paperback edition of his poetry book could be done by mail. Larry Marcus seemed almost relieved when Jim suggested a six-month layoff; Marcus had been given an assignment to write a screenplay for Arthur Penn. The poetry album could wait, or could be finished by the other Doors in his absence, as they had finished other albums without him.

In Paris Jim intended to stick to a more productive writing schedule, and with this in mind he called his literary agents to see if they thought anyone would be interested in an impressionistic autobiography. He was encouraged to put something on paper, at least in the form of a letter to show publishers.

Jim told Pamela she should leave for Paris as soon as possible and look for an apartment.

"Come on, Jim. You can't go to Paris looking like the Old Man of the Mountain."

Diane Gardiner was pointing at Jim's bushy beard. She, Pamela, and Jim were drinking wine in Diane's apartment. Pamela agreed that Jim would look better without so much hair.

"No," said Jim, "I, uh, no, I don't wanna do that. I feel better this way." He sat slumped in his chair.

"Well," said Diane, "Pamela doesn't think so, and if you can't trust Pamela's opinion, whose *can* you trust?"

"So he got up on my dining table," says Diane today, "and Pamela trimmed his beard and mustache and he looked real swell."

In the final days before Pamela left, they visited her birthplace in Weed, driving eight hundred miles north in the Mercedes with Sage, then went to see Pamela's parents in Orange, where they left Sage. On February 14 Jim drove Pamela to the airport. The next day in a cold, rainy Paris she checked into the Georges V Hôtel, the one Jim had told her looked like a "red-plush whorehouse."

"You can come over now," said Diane into the telephone. "She's gone."

Diane was talking to Patricia Kennely, who had arrived in Los Angeles two weeks earlier and seen Jim briefly. She was now staying at a friend's house. Diane told her that Jim had only been waiting for Pamela to leave before calling her—why didn't she come over and surprise him? "Well," said Diane after Patricia arrived and a bottle of wine was brought out, "our dear friend Grace Slick says you gotta have more than one person. Just think of Jim as some sort of male Justine."

Moments later Jim arrived and went upstairs to Pamela's apartment. All the furniture was in storage except for a mattress, a full bookcase, the TV, a small glass table, and Jim's big purple reading chair. Patricia waited only minutes before knocking on the door. When Jim opened it she said, "I have this bottle of wine that I can't open and I was wondering if you—" He folded her into his arms and she stayed a week.

Patricia remembers the final day. "It was pure hell. It started at four at some topless-bottomless coed bar where we had so many tequilas with beer chasers that the bartender was sending every third drink over free. Last I remember I'd had fourteen. Then we went to Jim's recording session with the friend with whom I'd been staying, and she made a play for Jim. I was furious, and I told her 'I don't care what you do after I go home, but at least have the grace to wait until then.' "

Jim was the compleat polygamist and the friend was really hot, so he was easy to lure away. They were at Poppy Studios, where they were mixing the Doors' album, and the friend went to the john. Five minutes later Jim left. And five minutes after that Patricia found them embracing outside on the lawn.

"*Get up!*" Patricia snapped, standing over them.

Jim looked up at her sleepily, smiling.

"C'mon! Up! Both of you! Up!"

The friend reached up and pulled Patricia down. For a moment three bodies reshaped themselves to absorb the flesh and bones of the others. Patricia regained her composure and said steadily, "Let me talk to Jim alone."

The friend left and Jim said, "Listen, honey, you know I'm too drunk to screw tonight, just let me sleep with her."

"Look," said Patricia, "it's my last night in L.A., I'm going home tomorrow and I'll probably never see you again."

Jim bristled at the possessiveness. "Well, I'm not gonna spend another night with you."

"Fine. But you're bloody well not going to spend it with her."

Back at the apartment, Jim began a search of the cupboards and kitchen drawers. The girls asked why.

"Oh," said Jim, "I'm looking for knives and scissors, so you can castrate me. One of you gets my cock, the other my body."

"Who gets your soul, Jim?"

"Oh, I'm going to keep that, if you don't mind."

The girls watched Jim collect all the sharp things, then place them under the living room couch. He then lay down and went to sleep.

"He looked waxen, rigid—horrible," Patricia recalls. "He looked already dead, lying there with the couch framing him like a coffin. I knew then I'd never see him alive again."

The next day Patricia returned to New York and Tom Baker came back from eight months in London. It had been at least that long since Jim and Tom had last seen each other. Now they fell on each other as brothers, and by the end of the day Jim had become so drunk and obnoxious that they were thrown out of one of the Santa Monica Boulevard clubs.

With Pamela in Paris, Jim was playing the role of the carefree bachelor. He had returned to the tart he called "L.A. Woman" to say his many farewells. He began hanging out at

Marshall Brevitz's new club and at the Palms and the Phone Booth, usually with Tom, Babe, and Frank.

The pace increased as Jim saw one old girlfriend through an abortion (he had asked her to have the baby and she had refused), spent four one-nighters with four others; and called every other telephone number he could find as he cleaned out his desk at the Doors' office.

On March 3 Elektra gave a party to celebrate the opening of its expanded Los Angeles office, and after putting in a token appearance ("I paid for the place, I may as well see what it looks like"), Jim went to Fred Myrow's house where they drank and talked, returning again and again to their show idea.

"What we wanted to crystallize or capture," Fred recalls, "was that moment of transition when we all felt so strongly in Los Angeles in the late sixties and early seventies. What'd Huxley say: 'Between the evergreens and the garages, something was lurking.' It was a weird environment. Los Angeles—whatever the fuck that means—that's what we were gonna explore on the show. The place, Los Angeles, in one POW's head, which was sufficiently removed by distance, and sufficiently familiar by background, to cope with both the overt and the covert, the obvious and the less obvious of this city that is not a city. That was the basis of the show: how you see something you know very well when you see it again, coming back after a long time, as if coming back from the dead."

They scribbled an outline for the show that filled four pages. Jim kept saying he had to go to Paris. "Well, look," he finally said, when Fred began to press again for Jim to stay, "tomorrow I'll either go to Paris or go to Catalina."

Jim and Babe already had been out in the Doors' boat once that week, a day trip along the coast to Palos Verdes. On March 4 they went to Catalina with two girls. "Very rough trip over, Babe wrote in his diary. "Coked and drunked out. Next morning very beautiful and clear and our hotel rm.

overlooking Avalon Bay. We went to Big Mike's and had a rousing breakfast of scrambled eggs, sausage, ham, sardines, olives, potatoes, chili, cold cuts, toast, and beer! beer! beer!''

Jim stayed close to Babe in the days that followed, stopping a fight that started in a pool room, going to the Muhammad Ali–Joe Frazier fight, walking the Venice beach. While at the beach, they went to the Santa Monica Pier for lunch and, Babe wrote, "clowned around in the arcade a while then came back into town."

Jim went to Paris the next day.

CHAPTER

12

The way Pamela told the story afterward, their brief exile in Paris was idyllic. Gone were the pressures that had led to decadence. Jim nearly stopped his drinking. He was writing huge quantities of fresh, exciting poetry, a book about the Miami trial (or an autobiography—her story varied), and, after they saw an opera, a symphony. Jim and Pamela were like newlyweds, compatible as never before.

That was Pamela's fantasy.

There was one story in particular she liked to tell about a journey they'd made to Morocco. "I woke up one morning and saw this handsome man by the hotel pool, talking to two young American girls. I fell instantly in love with him. Then I realized it was Jim. I hadn't recognized him. He had got up early and shaved his beard and he was so lean from losing so much weight, he seemed a new man. It was so nice to fall in love again, afresh, with the man I was already in love with."

At "home" in Paris, sometimes at the Georges V, more often in a third-floor apartment on the Right Bank, it was calm, at first. Most of their time passed in the large, sunny flat in Le

Marais, an old and distinguished residential section near the Place de la Bastille. They subleased it, paying 3,000 francs a month.

A young French cover girl, Elizabeth (ZoZo) Larivière, and her sometime boyfriend, an American television producer, had the place, but they planned to leave soon—he to return to America where he had a family, she to the south of France to make a movie—so they offered Pamela one of their spare bedrooms, telling her that when they left, she and Jim could take the place for at least two months.

For two weeks, until April 10, ZoZo remained in the flat, watching this odd couple adjust to Paris and readjust to each other. To ZoZo, it seemed a peculiar relationship. Whenever she talked with Pamela, Pamela spoke only of Jim and how wonderful he was, "everything was Jeem, Jeem, Jeem." But then when Pamela stayed out all night with some of the French friends she'd made through the rich count, in the mornings on the telephone she begged ZoZo to tell a lie for her. " 'Oh, please say to Jeem I was in your friend's house all the night and I'm going to come back at twelve.' I always used to have to say that to Jeem."

Jim would silently make breakfast for himself and ZoZo, serve it to her in bed and sit and talk with her as they ate. Some mornings he would then go into the smallest of the flat's three bedrooms, where he had moved ZoZo's desk, and sit and write—or rummage through one of the cartons of papers and notebooks, tapes, clippings, photographs, fan mail, and manuscripts he'd brought with him, searching through the relics and records of his past, trying to determine exactly what it amounted to. Later in the day, when the light that came through the courtyard window changed, he would sometimes move to the dining room table with his notebooks. Other mornings he went for long, solitary walks.

For hours he walked the Paris streets, first one neighborhood, then another, just as he had done in Hollywood. Heading north on his street, the narrow, treeless rue Beautreillis, a block of apartment buildings, a news agent, a bookshop, three small restaurants, a judo club, a boys' barbershop; then west along the rue St.-Antoine, past the open-air meat markets with rabbits hanging, mounds of red cherries, trays overflowing with fish and shrimp, cauliflowers big as basketballs; finding his way slowly to one of the city's thousand attractive and famous spots. Jim especially enjoyed the Louvre, the legacy of his teenage interest in art.

Many other mornings he headed south on the rue Beautreillis, only five blocks to the Île St.-Louis, which became one of his favorite neighborhoods in all of Paris. It was here, on the Quai d'Anjou, that he visited the Hôtel de Lauzun, once the meeting place of Baudelaire's and Gautier's beloved Hashish Club.

"It is so beautiful here," he would tell ZoZo or Pamela when he returned to the flat. "They threw the blueprint away after they made this city."

But contrary to Pamela's fantasy, Jim was still drinking—and heavily. It was with great pleasure that he discovered two of France's most traditional types of bars: the wine bistro and the sidewalk café. There was still a Hollywood/Hemingway/Fitzgerald feel to Paris, a foreign familiarity. A stop at a bistro or café was not just natural, it was *de rigueur;* not to raise a toast in praise was blasphemous.

Jim was keeping blasphemy at arm's length one day the first week of April at the Astroquet, a small club on the Boulevard St.-Germain. It took its name from the French word *troquet* (café), and the American reference to outer space, Astro; the interior was done up like a Buck Rogers cartoon.

Jim had been drinking alone when his attention was drawn to some young people who entered carrying guitar cases. After a while he walked to their table. "Are you guys Americans?"

"Sure are. Where you from?" No one recognized him.

"California."

"Me, too. Where'd you go to school?"

Hervé Muller

Pamela and Jim in Paris

"Uh . . . UCLA."

"Wow, me, too! When were you there?"

Jim thought a moment, said 1964 and 1965. Again the youthful American said, "Wow, me, too. What school were you in?"

"Uh, cinematography."

The young American paused. It was a game of Twenty Questions, or What's My Line? "Uh . . . uh . . . do you sing? With a group?"

Jim admitted that he did.

"Oh wow, Jesus, I'm embarrassed, I didn't even . . ."

Jim bought them drinks, straight whiskey with a beer chaser, the same thing he was drinking. The young man introduced himself: "Phil Trainer. These guys are my friends and we have a band called Clinic, we're all Americans, my dad's with the American Embassy here."

In the hours that sloshed toward dawn the guitars came out and Jim sang "Crawling King Snake." He told his new friends that he'd done that on the new album that would be released that week in America. He was smoking constantly and his voice was heavy and rough. Between songs they talked about music and stardom. Jim told them he had gotten everything out of it that was possible to get. They were amazed when he said he'd taken acid 250 times. Jim impressed them again when he told them about the night he had destroyed the recording studio. He said he really loved the other Doors, and thought Robby Krieger never got the credit he was due.

By dawn, all but Jim and Phil had gone. Jim was chain-smoking and inhaling so deeply he'd force a bronchial cough. Phil was a singer, too, and he says, "I thought Jim was destroying his chest and throat. He was taking these huge drags on the cigarette, really, oh man, if I have any image of him at the time it's him going *sssssuuuuuuuccccccckkkk* on the cigarette and then *cough, cough, cough.*"

They were both terribly drunk, and as they staggered out of the club and into the early morning, Jim unzipped his pants and took a leak. "Do da funky chicken," Jim said, "do da funky chicken." Then, zipper back up, he suggested they hire a cab to go looking for Pamela. "Do da funky chicken."

When they discovered that Pamela hadn't returned to their Marais apartment, Jim knew where to go—to the Latin Quarter to the flat of a woman photographer. He let himself in (he knew where the key was kept), and once he'd checked that Pamela was asleep with the photographer, he assaulted the liquor supply. First vodka. Then rum. Then whatever he saw, straight from the bottle, no chaser, no mix. After an hour of that, he sent Phil to wake Pamela.

At breakfast in a nearby café Pamela ordered for Jim: spaghetti and a glass of milk to line his stomach. "You're not gonna drink any more, are you, Jim?" Pamela began to beg. "Jim?"

Jim sat silently, staring into the busy boulevard. "Do da funky chicken," he finally said.

A few days later they rented a car and drove southwest through the French wine country, through Orléans, Tours, Limoges, and Toulouse, crossing into Spain through Andorra, visiting the Prado in Madrid, where Jim sought out "The Garden of Earthly Delights" by Hieronymous Bosch, his masterwork that included a mysterious face thought to be that of Bosch himself. From there they went south to Granada, where Jim was most impressed by the Alhambra, a Moorish palace generally conceded to be the most beautiful example of Western Mohammedan architecture still standing: a citadel of sunlit arches and exquisite blue tile.

Jim and Pamela were getting along well, nearly as well as she'd one day boast. Living together for an extended period in a car and in small hotel rooms provoked small arguments, but the distractions were numerous and marvelous. Not even when they were jived out of a hundred dollars by an English-speaking Arab who promised a large lump of hash were Jim or Pamela seriously disturbed.

From Tangier they drove south along the Atlantic coast-line to Casablanca, then inland to Marrakech. They ate well, drank the local wines, and recorded everything with a Super-8 movie camera they'd bought before leaving Paris. When they turned in the car and flew back to Paris the first week of May, they had been gone approximately three weeks.

Their flat was unavailable for a few nights so they moved into L'Hôtel, an exclusive Left Bank hostelry whose twenty-five extravagantly appointed rooms were becoming much in demand among visiting rock stars, who were attracted to the one-time residence of Oscar Wilde. Soon after, there were stories of another of Jim's binges and the accompanying fall from one of L'Hôtel's second-story windows. He apparently landed on top of a car, bounced once, and, dusting himself off as if nothing had happened, walked up the street for a drink.

Living on the Left Bank, in St.-Germain, in a way put Jim back on Santa Monica Boulevard, for here were all the famous bars. The Café de Flore and the Deux-Magots, where Sartre and Camus once did their drinking. La Coupole, with the works of Picasso, Klee, Modigliani, and so many more on the pillars: Art Deco heaven, where Scott and Zelda once held court. (Jim said it looked like Ratner's, a delicatessen in New York's Lower East Side.) To the *au courant* French crowd, the hippest "underground" clubs were the newly opened Le Bulle, and Jim's favorite, a series of basement caves called the Rock 'n' Roll Circus.

Six to eight months earlier the Circus had been *the* club in Pairs, on a par with, say, the Whiskey in Los Angeles: loud, with good bands and a good sound system, expensive, drink-oriented, verging on show biz sleaze. But respectable. Led Zeppelin and Richie Havens and Johnny Winter jammed there, and so did some of the Beach Boys. By the spring of 1971, however, the club had become a heroin marketplace that was frequented by the professional underworld: the whores, the thieves, the pimps. The disc jockey who had played records at the club early in the year, and then switched to Le

Bulle, an American exile named Cameron Watson, described the Circus as "cold turkey on the dance floor." Jim loved that, of course. From phony sleaze to real sleaze. For Jim that didn't necessarily represent a step down.

The end of the first week of May, Friday the 7th, Jim was at the Circus drunk and belligerent and, finally, violent, throwing pillows and knocking over furniture. Apparently he was not recognized and was picked up and thrown out. A young French student named Gilles Yepremian discovered Jim engaged in a shouting match with the club's bouncer.

"*Niggerrr. . . .*"

Jim tired of screaming and went to jump in a cab. The cabbie turned him away. He went to a second cab and again was refused. He began to scream again. Gilles, who understands virtually no English, thought that what he screamed was, "I want meat! I want meat!"

Gilles recognized Jim and approached a third cabbie, convincing him to accept them. But as the cab crossed the Seine, Jim insisted he be let out. He wanted to go for a swim. Two French policemen were strolling past in the predawn fog, their capes and pillbox hats forming a familiar silhouette.

"Fuckin' pigs!" Jim spit. Then yelled, *"Fuckin' pigs!"*

The *flics* continued their practiced *laissez-faire* walk and Gilles hustled Jim into another cab, taking him to the flat of a friend, Hervé Muller, who lived in the seventeenth arrondissement, near the Étoile. The cabbie complained about the size of the tip and Jim threw a fistful of money at him. As they climbed the five flights of stairs, Jim said, "Shhhhhh . . . we mus' be quiet."

A sweet little Czechoslovakian émigré named Yvonne Fuka threw open the door. "Yes?"

"I have brought you somebody I found in front of the Rock 'n' Roll Circus," said Gilles.

Yvonne peered around Gilles at the rumpled figure hanging over the stair railing. At the time she was an art director for one of France's leading rock magazines, *Best.* Her boy-friend, Hervé, with whom she shared this large one-room, kitchen, and bath, was a writer for the same magazine. She recognized Jim and told Gilles to bring him in.

Jim wobbled through the door, his head moving slackly from side to side, absorbing everything, finding a bed. He wobbled over to the bed and crashed. Then he slept until almost noon, when everyone introduced themselves.

There wasn't much in the refrigerator, so Jim suggested they all be his guests at a restaurant he knew. This was the Alexander, near the Hôtel Georges V, with a menu to match the neighborhood. Jim was recognized as a regular customer, at least as one who spent and tipped freely, but was told the restaurant did not serve breakfast. Perhaps they'd care to wait for lunch.

Lunch started for Jim with two Bloody Marys, and then he ordered a bottle of Chivas Regal scotch. An hour later he was drunk and insulting a tableful of French businessmen in a language they blessedly did not understand: "You look stupid. . . . Tell me, are you motherfuckers? Are you assholes?"

"He was drinking twice as much as anybody else," says Hervé sadly. "At the end of the meal they came with two bottles of cognac and asked him which one he wanted. And he just grabbed one of them, tore off the top and raised the neck to his mouth. He began asking Yvonne to get him a girl. 'Can't you get me a chick?' After a while he paid for everything with a credit card. There were five of us and it came to seven hundred francs."

They began walking to their car, Jim leaning heavily on Yvonne for support. "You must get me out of here," he told her urgently, "you must get me out of here." After only fifty meters he said he could go no farther, he had to rest. They eased him onto a bench and Hervé went on to fetch the car.

Jim turned violent when Hervé returned and had to be wrestled into the vehicle, then dragged up the five flights of stairs to Hervé's flat. Midway, he slumped and refused to be

Jim with Hervé Muller in Paris, June 1971

taken higher. "Leave me!" he said, sitting down on one of the
landings.

Then he bellowed, *"You mother-fucking niggerrrrs!"*

Finally Yvonne and Hervé managed to get him into their
flat and onto a bed, where he promptly fell asleep. It was three
o'clock on a Saturday afternoon.

Hervé and Yvonne saw Jim again. This time he was with
Pamela. They had dinner at Hervé's and Yvonne's and talked
of poetry and film. Jim said he had brought copies of *Feast of
Friends* and *Hwy* with him to France and wanted to get them
shown. He also gave a copy of "An American Prayer" to
Hervé, who asked if he could translate it into French. Yvonne

said she'd like to do some illustrations. Jim was interested in the possibilities a collaboration posed.

Later that evening after quite a bit of wine, Jim told Yvonne, perhaps inadvertently, why he was in Paris. "I'm so sick of everything. People keep thinking of me as a rock and roll star and I don't want anything to do with it. I can't stand it anymore. I'd be so glad if people didn't recognize me . . . who do they think Jim Morrison is, anyway?"

The following week Jim and Pamela left for Corsica. They flew to Marseilles, where Jim lost his driver's license, passport, and wallet, necessitating a return to Paris to acquire duplicates at the American Embassy. They again flew to Marseilles and finally on to Ajaccio, the island's major port and capital city, as well as the birthplace of Napoleon. Corsica is also known for the inordinate number of recruits it provides for the Paris police force, its high red thrusts of rock, quaint villages at the bottom of a mountain as awesome as any part of the Rockies or the French mainland Alps, wet-eyed fishermen's widows shrouded in black, a lack of young people, and the pungent and pervasive smell of Corsican *maquis* (grass), which is eaten by the cattle and appears in the meat, cheese, and milk. Jim and Pamela toured the island for ten days. On every day but one it rained. Pamela said it was idyllic.

The Doors officially left Elektra Records, ending a relationship that had started four years and ten months earlier. The same week Jim's final album, *L.A. Woman,* and the next-to-last single, "Love Her Madly," were released, and both began a rapid climb up the charts. The cover photograph for *L.A. Woman* was a group shot, placing equal emphasis on each member. In fact, Jim had slunk down in a way to make himself appear even smaller than the others! In addition, because no one had been successful in persuading Jim to shave, for the first time he appeared full-bearded on an album cover, wearing a demonic, sly smirk. Jim had gotten his revenge for the *13* and *Absolutely Live* front covers.

The critics were unanimous in their praise for *L.A. Woman*. The rebound that had begun with *Morrison Hotel* was accelerating. The doubters and the detractors were vanquished—the Doors were definitely back. Eventually the album would reach the number five position, and the single would go to number seven. The record industry was abuzz with reports that the Doors were negotiating with Atlantic and Columbia Records for unprecedented amounts of money. John, Ray, and Robbie got together occasionally to jam in their rehearsal studio, with Ray handling the vocals, working up material for Jim's impending return.

It was about this time that Jim, who had little if any knowledge of the recent upswing, called the office and told Bill Siddons he was getting music back into his head, but he wanted to rest a while longer. Later that week he placed an early-morning call to John Densmore and asked him how the material was coming. When John told Jim how well the album and single were selling and how much the press liked the records, Jim was amazed. "If they like this, wait'll they hear what I got in mind for the next one," he told John.

Jim was looking somewhat healthier than usual. He was clean-shaven, had lost some weight, and a wardrobe change made a difference as well. When he wasn't looking, Pamela had thrown out his lived-in jeans and battle jacket and had nudged him into his collegiate past. Now he was wearing button-down shirts, khaki trousers, and a pullover V-neck sweater. His Frye boots, worn and nearly rotten, stayed.

On coming back from Corsica he had hired a private secretary, a tall, thin, modelish blonde from Canada who spoke fluent French, Robin Wertle. Robin had been keeping records and working as an agent and stylist for a fashion photographer. She recalls that they met when the photographer was leaving Paris for a couple of months, "which left me free so I said I'd do it. Neither Jim nor Pamela spoke French, so it was a bit difficult for them to get around."

As it worked out, the job included "seeing to the apartment—everything from getting the cleaning lady to come, to typing letters, making calls to America, buying furniture, renting a typewriter, trying to make arrangements for Jim to show one of his films."

Jim seemed to be taking certain conscious steps to resolve those old conflicting demons, stardom and selfhood. But the steps were slow and laborious and he avoided thinking about it if he could.

Hervé came over with Yvonne June 11 to go with Jim and Pamela to see *Le Regard du Sourd* (*The Deaf Man's Look*), a play virtually without dialogue, most of whose characters were deaf mutes. When Hervé and Yvonne arrived at the rue Beautreillis flat, Jim said Pamela wasn't coming—he was bringing his dear friend from America instead. The friend, then a house guest, was Alan Ronay.

Pamela went out that night with what are called *minets,* young androgynous French dandies who wore sunglasses and white duck pants and spoke English rarely and condescendingly. Pamela loved them. Jim hated them, and told Pamela he didn't like her seeing them.

Time passed. He saw his old friends Agnes Varda and Jacques Demy many times. Back in 1968, Jacques had tried to break through the Doors' barriers to get Jim to score his first American film, *Model Shop.* At the time he was a much-hailed filmmaker for his award-winning *Umbrellas of Cherbourg.* Agnes, his wife, called herself the grandmother figure of the New Wave and once tried to get Jim for her impressionistic documentary *Lions Love.*

The three had become close friends and over the years Jim had developed a sincere fondness for Agnes. She was a little woman, only five feet, two inches tall, but highly intellectual, with a husky voice and blunt personality. She identified strongly with the working class, deliberately drove an inexpensive automobile, and openly admired young radicals for their rejection of middle-class values.

Jim in Paris, 1971

Jim also ran into Rory Flynn, Errol's amazing beanpole daughter who had been one of the Doors' first groupies at the Whiskey in 1966. Rory was now a model. They had a sober lunch.

A friend of Pamela's came by, meeting Pamela at the Café de Flore. Afterward, at the apartment in the Marais, Jim told the friend he'd been offered the lead in the movie version of *Catch My Soul,* the musical adaptation of *Othello* that had been staged in Los Angeles with Jerry Lee Lewis playing Iago. He said others in the movie would include Tina Turner, Joe Frazier, and Melanie. He said he'd also been offered a part with Robert Mitchum in Norman Mailer's allegorical story of an Alaskan bear hunt, *Why Are We in Vietnam?*

"I'm turning down the play," Jim said, "and I don't think I'll do the movie because it'll take up too much time when I could be writing."

They had dinner at Le Coupole and on the way home passed a student riot in the St.-Michel district. The brick-throwing riots were going on every weekend, a holdover from the national strike and student riots of 1968. Jim and Pamela had been caught in the middle of one a few weeks before. They all agreed that the riot morbidly fascinated them, but decided not to stop and watch.

For *Crawdaddy* magazine, Pam's friend wrote the following:

> Jim looks better than he has for a while, certainly better than the Miami trial days. He claims to have quit drinking, has lost considerable weight, but the French food has taken some toll, and he hasn't quite regained the licorice leather-legged look of the gaunt shadow that prowled L.A. as the Lizard King.

It was the first day of July and Paris was blazingly hot. Jim had crashed into a slough of terrible and terrifying despondency. He had been drinking heavily and now was trying to quit once and for all. He was trying to write, trying to seize the depressing full-nelson and crank it into something creative, but to no avail. He sat slumped at the dining room table, waiting for words to come. The little he put down was not up to the Morrison standard and he knew it. He would stand in front of the mirror for minutes at a time, staring into his own eyes, searching for an answer there. Alan Ronay had never seen him so low and Pamela was frightened. They took turns trying to distract him, trying to cheer him, but with no luck. Finally on Friday night, the 2nd of July, Alan suggested the three of them have dinner at an outdoor café not far from the Morrison flat. Jim refused to saddle his friends with his condition. He remained unusually quiet while meal noises replaced the absent conversation.

After supper Jim may have shown his emotional hand when he sent a telegram to Jonathan Dolger, his editor, regarding the cover of Simon and Schuster's paperbound edition of *The Lords and The New Creatures*. He wanted Joel Brodsky's "young lion" photo dropped and Edmond Teske's bearded, more poetic, photo to replace it. He then took Pamela home, going on alone to a movie that Alan had recommended (*Pursued* with Robert Mitchum).

Where Jim went after the movie, or *if* Jim went to the movie, is a matter for speculation. The various reports of that evening are snarled with contradictions. Some say he went to the Rock 'n' Roll Circus, so steeped in depression that he bought some heroin and O.D.'d in the club lavatory, only to be carried out the back door and dumped at his flat, in the bathtub. Others say he left Alan and Pamela and headed straight for the airport, where he was seen boarding a plane. Or maybe he just walked all night. Or he went to the film and returned to the flat, where he soon complained he wasn't feeling well and was going to take a bath. It is this last version that has gained the most exposure, but whatever happened on the Friday night, by Monday morning, July 5, Jim was rumored to be dead.

On Monday the national newspapers in London began calling Elektra Records' English offices. No one there could verify that Jim was alive. The papers had heard that he had been discovered dead at his Paris apartment. How did the rumor start and was it true this time? Clive Selwood, who ran Elektra's English office, called the company's office in France for verification. Elektra France was not even aware that Jim was in France. Clive then called the American Embassy and the Paris police. Both denied any knowledge of the death of an American named Jim Morrison.

Clive decided to forget about it, it was probably just another false alarm. He had almost convinced himself when two of England's primary rock weeklies called him, one right after another. Clive told them what little he knew. He then decided to call Bill Siddons in Los Angeles. Because of the time difference, he woke Bill up.

"Bill," he said, "I can't substantiate it in any way, but we are getting reports that Jim died."

Bill almost laughed. "Oh, come on Clive." He said he was going back to bed. When he couldn't fall asleep again, he decided to call Jim himself. Pamela answered the phone and told Bill he'd better come right over, as if Bill had only to travel around the corner. Pamela wasn't crazy about Siddons, but she knew he'd take care of business. Bill called the airport to book reservations for the next available flight. He then called Ray and woke him.

"Listen, Ray, Jim *might* be dead. I don't know if it's the real thing or not this time. I just spoke with Pam and she was vague. She wants me to fly right over. I'm going to check it out right away."

"Oh, Jesus," Ray mumbled. "Well, go over there and let us know the minute you find out anything."

Bill assured Ray he would and asked him to call the other guys, but to be sure to tell them it might be no more than another false alarm.

"I'm on the next flight," Siddons said.

"Oh, Bill," Ray added, "I don't mean to sound morbid, but please make sure."

"Make sure of what, Ray?"

"I don't know, man, just make *sure.*"

Siddons arrived in Paris on Tuesday, July 6. He was met at the flat by Pamela, a sealed coffin, and a signed death certificate. Funeral arrangements were quickly and secretly confirmed. On July 7 Pamela filed the death certificate with the U.S. Embassy, identifying Jim as James Douglas Morrison, a poet. She said there were no living relatives. The official cause of death was listed as a heart attack.

Siddons was efficient, and on Wednesday afternoon the coffin was lowered into the ground at Père La Chaise, a cemetery Jim had recently visited as a sightseer, seeking the graves of Edith Piaf, Oscar Wilde, Balzac, Bizet, and Chopin. Five mourners were present: Pamela, Siddons, Alan Ronay, Agnes Varda, and Robin Wertle. They threw flowers on the grave and said their goodbyes.

Bill helped Pamela pack their belongings and on Thursday they returned to Los Angeles where Bill announced what little he knew. Pamela, reportedly, was in shock and resting.

Nearly a decade later people still ask: Is Jim Morrison *really* dead? And *how* did he die?

Even before he died—assuming he *is* dead—Jim was that rare sort of figure about whom death rumors often circulated. When Jim Morrison was at his heroic height, he "died" nearly every weekend, usually in a car accident, often by falling from a hotel balcony where he'd been showing off for friends, occasionally from an overdose of something alcoholic, hallucinogenic, or sexual.

How did he die? Over the years there have been countless theories, some of them arising from a weird disappointment. Many have claimed, with ample reason, that it was totally out of character for Jim to die the way Siddons reported it, of a heart attack in a bathtub.

The official story goes like this: Pam and Jim were alone at the flat (sometime after midnight, Saturday, July 3, 1971) when Jim regurgitated a small quantity of blood. He had done this before, Pam said, and although she was concerned, she was not really upset. Jim claimed he felt okay and said he was going to take a bath. Pamela fell asleep again. At five she woke, saw Jim had not returned to bed, went into the bathroom, and found him in the tub, his arms resting on the porcelain sides, his head back, his long, wet hair matted against the rim, a boyish smile across his clean-shaven face. At first Pamela thought he was playing one of his macabre jokes, but then she called the fire department's resuscitation unit. A doctor and the police followed, Pamela said, but all were too late.

One factor causing much of the initial disbelief was timing. Bill told his story to the media a full *six days* after Jim died, two days after the funeral.

"I have just returned from Paris, where I attended the funeral of Jim Morrison," Siddons said in a prepared statement (released by a publicity firm in L.A.). "Jim was buried in a simple ceremony, with only a few close friends present. The initial news of his death and funeral was kept quiet because those of us who knew him intimately and loved him as a person wanted to avoid all the notoriety and circuslike atmosphere that surrounded the deaths of such other rock personalities as Janis Joplin and Jimi Hendrix.

"I can say Jim died peacefully of natural causes—he had been in Paris since March with his wife, Pam. He had seen a doctor in Paris about a respiratory problem and had complained of his problem on Saturday—the day of his death. . . ."

In the days that followed, Siddons offered no more information because he had none.

Another factor causing much of the disbelief was the fact that Siddons never saw the body. What he did see at Jim and Pamela's flat was a sealed coffin and a death certificate with one doctor's signature. There was no police report, no doctor present. No autopsy had been conducted. All he had was Pamela's word that Jim was dead.

Why was there no autopsy? "Just because we didn't want to do it that way. We wanted to leave Jim alone. He died in peace and dignity."

Who was the doctor? Siddons didn't know; Pamela didn't remember. But signatures can be forged or bought.

At any rate, that is the official story of how Jim Morrison died. The other stories told are more bizarre and, perhaps, more believable.

The Parisians hold out for heroin as the cause of death. Jim had been a regular at the Rock 'n' Roll Circus, the French night spot then known as a haven for the local heroin underground. Jim had always liked degenerate environments, enjoyed the extremes society contained. He had visited the skidrow districts in both L.A. and New York several times. He had gone regularly to the Circus, people there knew him. However, Jim's curiosity was probably more that of a spectator than a participant. He drank on skid row, but chances are slim that he shot up at the Circus. For one thing, he had a long-standing fear of hypodermic needles. If he did fix that night in Paris, it would have been a first, although he had probably snorted smack before. Still, wasn't Jim found in the bathtub, usually the first place an O.D. victim is taken for attempted revival? Doesn't some of the graffitti at his Père La Chaise grave, "Have Mercy for junkies" and "Shootez," support the belief that it was an overdose and not a heart attack?

If Jim had O.D.'d, the doctor probably would have noticed the needle marks. However, if he had snorted the heroin, there would be no way to detect it without taking a blood sample. With no autopsy, we will never know. It is possible, though. The amount of inhaled heroin that is lethal is considerably less when combined with alcohol. The two act in concert to still the central nervous and respiratory systems, resulting in a quick, painless death.

Other theories abounded in one circle of Jim's friends.

Hervé Muller

Graffiti for Jim near Paris gravesite

One had him killed when someone plucked out his eyes with a knife ("to free his soul," as the story had it). Another had a spurned mistress killing him long-distance from New York by witchcraft. Still other theories claimed Jim was the victim of a political conspiracy aimed at discrediting and eliminating the hippie/New Left/counterculture lifestyle (actually this is supposed to have been a vast, pervasive, connected set of conspiracies that included the shootings at Kent State and Jackson State, the riots at Isla Vista, the Weathermen bombings, the stiff prison sentences given Timothy Leary and the Chicago Eight, the Charlie Manson murders—not to mention the deaths of Hendrix and Joplin and more than two dozen Black Panthers). Jim was certainly popular enough and, more threateningly, smart enough to cause the powers that be ample reason to take some sort of action to prevent his subversive influence. Certainly the authorities were wary of him, viz. the in-depth FBI investigation of his past following the Miami arrest.

Others, less conspiracy-prone, believe Jim overdosed on cocaine, a drug he certainly enjoyed, yet one that is much less lethal than heroin, even when taken in great quantity. Still others claim that Jim probably did die of "natural causes" but that Pamela wasn't there when he did. Perhaps she was gone for the weekend with the count, not returning until Monday to discover Jim dead, which would explain the delay in the announcement. Some people merely shrug and say that, excepting the murder stories, it doesn't matter exactly how he died— whether he overdosed on something, had a heart attack, or merely drank himself to death (as so many surmised from the start). The bottom line still reads "suicide." One way or another, Jim had died of self-abuse, and finding out how was only a matter of determining the caliber of the metaphorical pistol he held to his own head.

The truth is no one knows for sure how Jim Morrison died. If there was ever a man who was ready, able, and willing to die, it was Jim. His body was old and his soul tired.

On the other hand, there are those who won't buy any of this. Jim Morrison is *not* dead, they say. This is not as far-fetched as it might seem. If there was ever a man who was ready, willing, and able to disappear, this also was Jim. It would be perfectly in keeping with his unpredictable character for him to stage his own death as a means to escape his public life. He was tired of an image he'd outgrown but couldn't live down. He had sought credibility as a poet only to see his attempts foiled by his appeal as a cultural hero. He enjoyed singing and genuinely loved the talent the Doors were, yet he also desperately sought relief from the pressures stardom brought. Perhaps he had done nothing more the weekend of July 3-4 than drop out of sight to find the peace to write and the freedom of anonymity.

Certainly the seeds of such a hoax had been planted: At the Fillmore in San Francisco in early 1967, when the Doors still hadn't had a hit record, Jim suggested pulling a death stunt to bring the band to national attention. There was also his comment about using the name Mr. Mojo Risin' to contact the office after he "split to Africa." In addition, he told both authors of this book at different times that he could see himself changing careers radically, reappearing as a suited and neck-tied businessman. Steve Harris, Jac Holzman's assistant, clearly remembers Jim asking him after Brian Jones's death what would happen if he suddenly died. How would it affect business, Jim wanted to know. What would the press say? And who would believe it?

The seeds were planted even earlier in his life. When Jim was studying the life and poetry of Arthur Rimbaud, he was gripped by the fact that Rimbaud had written all his poetry by the age of nineteen and then disappeared into North Africa to become a gun runner and slave trader. With Mary Frances Werebelow, Jim entertained long conversational investigations into how the Disciples had stolen the body of Christ from the crypt, joking about the "Easter Heist" but dealing with it seriously and logically.

All Jim's closest friends agree (and some insist) that not

only is it exactly the sort of prank Jim would pull . . . but with Pamela's devoted help, could actually, incredibly, pull off.

Agnes Varda and Alan Ronay are not talking. Robin Wertle and Hervé Muller swear they don't know any specifics. Siddons only knows what he saw and was told by Pamela. And Pamela took the secret to her grave, when she died three years after Jim.

Going on a decade now, there's still no word from Mr. Mojo Risin'.

Patricia Kennely

Afterword

The poet Blake said, "The road of excess leads to the palace of wisdom." Jim Morrison understood that and he was excessive. Either poets arrive at wisdom because they are, in fact, poets, or they never get there because they are divine fools. It is one and it is the same.

Another proverb from Blake's *Marriage of Heaven and Hell* states, "Prudence is a rich, ugly old maid courted by Incapacity." Jim was not prudent and it follows that he seldom knew incapacity. Jim was a metamorphic hero who thrilled us with his energy and daring. He perceived with his senses and he altered them with alcohol (sacred to Dionysus, the god of drama and intoxication), with acid, and with the interior elixir of his own ebullience and exuberance. Jim was one of the brightest spirits that I've ever known, and one of the most complex—all of us mammal beings made out of meat and nerves are bound to be complex.

Jim was fascinated by the experience of his senses and was continually delighted by change in his nervous system. When he ceased being the leather-clad singer/sex symbol of the

Doors, he became the beautiful wreck who blossomed into a chunky, bluesy singer.

One of the things I like about this biography is that it shows that Jim knew himself to be a poet. That was the basis of my friendship and brotherhood with him. Also, the authors recognize that Jim was not a materialist, after the dollar, as are many artists of rock 'n' roll. The modality Jim loved was that of experience and action. He wanted the transubstantiation of material nature into the gold of discontented delight.

Jim and I got together in London to discuss a film of my play *The Beard*. Jim met me at the airport and I told him about imagining Romantic poets flying through the night sky around the plane. I showed him a new poem about Billy the Kid and he spontaneously wrote a poem for Jean Harlow in my notebook.

We made a poets' tour of the city through the strip joints of Soho to the Tate Museum, and then took a moonlight ride with poet Christopher Logue to see the hospital which now stands on the site where Blake lived. We became brief habitués of the music clubs, The Bag of Nails and Arethusa's, where we saw Christine Keeler, movie stars, and drank glasses of Courvoisier and had philosophical talks with film directors.

In London I saw Jim's poems for the first time. In the lucid mescaline-like light of a hangover, I found his manuscript of *The New Creatures* on the coffee table of his Belgravia apartment and was excited by what I read.

I know of no better poet of Jim's generation. Few poets have been such public figures or entertainers (perhaps Mayakovsky in Russia in the twenties and thirties) and none have had so brief or so powerful a career.

Everyone has heard the Doors' music and knows the public legend, but Jim was sensitive about the possibility that his poetry would be read because he was a rock star. He guarded his poems thoughtfully and carefully and worked on them in secret.

When I saw his manuscript of *The New Creatures* in London, I suggested that Jim do a private edition for friends only and then give the book to a commercial publisher if he chose. That's what happened. Jim was two artists in one man, the passionate and impassioned singer (I've seen Jim sing so long that the audience had to lie on the floor to listen) and the quiet, gifted young poet of the page. He was Mr. Mojo Risin' and he was James Douglas Morrison, a poet of Scottish-American descent.

I've given poetry readings with Jim and seen his nervousness and determination to be heard on that level. I've listened to Jim, after his death, on tapes in a game lodge that was once a German fort in East Africa. On all occasions I heard an artist.

When I read Jim I feel the friend whom I miss. I sense Jim there as a brother to talk to.

As George MacDonald said:

> Death alone from death can save.
> Love is death, and so is brave.
> Love can fill the deepest grave.
> Love loves on beneath the wave.

Jim's presence and artistry created a vibrant wave, and he is there as a bright, singing statue in the light-shows and amplification. But his poems and songs stand proving, in fineness, that *Death alone from death can save.*

Michael McClure
August 1979

Acknowledgments

The year following Jim Morrison's alleged death Jerry Hop-
kins was sent to Europe as *Rolling Stone*'s roving correspondent. This made it a simple matter for him to research the
details of Jim and the other Doors' only European tour and of
Jim's final months in Paris. While researching the rest of his
life, Jerry traveled from his Los Angeles residence to Jim's former homes in Clearwater and Tallahassee, Florida; Alexandria, Virginia; and Alameda, California; as well as to New
York, Atlanta, and Valdosta (Georgia), San Francisco, Mam-
moth, Monterey (California), and Miami, Florida.

Those to whom both authors are especially indebted include the three surviving Doors, Ray Manzarek, Robby
Krieger, and John Densmore; Bill and Cheri Siddons; Frank
and Kathy Lisciandro; Babe Hill; Leon Barnard; Paul Rothchild; Diane Gardiner; Paul Ferrara; Bruce Botnick; Gloria
Stavers; Michael McClure; Hervé Muller; Billy James; Denny
Sullivan; Ronnie Haran Mellen; Jac Holzman; Dorothy Manzarek; and Lynn Krieger.

Those who offered their valuable time and memories to
Jerry include: Patricia Kennely; Rosanna (White) Norton; Fred
and Ilana Myrow; Tandy Martin Brody; Vince Treanor; Gerard
(Fud) Ford; Phil Oleno; Mrs. Walter Martin; James Merrill;
Randy Maney; Andy Morrison; Bob Hungerford; Ralph
Turner; Sammy Kilman; Thad Morrison, Jr., and Thad Morri-
son III; Margaret Morrison Blumberg; Nick; Pamela Zarubica;
David Thompson; Mrs. Paul R. Morrison, and John DeBella.

Others whom Jerry interviewed include: Elmer Valentine;
Mario; Larry Marcus; Harvey Perr; Sylvia Romano; Mike
Gershman; Danny Fields; Jonathan Dolger; Judy Sims; David
Anderle; Digby Diehl; Russ Miller; Mike Hamilburg; Michael
Ford; Garry Essert; Julia (Brose) Densmore Negron; Gayle
Enochs; Charles Lippincott; Barry Opper; Eva Gardonyi; John
Ptak; Linda Kelly; Gay Blair; Bill Runyan; George (Bullets)
Durgom; Salli Stevenson; Jac Ttana (Joe Kooken); Anne
Moore; Bill Belasco; Ron Raley; Nina and Adam Holzman;

Todd Schiffman; Paddy Faralla; Bill Kerby; Renata Eder; Sue Helms; Pamela Courson; Stanton Kaye; Naomi Grumette; Clare (Sparks) Loeb: Marshall Brevitz; Anne Schlosser; Paddy Monk; Judy Huddleston; Samatha Spitzer; Ellen Sander; Bill Graham; John Harris; Alan Weber; Bill Thompson; Ned Moraghan; Robin Wertle; Patricia Charley; Leslie Gilb; Steve Wax; Trina Robbins; Philippe Paringaux; Elizabeth (ZoZo) Larivière; Yvonne Fuka; Dominique Lamblin; Phil Trainer; Cameron Watson; Hervé de Lilia; Arthur Dorlag; Charles Reimer; Ashley Ahl; Joe Burke; Luther Davis Jr.; Tom Reese; Frances Warfield; Hilton Davis; Diane Warfield; Deucalion Gregory; Ihor Todoruk; James Blue; Colin Young; John Tobler; John Morris; Clive Selwood; David Apps, Elliott Kastner; Chris Greenwood; Rory Flynn; Gus Dana; Terence McCartney Filgate; and Roger Tomlinson.

I'd also like to thank the following people: Rich Linnell; Kim Fowley; Iggy Pop; Alice Cooper; Patti Smith; Alan Lanier; Nigel Harrison; Jim Ladd; Shelly Ladd; Harvey Kubernick; Penelope Abrams; Mel Posner; Marty Fox; Bob Greene; Eric Rudolph; Elektra Records, N.Y. and L.A. (especially the girls in West Coast publicity); Marcy Rudo; Dave Marsh; and Todd Gray. Also my family; Barbara Reinhart; Ken Keyes; John Randell; and Shep Gordon, all of whom gave my mission inspiration and support in one form or another.

A debt is owed to the U.S. Navy Public Information Office at the Pentagon; Elektra Records International; the files of *Billboard* and *Cashbox* magazines; the *Miami Herald* and the *Miami News Leader;* the *Los Angeles Times*; *Melody Maker*; *New Musical Express*; Rogers, Cowan and Brenner in Beverly Hills and London; Gibson and Stromberg; Florida State University; St. Petersburg Junior College; George Washington High School; *Crawdaddy* magazine; *Creem* magazine; *The Village Voice*; *Rolling Stone*; and *Circus* magazine.

And Jerry and I would like to thank especially the Doors' fans everywhere who have proved that a good thing never dies, that Jim Morrison and the Doors live on through their words and music.

—Daniel Sugerman

Discography

45611   Break On Through
           End of the Night (Jan. 1967)

45615   Light My Fire
           The Crystal Ship (Apr. 1967)

45621   People Are Strange
           Unhappy Girl (Sep. 1967)

45624   Love Me Two Times
           Moonlight Drive (Nov. 1967)

45628   The Unknown Soldier
           We Could Be So Good Together (Mar. 1968)

45635   Hello, I Love You
           Love Street (Jun. 1968)

45646   Touch Me
           Wild Child (Dec. 1968)

45656   Wishful, Sinful
           Who Scared You (Feb. 1969)

45663   Tell All the People
           Easy Ride (May 1969)

45675   Running Blue
           Do It (Aug. 1969)

45685   You Make Me Real
           Roadhouse Blues (Mar. 1970)

45726   Love Her Madly
           Don't Go No Farther (Mar. 1971)

45738   Riders On the Storm
            Changeling (Jun. 1971)

E-46005   Roadhouse Blues
            Albinoni Adagio (Jan. 1979)

45 rpm "Spun Gold" Series

45051   Light My Fire
            Love Me Two Times (Apr. 1971)

45052   Touch Me
            Hello, I Love You (Apr. 1971)

45059   Riders on the Storm
            Love Her Madly (Sept. 1972)

33⅓ rpm albums

74007   *The Doors* (Jan. 1967): Break On Through, Soul
            Kitchen, The Crystal Ship, Twentieth-Century
            Fox, Alabama Song, Light My Fire, Back Door
            Man, I Looked at You, End of the Night, Take It
            As It Comes, The End

74014   *Strange Days* (Oct. 1967): Strange Days, You're
            Lost Little Girl, Love Me Two Times, Unhappy
            Girl, Horse Latitudes, Moonlight Drive, People
            Are Strange, My Eyes Have Seen You, I Can't See
            Your Face in My Mind, When the Music's Over

74024   *Waiting for the Sun* (July 1968): Hello, I Love
            You, Love Street, Not to Touch the Earth,
            Summer's Almost Gone, Wintertime Love, The
            Unknown Soldier, Spanish Caravan, My Wild
            Love, We Could Be So Good Together, Yes the
            River Knows, Five to One

75005   *The Soft Parade* (Jul. 1969): Tell All the People,
            Touch Me, Shaman's Blues, Do It, Easy Ride,
            Wild Child, Runnin' Blue, Wishful Sinful, The
            Soft Parade

75007   ***Morrison Hotel*** (Feb. 1970): Road House Blues, Waiting for the Sun, You Make Me Real, Peace Frog, Blue Sunday, Ship of Fools, Land Ho!, The Spy, Queen of the Highway, Indian Summer, Maggie M'Gill

2-9002   ***Absolutely Live*** (Jul. 1970) (a double album): Who Do You Love, Medley: Alabama Song/Back Door Man, Love Hides, Five to One, Build Me a Woman, When the Music's Over, Close to You, Universal Mind, Break On Through #2, The Celebration of the Lizard, Soul Kitchen

74079   ***13*** (Nov. 1970): Light My Fire, People Are Strange, Back Door Man, Moonlight Drive, Crystal Ship, Roadhouse Blues, Touch Me, Love Me Two Times, You're Lost Little Girl, Hello, I Love You, Wild Child, Unknown Soldier

75011   ***L.A. Woman*** (Apr. 1971): The Changeling, Love Her Madly, Been Down So Long, Cars Hiss by My Window, L.A. Woman, L'America, Hyacinth House, Crawling King Snake, The WASP (Texas Radio & the Big Beat), Riders on the Storm

2-6001   ***Weird Scenes Inside the Gold Mine*** (Jan. 1972) (a double album): Break On Through, Strange Days, Shaman's Blues, Love Street, Peace Frog, Blue Sunday, The WASP, End of the Night, Love Her Madly, Spanish Caravan, Ship of Fools, The Spy, The End, Take It As It Comes, Running Blue, L.A. Woman, Five to One, Who Scared You (You Need Meat), Don't Go No Further, Riders on the Storm, Maggie M'Gill, Horse Latitudes, When the Music's Over

EQ-5035   ***The Best of the Doors*** (Quadrophonic) (Aug. 1973): Who Do You Love, Soul Kitchen, Hello, I Love You, People Are Strange, Riders On the Storm, Touch Me, Love Her Madly, Love Me Two Times, Take It As It Comes, Moonlight Drive, Light My Fire

5E-502 *An American Prayer* (Nov. 1978): Awake, To
Come of Age, The Poet's Dreams, World on Fire,
An American Prayer (album includes a live
Roadhouse Blues in addition to Morrison recited
poetry & new music by the three surviving Doors)
(also 8-page color libretto)

All records Elektra Records

Books

The Lords
Privately published,
limited edition of 100 copies,
Western Lithographers, Los Angeles, Spring 1969

The New Creatures
Privately published,
limited edition of 100 copies,
Western Lithographers, Los Angeles, Spring 1969

The Lords & The New Creatures
Simon and Schuster
(hardcover), May 1970

An American Prayer
Privately published,
limited edition of 500 copies,
Western Lithographers, Los Angeles, Summer
1970

The Lords & The New Creatures
Simon and Schuster
(paperbound), Autumn 1971

Film

Break On Through:
16 mm, color;
Elektra Records promotional film made for TV;
2 min. 25 sec.

The Unknown Soldier:
16 mm, color;
Elektra Records promotional film made for TV;
3 min. 10 sec.

Feast of Friends:
16 mm, black and white and (mostly) color,
synch-sound documentary
photographed and designed by Paul Ferrara and
Jim Morrison;
edited by Frank Lisciandro;
sound by Babe Hill;
co-produced by the Doors:
40 min.

HiWay:
35 mm, color, synch-sound;
a film by Jim Morrison, Frank Lisciandro and Paul
Ferrara,
sound by Babe Hill,
title song: Georgie Ferrara, music: Fred Myrow;
50 min.

The Doors Are Open:
Television black & white,
live footage intercut with footage of political events
of 1968.
Four parts, filmed by Granada TV, London, England at the Roundhouse Theatre;
excellent performance, fair sound.
1 hr.

About the Authors:

JERRY HOPKINS: Jerry has been chronicling popular music since his graduation from Washington and Lee University in 1957. He has written for dozens of publications as a free-lance journalist and has had several books pertaining to rock music published. In 1971 Jerry published the first, and what remains the most definitive, Elvis Presley biography, *Elvis*. That book was dedicated, in part, to Jim Morrison "for the idea." After Jim's reported death in 1971, Jerry found himself moved to the point of deciding that his next project would be to write Jim's biography. Jerry had met Jim when he interviewed him for *Rolling Stone*, and again when he traveled to Mexico with the Doors to cover their south-of-the-border concerts.

From 1971 to 1975 Jerry researched Jim's life. It was during the investigation for this book that Jerry first met and interviewed Danny Sugerman, a friend and business associate of Jim's.

Today Jerry Hopkins lives in Hawaii with his two children. He covers the Hawaiian music scene and remains a contributing editor of *Rolling Stone* magazine.

DANIEL SUGERMAN: Danny is twenty-four years old and lives in Beverly Hills, where he operates a successful management/public-relations firm. He also serves as a confidant and aide to the surviving Doors, especially Ray Manzarek, whose career he has managed since the Doors disbanded. In the Doors' heyday he served as a management associate and was an integral part of the "Doors Family." At Jim Morrison's encouragement, Danny began writing when he was thirteen years old, first covering Doors concerts and later, in more depth, Jim's notorious Miami trial. The two became close, and after Jim's death in Paris, Danny continued to cover the rock music scene for various publications here and abroad.

After Jerry Hopkins provided the research and the first two drafts, Danny went to work assembling what would be the final manuscript, attempting to make Jim as real to the reader as only one who knew Jim intimately could.